The Game Designer's Playlist

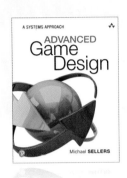

The Game Designer's Playlist

Innovative Games Every Game Designer Needs to Play

Zack Hiwiller

✦✦Addison-Wesley

Boston • Columbus • New York • San Francisco • Amsterdam • Cape Town
Dubai • London • Madrid • Milan • Munich • Paris • Montreal • Toronto • Delhi • Mexico City
São Paulo • Sydney • Hong Kong • Seoul • Singapore • Taipei • Tokyo

Many of the designations used by manufacturers and sellers to distinguish their products are claimed as trademarks. Where those designations appear in this book, and the publisher was aware of a trademark claim, the designations have been printed with initial capital letters or in all capitals.

The author and publisher have taken care in the preparation of this book, but make no expressed or implied warranty of any kind and assume no responsibility for errors or omissions. No liability is assumed for incidental or consequential damages in connection with or arising out of the use of the information or programs contained herein.

For information about buying this title in bulk quantities, or for special sales opportunities (which may include electronic versions; custom cover designs; and content particular to your business, training goals, marketing focus, or branding interests), please contact our corporate sales department at corpsales@pearsoned.com or (800) 382-3419.

For government sales inquiries, please contact governmentsales@pearsoned.com.

For questions about sales outside the U.S., please contact intlcs@pearson.com.

Visit us on the Web: informit.com/aw

Library of Congress Control Number: 2018946904

ISBN-13: 978-0-13-487326-8
ISBN-10: 0-13-487326-2

1   18

Editor-in-Chief
Mark L. Taub

Acquisitions Editors
Laura Lewin
Malobika Chakraborty

Development Editor
Christopher Zahn

Technical Reviewer
Dax Gazaway

Managing Editor
Sandra Schroeder

**Full-Service
Production Manager**
Julie B. Nahil

Project Editor
Dhayanidhi Karunanidhi

Copy Editor
Stephanie M. Geels

Indexer
Cheryl Lenser

Proofreader
Abigail Manheim

To Gloriana, my {^C testingcheats on Sims.add_Buff e_Buff_Happy}

Contents

PREFACE

Kids these days, let me tell 'ya. Back in my day, if you wanted to rent a game, you went to the video rental place and...What's that? Oh, it was a building that had tapes of the movies you could watch...Tapes. They came on tapes. Quiet, let me finish. You had whatever was in stock to choose from. If all they had on hand was ActRaiser for the Super Nintendo, then you rented ActRaiser again, by God.

There were 721 Super Nintendo (Super NES) games released over the 8-year lifespan of the system in North America. If you had access to every game, then you would have the possibility of playing a new game every 4 days. This was a little better than the Nintendo Entertainment System (NES). That console had 679 games released in North America over a 10-year lifespan, or a new game every 5 and a quarter days, give or take. Assuming that you were savvy enough to avoid the truly terrible releases (I, for instance, was not savvy enough to avoid Where's Waldo in my cartridge rental days), you could feasibly play every game worth playing.

Fast forward (to continue my tape references) to 2017. There are few rental locations as we have digital distribution networks that put entire catalogs of games ready at a moment's access. Steam, a service run by Valve, is the 800-lb gorilla in the PC game distribution arena. SteamSpy, an independent site, claims that 4,859 games were released on Steam in 2016 alone. That averages out to over 13 games per day, not counting other services that provide games like itch.io or web game portals. And let us not forget about those old console games. They keep a steady business.

Of course, we no longer only play games on dedicated hardware. Phones and tablets have taken over as a pillar of the gaming ecosystem. PocketGamer.biz estimates that Apple's App Store added 280,595 games submissions in 2016 for its iOS devices. This amounts to a paltry 768 submissions per day. There are more games submissions per day on iOS than there were games for the NES or Super NES's entire lifespan. Naturally, this number ignores games unique to the Android or Windows Phone environments exclusively.

Many game players these days forget about board games, which are in a renaissance of their own. The site BoardGameGeek.com lists over 400 games with a ranking in their database among 2016 releases and has many more 2016 releases without a ranking. One of the world's biggest board game fairs, the *Internationale Spieltage* or "Spiel" in Essen, Germany, had more than 1,000 exhibitors in 2016.

And that is just 2016. Woe be to you to keep up if you take a year off from gaming. Personally, I find it easier to buy games and never play them. I have more than 600 games in my Steam library, and steamdb.info reports that I haven't played 216 of them. Money well spent.

Understandably, efforts exist to curate this tsunami of game releases into something manageable for players bound by human timescales and wallets. This curation cuts down player attention to the largest releases. No Zelda or Mass Effect is going to sneak under the radar. Mobile games, especially, are curated in part by a kind of leaderboard that shows the games that have the most downloads or revenue. This forms a rich-get-richer marketplace where the only way to be noticed is to already have been noticed and successful.

Curation itself has issues for game players who just want to "keep up." "Let's Play" reviewers have exploded in number on YouTube. Live streaming viewership is up. Amazon's billion-dollar purchase of the live streaming service Twitch seems prescient given Twitch's 2 million broadcasters and 10 million daily active users. How do you find a good YouTuber or Twitch streamer? Well, you could look at a view count or other leaderboard, but these have the same positive feedback loop problems as the mobile games leaderboards. Or you could find a curated list of approved streamers. *Quis custodiet ipsos custodes?* Who curates the curators?

In many fields, we've delegated the task of curation to algorithms. Music is a field that has experienced a similar explosion of production over the last two decades. Many of us trust services like Pandora and Spotify to act as curators. To some extent, they are successful. But they tend to give us more of what we already said we liked. Netflix will not stop recommending superhero shows (which I really don't like in general) because I watched Jessica Jones on my account.

The extent to which we have knowledge of what will actually be best for us and algorithms can capitalize on that is debatable. Only 7% of marriages in 2015 had their relationship paired via an online dating algorithm. Facebook and Twitter have helped sort us into political echo chambers by suggesting that we follow people who confirm our existing biases and thus seem like effective news sources. In games, metrics-based design is a type of algorithmic conformity that values what is already popular as what should be designed. It is why every successful mobile game seems to require a screaming guy as its app icon (see Chapter 12, "The Clone Wars").

Before Gutenberg's printing press revolutionized publishing, it may have been possible to read every book that was released. In the 15th century, it became impossible to confidently stay abreast of all published knowledge. By the 19th century, Alexander von Humboldt and Goethe were said to have been able to hold all collected human knowledge, although that is certainly disputable. Here in the 21st century, we've given up on the proposition that one person should know about every issue and every field (except in election years).

In place of that, we've specialized ourselves. It is still possible to know everything there is to know about small subcategories of human knowledge. I feel confident that the top brain surgeons keep up with all of the burgeoning information regarding their field. I know that on the Internet there exists someone with a complete understanding of every episode of "Bob's Burgers." Somewhere else exists the definitive champion of all information regarding the Kennedy assassination. The deluge of human knowledge gets channeled out into a wide delta of specialties, and that's largely okay.

Our understanding of games is a microcosm in that delta. Where one could previously keep abreast of every interesting development, so too will we need to specialize. Just as the Kennedy assassination expert only really needs to care about the works that touch her sphere of interest, we too can pare down our diet of information consumption to fit our interests and needs. My specialty is game design. I examine all kinds of subjects through that lens but do not limit myself to only works directly about my specialty. When I read a book about social psychology, I'm usually thinking about how that applies to games. But more importantly, when I play games, I am thinking about how the design of the game can teach game designers.

The game design students I teach are a wide range of ages. Many are older than I am. So when I reference classic arcade or console games, I used to take it as given that the class knew what I was talking about. Recently, one of my staff came to me and told me that he was talking to a class about the constant health drain mechanic in Gauntlet to a sea of glazed expressions. When he polled his class, not a single student had played a Gauntlet game. That was surprising. More recently, I was discussing with a class the tank-style controls in Katamari Damacy and received the self-same expression indicating lack of understanding. Surely, they had played Katamari Damacy. It was one of the more clever titles of the 2000s. Then I remembered that while it had recognition among game designers of the 2000s, my students that were right out of high school were 5 years old when it was released.

This book exists as a narrow type of non-algorithmic curation. Which games should game designers be playing in order to further advance their knowledge that is instrumental in the craft? I give a wide variety of examples in the following pages. However, like the polymath born after the proliferation of the printing press, I can only pull from examples that have been visible to me through my own use of curators. That will necessarily leave holes. I welcome anyone who has a game or an experience that would help illustrate the practice of game design to get in contact with me so I can add it to this ever-growing playlist of games worthy to teach game designers.

What This Book Is and Is Not

For this book, I want to highlight games that have something to teach current and upcoming game designers or those who are simply curious about game design. Some of these games will be among the most popular games of all time. For these, I will explain what aspect or aspects of the game novice designers might not necessarily appreciate. Other games will be obscure and will be worth mentioning because of their novelty, or even a gimmick that may be able to be reappropriated in a different context. It is my hope that after reading about this collection of games, you will attempt to play as many as possible and use the experiences to broaden your approach when faced with your own game design problems.

It is perhaps as important to explain what I do not intend to use as selection criteria for the games listed.

First, this book is not a collection of good games, whatever that means. I think many of these games are good. Some are my all-time favorites. Others I really do not like to play. Many lists that attempt to collate "books writers must read" and "movies film students much watch" are just lists of what the author thinks are good works to consume. That kind of list would be sufficient if my goal were to simply provide you with sources of good play experiences, but as I have stated, that is not my goal. I want to separate the notion of a game that is good because it is fun to play or aesthetically pleasing from the notion of a game that is good at teaching game designers a particular element of craft.

Additionally, I want to eliminate the inclusion of games solely because of their historical significance. Spacewar! is, of course, a natural part of any list of the most important games of all time. However, playing Spacewar! in the present day is not a particularly enlightening experience in terms of how play should direct the design of modern games. We've simply come a long way since then. However, playing Centipede is helpful to modern designers because of its use of triangulation and how it addresses hardware limitations, evergreen topics for those wishing to solve similar problems.

An entire encyclopedia could be filled with great design examples from older games. However, I've chosen to shy away from games that had fantastic design innovations or implementations that have largely become a part of the design zeitgeist over time. Deus Ex, for example, has its prints all over nearly every 3D action game of the past two decades. But if you go back and play the original Deus Ex, you will see how iteration has improved upon those huge first leaps since. Thus, while Deus Ex is one of the greatest games of all time because of what it was in 2000, a modern designer can better learn about stealth mechanics and level design from 2016's Dishonored 2.

While some of the entries will be included largely based on what they represent thematically, I want to stress how those thematic choices foment a game where a player makes meaningful decisions in context. It is the player's decisions that form the crux of his playing experience (see my previous book, aptly named *Players Making Decisions*), and so a game designer's work should be largely about creating the decision space in which the game operates.

Finally, while I reserve the right to make some exceptions, I do want the games listed to be largely playable by you, the reader, if what I explain sounds interesting. It is of no use to you if I tell you about a game that is really informative but is no longer playable in any reasonable way.

I am not a game historian. There are many scholars and enthusiasts who spend their professional careers on the Sisyphean pursuit of the preservation and cataloging of a small fraction of the games that exist. Preservers of books have it easy in comparison; an 80-year-old copy of *The Hobbit* is readable as is. But if you want to play The Hobbit 1982 text adventure game for the ZX Spectrum, you first have to find a way to emulate the entire hardware of the ZX Spectrum itself. It's as if you would have to create an artificial eye to read an old book.

Not being a game historian means that I am largely pulling from my own limited experience and that of my friends and colleagues. This work is not intended to be a *corpore ludos,* or a complete curriculum of games. Hopefully, it serves to guide you toward experiences that challenge, teach, confuse, and, of course, entertain.

Game Awareness Survey

As part of my research for this book, I conducted a non-scientific survey that included hundreds of game design students, faculty, professional game designers and lay persons. I asked them to rate approximately 100 games on a scale of familiarly from "I have played this game" to "I have not heard of this game."

This entire project started when one of my staff at the university at which I teach told me that he was trying to use the classic arcade game Gauntlet as an example in his Game Mechanics course, and when he polled his students, 0% of them had ever heard of Gauntlet. This was surprising to him and to me, and I wondered why. It couldn't be a generational effect because we have a pretty diverse distribution of students by age. Was it just a thing game designers of a particular age knew and everyone else didn't?

In my survey, I collected demographics on age and professional status along with the familiarity of various titles in the hopes of isolating some sort of explanatory factor. I was unsuccessful along those lines. Neither age nor professional status had any statistically significant explanatory power over the familiarity of respondents to titles. However, I did receive enough data to glean a spectrum wherein I could classify a game's level of obscurity in the popular culture.

Two of my entries were inspired, in part, by a 2016 Chapman University study on conspiracy theories. They wanted to investigate which conspiracy theories Americans believed and what factors implied higher susceptibility to conspiracy belief. They found, for example, that 54.3% of Americans surveyed agreed or strongly agreed that the government was concealing information about the 9/11 attacks. And 30.2% believed that the government was concealing information about then-President Barack Obama's birth certificate. But most interesting was a control element that they added. They asked whether respondents believed the government was concealing information about "the North Dakota crash," a conspiracy created specifically for this survey. With that statement, 7.5% of respondents strongly agreed and 32.5% agreed or strongly agreed.

Similarly, I decided that two of my hundred examples in the Game Awareness Survey would also be made up. The first, "Fantasy Guild Online (2006)" sounds pretty real. Surprisingly, putting those words in that order only results in five Google hits. Approximately 3% of my respondents said they had played it. Approximately 20% said they were familiar with it in some way.

My other fake entry was "Polybius (1981)." This was a risky fake entry because it does have some cultural validity. Polybius was the name of an arcade game in a 1980s urban legend. Supposedly, it appeared in Oregon arcades, where it caused players to become addicted and entranced. Then, black-suited anonymous figures from a vague yet menacing government agency would collect information from the arcade machines every night, taking the data back to analyze the game's psychoactive properties or to recruit high-scoring players a la *The Last Starfighter*. Another 3% of my respondents said they had played Polybius. (But a different 3% from the Fantasy Guild Online players! No one said they had played both games.) Approximately 16% said they were familiar with Polybius in some way. I obviously didn't ask about the urban legend aspect of it, but if 20% said they were familiar with Fantasy Guild Online, which has no online references at all, the urban legend effect is likely minimal.

From the survey results, I constructed a measure of a game's awareness. Games with a score of 33.3% or lower, I considered to have a high cultural awareness. These included a diverse range of games for different audiences and media such as Metal Gear Solid, Bejeweled, Sudoku, Dungeons and Dragons, and The Settlers of Catan. I only cover these games in the book if a particular aspect about them deserves attention. Games with a 66.7% or higher I considered to have a low cultural awareness. These games receive much more specificity with regard to their rules and systems in the text of this book. My fake entries received scores of approximately 94% by this metric—10% of games included in my survey are considered more obscure than these fake titles. I've included each one of those super obscure games in this book. I'll leave it as an exercise for the reader to figure out which games these are.

What This Book Covers

To give you a preview of what the book covers, I provide a short description of each chapter.

Chapter 1, "From Simplicity, The Universe," covers Go, one of the most elegant and beautiful games humankind has ever created, and how humans are no longer the pinnacle of its play.

Chapter 2, "Randomness and Cholesterol," discusses the role of randomness in games and how designers consider randomness.

Chapter 3, "Pushing One's Luck," discusses games in which the player controls the influence of luck to some extent.

Chapter 4, "Piecemeal Perspectives," discusses games that deliver experiences with interesting narrative techniques.

Chapter 5, "Permanence," discusses games where challenge is front and center, often to the player's consternation.

Chapter 6, "Mechanics as Message," discusses games that have authorial meaning communicated through the game's mechanics.

Chapter 7, "Requiem for a Pewter Shoe," discusses games that change their own rules.

Chapter 8, "The Second Chance Phenomenon," covers Magic: The Gathering—one of the most referenced games for game designers—and how aspects of that game appear in a vast array of different types of games.

Chapter 9, "Challenging Complexity," discusses games that have simple rules but deep dynamic play.

Chapter 10, "Learning to Walk," discusses the bane of players everywhere: the game tutorial. Every game needs to teach players how to play it, unfortunately, so games that do this in a transparent and effective manner are worthy of discussion.

Chapter 11, "Mechanics in Milieu," discusses games in which the mechanics cannot be considered in isolation but instead as part of a cultural whole.

Chapter 12, "The Clone Wars," discusses the dicey topics of game cloning and originality.

Chapter 13, "The Discipline of Game Design," discusses games that have something to say about the process of game design itself.

Chapter 14, "Winning and Losing," discusses games that do not use a traditional one-versus-all structure and dynamics that result from that decision.

Chapter 15, "Inputs and Outputs," discusses games where play is not directed by traditional joystick inputs or button presses.

Chapter 16, "Whose Stories?" returns to themes from Chapter 4 but focuses on narrative experiences that extend the concept of narrator.

Chapter 17, "Cheat Codes," focuses on the concept of cheating. But then I cheat and talk about some games that I couldn't fit in any other chapter. This is your warning.

Chapter 18, "Conclusion and Final Playlist," is a short conclusion of sorts with an aside about designer mindset.

Register your copy of *The Game Designer's Playlist* on the InformIT site for convenient access to updates and/or corrections as they become available. To start the registration process, go to informit.com/register and log in or create an account. Enter the product ISBN (9780134873268) and click Submit. Look on the Registered Products tab for an Access Bonus Content link next to this product, and follow that link to access any available bonus materials. If you would like to be notified of exclusive offers on new editions and updates, please check the box to receive email from us.

ACKNOWLEDGMENTS

You would think that second books would be easier than first books, but I work hard to make things difficult for myself.

As always, I first have to thank my wife Gloriana, who picks me up when I need it most. Which is basically all of the time.

Thanks to all the folks with whom I've discussed the book and who have helped by reviewing drafts, especially Dax Gazaway and Kingsley Montgomery. Everything that is professional about this book is due to the work of the good folks at Pearson, Laura Lewin and Malobika Chakraborty, and my development editor, Chris Zahn.

Also, thanks to all the folks out there who warmly received my first book, *Players Making Decisions,* and have used it in their classes or studios. Say nice things to authors whose work you like. It really makes a difference to hear.

ABOUT THE AUTHOR

Zack Hiwiller is a game designer, educator, and author living in Orlando, Florida. He has been a game designer for large publishers and small, independent developers. He is also a department chair in the game design program at Full Sail University and is the author of *Players Making Decisions: Game Design Essentials and the Art of Understanding Your Players.*

CHAPTER 1

FROM SIMPLICITY, THE UNIVERSE

"Man is not born to solve the problem of the
universe, but to find out what he has to do;
and to restrain himself within the limits of his
comprehension."

—Johann Wolfgang von Goethe

In a commencement address in 2005, writer David Foster Wallace
relayed this parable: "There are these two young fish swimming along
and they happen to meet an older fish swimming the other way, who
nods at them and says, 'Morning, boys. How's the water?' [...] [T]he two
young fish swim on for a bit and eventually one of them looks over at
the other and goes, 'What the hell is water?'" One needs awareness of all
the things around us that are so taken for granted that they are invisible.
We start our examination of games with one of the most popular games
of all time, one that few in the West bother to explore.

A Universe, Conquered

Imagine for a moment that your life to this point took a different path. Imagine instead that since the age of five you were enrolled in a school specifically to train you to be an expert doctor. Your country, small on the world stage but important nonetheless, venerates the skills of doctors fervently, especially their ability to diagnose troublesome cases. Competition among medical students is cutthroat, and only the most rigorous study habits and keenest intuitions can vault a small percentage of students into the ranks of professional diagnosticians. People with lower skill levels still work, of course, but only the best can make a living on just their ability to diagnose. Imagine further that this skill is so venerated that it becomes a bit of a national pastime. Diagnosing is medicine, sure, but it also fills part of the cultural identity—a combination of philosophy and art.

You, after years and years of hard work, have become the world leader in diagnosis. This isn't braggadocio; it is fact. A world ranking system makes this explicit. You spent a few years at the amateur level and have since climbed rank after rank of professionals. You are now a Rank-9 professional and the best in the world. Your services are in high demand, and you have obtained celebrity status. At only 33 years old, you look forward to decades in which to practice your craft at the highest level.

Then you get an odd invitation. A computer company thinks they can make a program that out-intuits the best doctors and they will give you a bunch of money to go head to head. That is fine—many have tried in the past. But the task of diagnosis is just too vast for computers to master. They do fine, certainly. One would take the diagnosis of a specialized computer program over the random guess of a guy on the street, but the art of diagnosis is too nuanced and vast for a computer to compete with the best. Maybe in a generation or two when artificial intelligence (AI) approaches the level of human complexity it will be possible, but right now? No. Easy money.

You accept. The competition is shown live on your country's television networks and streamed to enthusiasts around the world. Expert panelists come on before the competition to repeat what everyone already knows: The human body is too complex. While computers do a good job at approximating human performance, it will be a long time before they can exceed it.

The point of all of this confidence leads to an obvious narrative conclusion. You lose to the computer. In front of your adoring countrymen, in front of the world, your entire worldview must change. Everything for which you've trained your entire life and everything you've believed about the intuitive nature of diagnosis is about to change. Where once you could be confident that your skills had worth, now it is possible with a little infrastructure that anyone could have access to the same (or greater!) power through their phones. What would you do? What would the country do? What would the world do?

To an extent, this is the story of Lee Sedol. In 2016, he, as a Go world champion, was beaten in a best of five series by an AI developed by DeepMind called AlphaGo. And to a shocked community of Go players, it wasn't even close.

In Lee's home country of South Korea, Go is part of the cultural identity. There are Go academies that train hopeful prodigies from their kindergarten days to become professional Go players. A rigid hierarchy of Go castes clearly delineates skill levels, and only four players each year become professionals.

Lee was supposed to win. In interviews before the match, Lee stressed that he was not considering the possibility of losing the five-game series, only that he had to focus on not losing one of the five games. Among online Go communities (at least the English-speaking ones I can find), the outlook was curious confidence. Estimates of Sedol losing one game ranged from 50% to 80%, but odds of Sedol losing three or more of the five-game series tended to be at 10% or lower. Professional gambling outlets had a more even outlook, putting an AlphaGo series victory at around 50%.

Lee lost game one. Then the next day, he lost game two. Then two days later, he lost game three and the series. Game four, Lee won. AlphaGo finished the series winning game five.[1] Lee never won as black, considered the more challenging color.

Journalists made much hay comparing the match to a 1997 match between world Chess champion Garry Kasparov and IBM's Deep Blue AI. Deep Blue won the 1997 series, which was then heralded as a watershed in the human-computer relationship. *Time*'s article about the match at the time had the headline "Can Machines Think?" The similarities are there: the confident human champion, the skeptical enthusiast community, the valuing of human adaptability versus algorithmic power. However, there is a key difference that makes AlphaGo's victory much more interesting, and it has to do with the nature of the game itself.

The Simplicity and Complexity of Go

Go is an ancient game, assumed to be one of the most ancient board games in continuous play. It is a strategy board game for two players. In the form played by Lee and AlphaGo, players sit on opposite sides of a board that has a 19 × 19 grid. More casual versions of the game use a smaller grid. One player has a pool of black stones, the other white. Players take turns placing stones on the grid's intersections in the hopes of capturing opponent's stones by positioning and increasing the amount of board territory they control.

Key to the game of Go is the concept of *liberty*. A stone has liberty if there is an empty space horizontally or vertically from it on the grid. A stone with no liberty is removed from the

---

1. While Sedol was a world champion, he was ranked #5 in the world. AlphaGo later beat the world-ranked #1 player in three straight games to much less fanfare in 2017.

board. In the Figure 1.1, white's stone marked #1 has liberties at A and B. Since C is diagonal, it doesn't count as a liberty. White's stone #2 has only one liberty: A. If black plays at A, stone #2 will be captured. In Go terms, stone #2 is in *atari*.[2]

Stones of the same color placed horizontally or vertically become a chain, or essentially one big connected stone. A stone within a chain can have liberty and stay on the board, but the chain must have liberty somewhere. In Figure 1.1, black's stone #3 has no liberty itself, but is connected to the stone to its left, to the stone above it, and through that stone to the stone above and right. That chain of stones acts as one and has only one liberty: D. Thus, the whole chain is in atari.

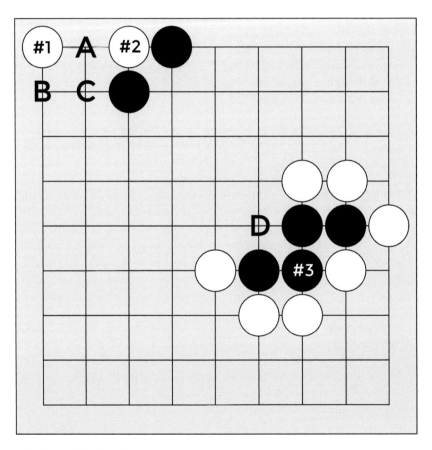

Figure 1.1 A sample Go board

The only other rule of note is that you cannot make a placement that reverts the board back to the state that it was before your last turn, a fix to eliminate infinite loops. Players go back and forth capturing or protecting territory by placing stones. The goal is to hold as much territory as possible.

---

2. Nolen Bushnell named the pioneering game company Atari after this bit of Go terminology.

What seems strange to players familiar with Checkers, Chess, or other abstract strategy games is that the game has no capture that marks the end of the game. Instead, the game continues until both players pass. Practically speaking, the game continues until one player resigns feeling he is in too weak of a position to come back.

We will come back time and again to the comparisons of Go to Chess for a number of reasons. First, Chess is well understood by western audiences. Second, the similarities between Kasparov's loss to Deep Blue and Lee's loss to AlphaGo are significant. Finally, Chess is aesthetically similar enough to Go that it has relevant parallels.

Go is a conceptually simple game: The only weapon in the game is where to place a single stone. Compare this to Chess, in which each piece may have a different means of capture. While there are no "piece types" in Go, a position in Chess matters for both its location and the type of piece there. If you can capture a queen in Chess, it is often a good idea, no matter its location on the board. Go is more egalitarian. Every piece is not of equal worth, but it can certainly look that way on the surface.

Combinatorics illustrates the large problem spaces of both Chess and Go. For a trivially simple game such as "What hand is the penny in?" the "board states" there can only be: {left hand:penny; right hand:nothing} or {left hand:nothing, right hand:penny}.

Tic-tac-toe is a comparatively simple game that actually contains some level of strategy as compared to the pure luck of our penny game. There are nine locations on the board. Each location can have an X, an O, or be empty. Thus, there are 3^9 or 19,683 possibilities. Of course, since some of those boards can never exist because of the rules (all 9 Xs, for example), we can reduce that down to 5,812 legal board states[3] in a 3 × 3 game of Tic-tac-toe. By this measure, Tic-tac-toe is 2,500 times more complicated than the penny game.

Chess has a board with 64 locations. However, each location is more complex than just white, black, or none. We must consider whether a space has a white pawn, a black knight, or a promoted white queen. Just like we reduced our Tic-tac-toe space to a number of legal boards, the restrictions for legal boards in Chess is more stringent. Not only can we not have 64 white pawns, but we must be careful that a board doesn't put one of the kings in check, among other conditions.

This problem is not trivial. In 1950, mathematician Claude Shannon estimated the number of Chess states as 10^{120}. Later estimates reduced this number to approximately 10^{50} or 100,000,000,000,000,000,000,000,000,000,000,000,000,000,000,000,000. This is considerably larger than our Tic-tac-toe space.

---

3. From http://brianshourd.com/posts/2012-11-06-tilt-number-of-tic-tac-toe-boards.html.

Go strips the location states back down to three. At each location, there can be a black stone, a white stone, or no stone. This makes the upper boundary of the possible Go boards simple: 3^{361}. But like in our previous examples, we have to remove boards that aren't legal. For instance, any board that contains a stone with no liberty must be removed from consideration. In 2016, researchers were finally able to calculate the number of board states. Rather than give you their exact number, it will be easier to think about a nice round estimate of 10^{170}.

We humans have a hard time thinking about exponentials. How much larger is 10^{170} than 10^{50}? For some reason, when we look at these numbers we want to multiply and say that the Go estimate is 4-ish times larger. On the contrary, it is **10^{120} times larger.** If you had a normal-sized Go board that represented each board state, you could fill the entire observable universe with Go boards and still have plenty of boards to place. If you shrunk each Go board down to a single atom, you still wouldn't even have a chance. The universe would run out of room.

The number of game states is large, sure. But that is just one way to look at a game's complexity. Discussing it more would belabor the point. More than just the vastness of the game space is how interconnected it is. If I choose not to make a move because it will give you a better position next turn, I'm said to be looking one move ahead. If I am able to reject a move because it will open up a good position for you in two moves, I can be said to be looking two moves ahead. Depending on how many possible options I have when it's my turn, each move ahead gets exponentially harder. If I had 10 options for next turn, then I have to consider 10×10 options two turns from now. If a move puts me in a bad spot 10 turns from now, I need to be able to see that one of 10,000,000,000 moves. Even if I was to pare that tree down to "reasonable" states, it would still be massive. A turn in Go can have real lasting effects 100 turns later. Few Chess games reach 100 moves in total.

Cognitive theorists debate how many "moves ahead" the human brain is realistically able to hold. There are real limits to the amount of information we can consider. Computers, while faster thinkers than us, have real limits as well. And much like humans, they use the past as a shorthand.

More Than Thinking, Learning

In the late 18th century, audiences marveled at the "Automaton Chess Player," also called the "Mechanical Turk." It was purportedly a mechanical man that could play expert-level Chess. It played against Catherine the Great, Benjamin Franklin, and Napoleon Bonaparte. Charles Babbage, who would later be considered the father of the computer, lost to the Turk twice. Edgar Allen Poe wrote about the machine, purporting it to be a hoax because a "pure" machine should always win.

Poe was right. The Turk was a hoax. Reportedly, during its match with Napoleon it swept the pieces off the table in a rage after Napoleon tested it with a series of illegal moves. That should have been a hint to its mechanisms. The trick was that a grand master Chess player controlled the movements of the automaton using magnets and strings while hidden beneath the Chess board. The clever part of the con was how the human player could be hidden when the mechanisms underneath were opened and examined.

For a long time, the pursuit of a machine that could beat a human was focused on isolated computation. If the best human could look seven moves ahead and a machine eight, then the machine should be able to capitalize on that advantage. However, it turns out that looking farther ahead isn't how high-level players actually play the game well.

Psychologists William Chase and Herbert Simon published a study in the 1970s in which both Chess novices and Chess experts were given patterns of Chess pieces on boards to memorize and recall. Some of the boards were examples from real matches; others were random assortments of pieces. Chess experts were able to recall the patterns from real matches better than the random patterns, whereas novices had equal trouble with both. This lead to the conclusion that at least part of a Chess player's expertise is the ability to compare a current situation with one they have encountered before.

If an expert player plays 10 games of Chess a day every year for 40 years, she could end up with a library of experience of 150,000 games. Her recall would not be perfect, but this could provide a broad range of experience from which to say, "I remember a game like this; I made this move and lost," or "I remember another game like this; I made this move and won." Comparing the two experiences, she could then make the latter move.

The ability to draw on past experiences was essential to one of Kasparov's early victories over Deep Blue. He was able to switch styles on the fly while Deep Blue was using the same hard-coded strategy of what makes for a "good" move. In Kasparov–Deep Blue I, it was not relevant that Deep Blue could evaluate 200 million positions in a single turn if the criteria to determine which of these moves was best was flawed.

AlphaGo benefitted from 20 years of technological advancement in the speed of computers since Deep Blue's victory. But as we've seen, Go itself is exponentially more complicated, and brute force alone would not be the key to winning the game. Instead, AlphaGo does what Kasparov did to succeed: It uses what it knows from the past to determine what the value of a move in the present game might be.

Let's use a trivial Chess example. You have two pawns, a rook, and your king; the opponent has one queen, two pawns, a rook, and her king. Who is more likely to win? Your opponent has more pieces, and those pieces are worth more using standard Chess scoring. But what if your pawns are positioned in a way that you can mate the opponent in the next move? Then we need to revise what the opponent's queen is worth in that particular situation. We do that using heuristics. The algorithms that do the evaluation of specific moves are called *value networks*. The networks that determine what to do given the value of the game state are called "policy networks."

The AlphaGo team "trained" its policy algorithms by showing it 30 million examples played by real Go masters to suggest what real masters would do in numerous situations. This would be sufficient if the goal of AlphaGo was to play like a human master, but the goal was to be better than the human masters. So AlphaGo uses what it knows from that database to play the current game against itself a vast number of times, refining its value network—the rules that identify what a particular position is worth—to generate a recommended move.

Here, then, is the relevant difference between Deep Blue and AlphaGo. We told Deep Blue what a good move looked like and it found the best move it could, given time. AlphaGo *tells itself* what a good move looks like given the circumstances and finds the best move it can, given that. And each time it plays, it has more information to guide better and better decisions.

Because what AlphaGo does is now firmly in its black box, we don't really know what the criteria are that guide its search at any given time. We don't tell it that a queen is nine times as valuable as a pawn. We just show it enough games and give it enough time for testing, and it figures that out. In Game 2, Move 37 of the AlphaGo–Lee match, AlphaGo chose a move that its own predictive model, based on its library of professional Go games, identified as having a probability of 1 in 10,000 of being the best move. That is, a professional Go player would almost never consider the move. Lee, shocked by the move, rose from his chair and left the room for a few minutes. AlphaGo went on to win that game.

DeepMind has already created an AI that can play Atari games with only the raw images from the screen as input. The AI is not told the rules of Space Invaders, only that the goal is to maximize the score. Off it goes, playing millions of games, bettering itself, without ever really knowing why Earth needs to be saved from those invaders. While I write this, DeepMind is working on solving StarCraft II using techniques similar to those used by AlphaGo.

To emphasize the speed of developments in the AI world, in the time between writing the first draft of this chapter and my first revisions of it, DeepMind created a derivative AI that taught itself Chess and Shogi (a Japanese cousin of Chess) that could beat the reigning best AIs. And it accomplished this after only being told the rules and simulating games with itself for less than 24 hours.

Play to Win

In October 1990, newspapers across the country ran a panel of Gary Larson's famous *The Far Side* comic called "Hopeful parents." In it, a child plays video games, rapt, while his proud 1950s-style parents look on from behind, sharing a thought balloon of a "Help Wanted" ad in the far future of September 2005. The ad is loaded with pleas for game players: "Do you laugh in the face of Killer Goombas? Call us. $80,000/yr plus a free house."

Philosophers have engaged with the question of humor for centuries, but one explanation that is popular is the benign violation theory. It posits that what we find funny is a violation of expectations with a benign outcome. For instance, seeing someone unexpectedly getting hit with a pie is funny because it is unexpected and has no real consequence. Larson's "Hopeful parents" panel was funny in 1990 because it was unexpected and benign. It was unexpected because who expected someone to get paid to play video games? It is benign because if they are wrong, it isn't like the little boy's friends are all out learning plumbing and accountancy at that age (and even if they were—it is just a cartoon).

But Larson's joke isn't that unexpected anymore. In September 2005, the date the cartoon looks forward to, I was employed as a game designer and my parents had the cartoon hanging in their home. We were stretching the joke a little—being a game designer is about playing games as much as being a chef is about eating food. Skip forward a few years and the unexpected aspect of the joke loses even more focus.

Market intelligence firm Newzoo estimates that eSports will be a $1.4 billion field with an audience of more than 300 million people by 2020. Defense of the Ancients 2 (or Dota2) player Saahil "UNiVeRsE" Arora is reported to have made $2.7 million in tournament prizes (not counting sponsorship revenues). And like any popular sport, betting exists on the periphery. Numerous sites let you bet on popular games like Defense of the Ancients 2, Counter-Strike: Go (not the same Go we covered above, thankfully), or StarCraft II.

The 2006 World Chess Championship was marred by controversy when the manager of one player accused the other of excessive and frequent bathroom breaks, the implication being that when he got into a tough spot, he'd head to the bathroom and receive assistance from a Chess program. As evidence, the manager showed that upon returning from the bathroom, the player's moves corresponded with the recommended move from a popular Chess program 78% of the time.

Whether there was cheating at the event is not particularly relevant here. Samsung received a patent in 2016 for augmented-reality contact lenses that can overlay real vision with computer-generated information. What happens to human Chess competition when those are readily available? Do you ban contact lenses in general? What if the equivalent becomes implantable?

Doping is a constant concern in all sports. Yet doping alone won't make for a great athlete. It simply separates the already elite. A DeepMind-powered AI wiring directly into your vision could allow anyone to compete with the best. When DeepMind's StarCraft II AI is complete, how will eSports audiences know what they are watching is real human performance and not AI driven or AI augmented? What will that do to the viewing experience? If DeepMind can use its techniques on games as wildly different as StarCraft II, Space Invaders, and Go and master them all in a decade, how long will it be before it can at least help with every type of human game?

While Deep Blue was a true supercomputer, consumer-level hardware can now run Chess programs that can beat every player on Earth. Human-versus-human Chess championships are now quaint junior varsity leagues in comparison to the AI versus-AI tournaments.

This can go one of two ways. The first is the optimistic approach. Long ago, we developed machines that can transport us at great speeds and great distances, yet we still have sprinting and distance running. Players aren't using Segways during soccer matches. There is a burden on professional leagues to adhere to a strict set of performance limitations to uphold the sanctity of the game and, while there are some challenges, it works fairly well. The fact that elite cyclists have a high incidence of doping has done nothing to dissuade bikers from hitting the road in cycling contests all over the world. Chess tournaments draw steady participation in this post Deep-Blue-in-your-pocket world. As much of a cultural touchstone as Go is in east Asia, it would be hard to imagine a 2,500-year streak of popularity melted by recent developments.

Even largely technical sports draw a line on what is acceptable. The "formula" in Formula One racing refers to the set of rules for what teams are and are not allowed to include in their car in a given season. Formula One racing is extremely popular despite the reality that it isn't the pinnacle of what is possible in terms of automobile speed; it is the pinnacle of what is possible given a distinct set of rules. These guidelines will help us define the role of sports and games in an increasingly augmented world.

The pessimistic approach ranges from economic dystopia to Armageddon. In 2016, billionaire Elon Musk said that increases in AI and automation will soon make most current jobs obsolete. He should know; his Tesla company is one of the companies developing self-driving trucks that aim to put the world's 20 million truckers in a new career. A 2016 McKinsey study examined the automatability of over 800 careers. It found that 51% of the U.S. economy's activities were susceptible to automation. I, for one, welcome our new robot overlords.

Futurists have gone further. Many estimate that based on past increases in computing power, we should have the ability to digitally simulate the human brain sometime in the next 15 years. After that, who knows? In the 1950s, the great computer scientist Alan Turing said that when machines become more complex than the human brain, the machines would be in control. Others have stated that once machines are artificially intelligent in the general sense, that they would be able to build smarter and smarter machines that we cannot yet imagine. In *Darwin Among the Machines,* George Dyson wrote, "In the game of life and evolution, there are three players at the table: human beings, nature, and machines. I am firmly on the side of nature. But nature, I suspect, is on the side of the machines." I. J. Good, the mathematician and contemporary of Turing, was one of the people responsible for helping popularize Go in the West. He also believed that a smarter-than-human machine would eventually lead to the extinction of mankind.[4]

Summary

We've gotten into some interesting topics. And while they are certainly game related, what do they have to teach game designers? Let's come back for a moment from the world of Godlike machines to the realm of simple game design.

If you exclude basics like the term definitions and end state, Go really has only three rules: adjacent stones of the same color are considered one stone, stones that have no liberty are removed, and you cannot recreate a former board position. A fourth rule can be employed that allows a weaker player to start with additional stones, but this is optional. No other game wrestles such a great amount of complexity of play from such a simple rule set.

Go has no weird rules or edge cases. Even Chess has *en passant* capturing and *castling*, special asterisks that flummox new players for their rare application. Go remains beautiful because of its combination of simplicity and depth.

When designing a game, you will be constantly bombarded by your subconscious with possible additional ideas. Wouldn't it be cool if my main character could fly? Or walk on the ceiling? Wouldn't it be great if my card game had one extra card type? Or my turns had one more phase? So many possibilities could be created! However, there are also bugs and unintended consequences that creep in with new features. Games with more complex rulesets are harder to teach to new players and harder to develop and test. If Go can be described in a paragraph, played for three millennia, and considered the pinnacle of AI development, then does your game *really* need that extra feature?

I've never created a game as simple and as elegant as Go; almost no one has. But understanding Go helps a designer to understand the interplay between rules, systems, and play experience in a way that is difficult to put into words. It is everything essential about game design freeze-dried and preserved for eternity: decision making, aesthetics, tactics, strategy, psychology, philosophy, risk, reward, intuition, and mathematics. It is the essential start for any game designer playlist.

---

4. A really great takedown of this position is at the following link, but is too out-of-scope to cover here: https://backchannel.com/the-myth-of-a-superhuman-ai-59282b686c62

Additionally, and while it seems strange to talk about this given the quintessentially analog nature of the games discussed, AI is a large part of most digital games. Understanding the complexity of how an algorithm plays a simple game like Tic-tac-toe, Nim, or Battleship is a good first step. Understanding how to tackle more complex games like Othello or Backgammon is next. When you consider the complexity of acting humanlike in a game as simple as Checkers, it will help clarify the algorithms required in any other design you may create.

GAMES COVERED

Playlist Game #1: Go

Designer: Unknown

Why: Simply put, Go is one of the most sublime games ever created. A designer that cannot appreciate the game's depth based on the dynamics created by simple rules is a designer that will have trouble understanding complex interactions in even relatively simple game systems.

CHAPTER 2

RANDOMNESS AND CHOLESTEROL

"Creativity is the ability to introduce order into
the randomness of nature."

—Eric Hoffer

We live in an unfathomably complex world. It is tough to appreciate in
modern times how humanity lacked the understanding of basic natural
phenomena when their entire livelihoods may have been determined by
those same phenomena. If crops failed, an entire village could starve.
To avoid that, there needed to be a cause-and-effect relationship
between a farmer's behavior and the odds of a successful harvest.
Without understanding of the mechanics of weather, chemistry, and
botany, human societies improvised.

A Short History of Randomness

Modern humans have developed greater and greater tools over the centuries to help in our understanding of seemingly incomprehensible relations of cause and effect. Ancient humans (and some modern people as well) often presumed all mysterious phenomena were related. Thus, the unfathomable motions of celestial bodies were used to predict the equally puzzling results of the fertility of livestock or the fortunes of kingdoms. As these outcomes were seemingly random, many religious practices were based on equating the results of an unrelated random process to the natural order. Ancient Germanic tribes would mark wooden sticks with symbols and scatter them on a cloth. The local priest would blindly pick three sticks to reveal the will of God. In an ancient practice called *belomancy,* a person would mark arrows with different possibilities and then shoot them. The arrow that flew the farthest would be the favored result. In a Shinto practice still widely performed today, a parishioner receives a random scrap of paper, called *O-mikuji,* that reveals her fortune.

One method of revealing the mystery of the will of God was through the uncertain rolling of dice in a practice called *cleromancy.* In the saga of Olaf Haraldsson, the medieval Norwegian king challenged a rival ruler to a game of dice casting for the possession of a disputed island. The rival rolled first and rolled two sixes (two six-sided dice being the dominant random determinator long before Monopoly). King Olaf, undeterred, citing his faith in God to win against even a twelve, rolled the dice. The first die showed a six. The second die split in two, showing the six side and the one side. Since King Olaf was then showing thirteen, he won the island.

Before we get too high and mighty on the progress of modernity in cleansing us of these superstitions, a 2016 Chapman University survey found that more Americans believed that rooms could be haunted by evil spirits than believed in the efficacy of vaccines. Almost certainly, we hold a collection of interpretations regarding the incomprehensible elements of our lives, and many of these will turn out to be hogwash.

Random number generation was not always simply used as a means to understand the world. Senet, considered to be the one of the most ancient board games, involves throwing two-sided sticks to randomly determine piece movement toward an end goal (perhaps as an ancient precursor to Backgammon). While Senet had religious connotations, historians believe it was played as a game rather than as a divination exercise.

Pass the Chips

In my introductory game design classes, I often ask students to play LCR. LCR is a dice game where the goal is to be the last player remaining with points. Each player starts with three point chips. On your turn, you roll three dice. These dice have one side that says, "L," one side that says, "R," and one side that says, "C." If you roll an L, you pass a point chip to the player on your left. The roll of an "R" means you pass a chip to the player on your right.

And a "C" means you drop a chip into the center pot, essentially removing it from the game. The remaining three sides of each die contain a dot, meaning that die has no effect. On your turn, you roll a number of dice equal to the number of point chips you have (but no more than three) and pass your chips according to the results. If you have no chips, your turn is skipped, but you can re-enter play if another player gives you chips. The game continues until only one player has chips. As the game is negative-sum (i.e., the center chips never come back), the game has a finite length.

I will skip my pedagogical journey in which I lead students to tell me that the reason the game is enjoyable for the audience (to those who like the game) is not in the game itself, it is in the experience of uncertainty. Players themselves often do not find the experience rewarding as play, but as a communal activity. "It would be a good drinking game," they say. When I probe that line of questioning, I ask them to compare it to drinking games with uncertainty that also give the player some agency; games like Beer Pong, Flip Cup, Cards Against Humanity, and even Jenga all rate higher as games to play while drinking.

LCR entirely plays itself. While my students are not a representative sample of the market at large (they are certainly demographically different), it does not take long for them to discover that a game of pure luck needs something else (e.g., physical stakes, chemical impairment) to remain viable.

There is a dichotomy, especially among games enthusiasts, that since a game of luck on its own offers little for any normally developed adult, then luck and skill exist on a spectrum. In this view, skill-based mechanics are pure and luck-based mechanics are strictly inferior—the more luck you add to the game, the more diluted the solution becomes. Given this view, FreeCell is essentially superior to Klondike Solitaire. They have nominally similar mechanics, but one (Klondike) adds an element of luck that makes it less pure. That dichotomy can only hold if there is only one kind of luck that stands opposed to skill.

As a purely normative counterexample, we would expect if games of skill were *a priori* better than games of chance that we would see those preferences revealed in the market. In documents pertaining to a 2009 lawsuit, the company behind LCR revealed that it sells 500,000 copies of the game *per year.* This is an astonishing number for any game, let alone a game that offers no player agency or decision making.

Mate

Sid Sackson was a prolific board game historian and designer. His collection on his death in 2002 was estimated at 18,000 games. In his 1969 book, *A Gamut of Games,* he details one of his great finds, called Mate. Sackson translated an otherwise lost 1915 German pamphlet written by G. Capellen and brought the game to wider attention.

In Mate, players play with only 20 cards out of the standard 52-card French deck. They use the ranks of aces, 10s, kings, queens, and 7s. The ranks have power in that order: Aces are strongest and 7s are weakest. The object of the game is to force the opponent into a position in which he cannot play a card in response, which is called *mate.* Suits are ranked with clubs as the highest, followed by spades, then hearts, with diamonds at the bottom.

To start, players shuffle all 20 cards together and deal 10 to each player *face up.* It is always known what the other player has. A starting player is randomly chosen. That player chooses and plays one of the cards. The opponent must match the suit played. If he cannot, he must match the rank played.

If both players play a card, then the higher-ranking card leads the next pair of cards to be played. For instance, you lead a 10 of spades. I have no spades, so I must play a 10. I play the 10 of hearts. Since spades outrank hearts, you get to start the next pair. If I had no 10s and no spades, you would win the round.

If players play 10 pairs (and thus run out of cards) the round is a draw.

When a player wins a round, the winning player scores based on the rank of the card that caused mate. Aces are worth 11, 10s are worth 10, kings 4, queens 3, and 7s 7. Multiply this by the pair in the round. For instance, if above was the seventh pair of the round and you mated me by playing a 10, you would score 7 × 10, or 70 points.

For the second round, players *swap their hands of 10 cards.* What you had to work with in the first round, I now have to work with and what I had you now have. After the second round, the player with the most points wins.

By swapping hands, the luck of the initial draw is completely evened out. Additionally, since a player can see his opponent's cards, he knows exactly before playing if a player can follow or be mated. Thus, it becomes a game of baiting a player into giving up a card that he will need for his defense later.

On my first play of Mate, I personally found the ranking system a bit confusing. 7s are worth 7 points but are ranked lower than a queen that is worth 3 points? I provide two solutions for this. Either keep the table in Figure 2.1 handy, or you can use a special deck of cards I made for playing Mate that is available through DriveThruCards at http://www.drivethrucards.com/product/206868/Mate.

For my redesign, I got rid of the standard French deck suits and numbers (see Figure 2.2). Suit is replaced by the height and color of the square in the left column. If that cannot be matched, compare the position of the icon on the right column. The score multiplier is printed on each card. Since the queen/king is represented by a cup/meditating person, there is no cognitive dissonance as there is when battling with the concept that a queen and king rank between a 7 and a 10. I have submitted this redesign to the Mate entry at Board-GameGeek.com and have it available as a pay-what-you-want title at DriveThruCards.

	Best				Worst
Best	A♣	10♣	K♣	Q♣	7♣
	A♠	10♠	K♠	Q♠	7♠
	A♥	10♥	K♥	Q♥	7♥
Worst	A♦	10♦	K♦	Q♦	7♦
	11 pts	10 pts	4 pts	3 pts	7 pts

Figure 2.1 Mate scoring

Figure 2.2 Revised Mate card

Once you have played a few rounds, you may add the rule of *foreplacing.* In foreplacing at the start of a round, you show your opponent a card that you will remove from your hand for the rest of the game. Either player may do this, but it will limit the amount of cards you have available and make it easier for the opponent to mate. As compensation, your pair multiplier will increase by one during scoring if you win. In the above example, you won on the seventh pair, so you would get $(7+1) \times 10$ or 80 points if you foreplaced a card.

If you ever cannot play because you lack a card due to foreplacing, you may use your card from the last pair as your card.

An additional advanced rule is the concept of *overmating.* An overmate is a mate done on the last possible turn after foreplacing. In that case, your score is doubled. Say that you mated with an ace of clubs on the tenth pair after having foreplaced. You would receive $(10+1) \times 11 \times 2$ or 242 points.

Both foreplacing and overmating add additional strategic tension to the game.

Stranger and Stranger Danger

After playing a few games of Mate, try changing up the rules. I call this variant Stranger. Stranger keeps all the rules of Mate except the following:

- Secretly remove two cards at random before dealing. Each player receives only nine cards.
- Hands are secret information.

What is the experience of playing Stranger versus playing Mate? Try it before reading further.

The dynamics of Stranger are immediately different. Because two cards are removed, you cannot always know precisely what is in your opponent's hand. The only way to know that a player is out of spades is to either have all remaining spades in your hand or to play a spade and have your opponent follow rank instead of suit. The strategy of the game relies more on guesswork than in luring your opponent into a trap. This guesswork makes the scoring seem arbitrary. Where in Mate, you can achieve a high score by timing your coup-de-grace at the latest moment, in Stranger your winning moves tend to come by surprise. This makes the game less strategic and more reliant on good fortune. In Stranger, the second round has more information than the first as a player with an excellent memory should be able to deduce which cards are removed when he sees his second-round hand.

Stranger isn't necessarily a bad variant, but it is less a game of pure strategy. It feels more like a two-player variant of Hearts in which some skill is required, but poor estimations of hidden information and poor starting positions may weigh the odds in one player's favor before the first turn has commenced.

Now let's try a further variant I am calling Stranger Danger:

- Deal ten cards to each player *face down* as their deck. There is no foreplacing of cards.
- Players draw the top two cards as their hand from their deck. These are public information and are shown face up.

- When players lead a pair, they play a card from their hand.
- When players respond to the opponent, they must match the suit from a card in their hand. If they cannot, they must match the rank with a card in their hand. If they can do neither, they play the top card from their deck. If the top card matches suit or rank, play continues. Otherwise, the round is over. Score as in Mate.

Stranger Danger, on its face, looks like Mate but plays like War and is much less satisfying. There is some level of decision making; you look at the opponent's hand to determine which, if any, of your hand cards will cause the opponent to need to have a lucky card draw. Sometimes your opponent will be saved by the luck of the draw. It is the paean to uncertainty that students saw as a virtue in LCR but seems hollow and unfulfilling after playing Mate.

Stranger and Stranger Danger are small variants mechanically. They offer a few bullet points of changes each. But removing information in Stranger and agency in Stranger Danger weakens both experiences. Mate has randomness. There can be challenging hands. But even without hand-swapping between rounds, Mate provides a strategic experience that is lost in the listed variants. Stranger Danger isn't worse than Mate because it is a game more dependent on luck than Mate. It is worse than Mate because its decision making is less interesting. Tic-tac-toe is less dependent on randomness than Mate, but few would find Tic-tac-toe to be the superior experience. Mate is a trick-taking game in the family of games like War and Spades. To the luck-skill spectrum believers, a trick-taking game with even less randomness than Mate is Goofspiel.

Goofspiel

Goofspiel is a trick-taking game designed by American mathematician Merrill Flood in the 1930s. Each player receives every card of a suit, ace (low) through king (high). An unplayed suit becomes the prize deck and is shuffled. Each turn, one of the prizes is revealed. Each player chooses a card and simultaneously reveals it. The higher card wins the prize card. After 13 rounds, every card from the prize deck will be divvied up and every card in the players' hands will have been played. Each prize card is valued at its face (aces are 1 point, 2s are 2 points...up to kings at 13 points). The player with the most points wins.

The only randomness in Goofspiel is the order of the prize cards. Everything else is up to the players. Knowledge of what cards players have remaining is perfect since each player knows what cards their opponent starts with and what cards they have played. It merely becomes a game of chicken, hoping your opponent will choose a card only slightly lower than your own. If your opponent chooses a higher card, then she wins the trick. If she chooses a much lower card, then you win, but she keeps her higher cards for later.

The form of Goofspiel is what mathematicians call a "Colonel Blotto game" or a "Blotto game." In the original Blotto game, the Colonel has an army of X units and has to go up against his opponent who also has X units on a number of battlefields. He can divide up his X units in any way. If any battlefield has more units of one army than its opponents, the army takes that battlefield. A player wins if his army takes more battlefields than the opponent. This form is seen in many modern board and card games like Battle Line and Hanamikoji.

Is Goofspiel a better game than Mate because it has less randomness? Would Goofspiel be a better game if you played the prize cards in order from king in the first trick to ace in the thirteenth, thus removing all system randomness from the game? What makes one kind of randomness exciting and another kind stultifying?

In the example of a Blotto game depicted in Figure 2.3, each player has ten soldiers to split amongst five battlefields. The two players secretly decide and reveal simultaneously. The angel player wins the first battlefield 3-2 and the second battlefield 1-0. The devil player wins the third battlefield 5-2 and the fourth battlefield 2-1. The angel player wins the fifth battlefield 3-0 and wins the overall game by having three battlefields to the devil player's two.

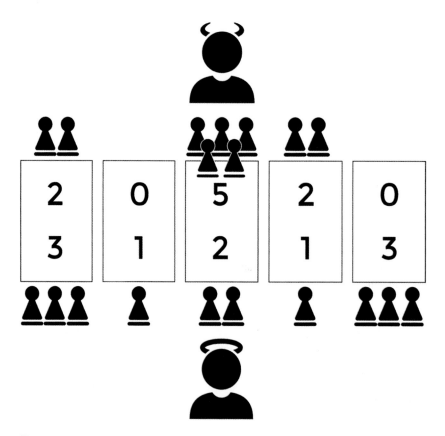

Figure 2.3 A Blotto game

Agency and Uncertainty

On April 15, 2011, the FBI raided the offices of three major businesses, seized $3 billion worth of assets, and arrested the businesses' leaders on charges of fraud. Subprime lenders? Inside traders? Timeshare hucksters? No, the three companies were PokerStars, Full Tilt Poker, and Absolute Poker/Ultimate Bet. Together they served a large portion of the online poker market in the United States. Authorities charged these companies with violating the 2006 Unlawful Internet Gambling Enforcement Act, a law which targets online sports betting.

The next year, Lawrence DiCristina was arrested for running a for-profit poker club in a New York City warehouse. In his case, lawyers argued that since poker is a game of skill, statutes forbidding profiting on games of chance did not apply. A district court agreed. A higher court overturned that ruling, stating that poker contains "a sufficient element of chance to constitute gambling under that state's laws." How much chance or randomness is sufficient? The question of luck versus skill has major real-world implications.

Golf is a sport enjoyed by millions with a solid professional circuit. Dustin Johnson, the 2016 PGA Player of the Year, won over $9 million in tournament prizes that year (not including earnings from sponsorships). Despite Johnson's obvious overwhelming skill, golf is still a game of great uncertainty. Golfers will not be able to anticipate every slight wind gust, every minuscule depression in a green, or every slick blade of grass that ends up affecting the trajectory of their shots. Great golfers, like great poker players, have to play in a way that manages that uncertainty better than their opponents.

I've purposely been playing fast and loose with two terms to this point: Luck and unpredictability or randomness[1] are far from the same thing. A spectrum between luck and skill is possible, but not in the way that most use it. The luck-skill spectrum is not a measure of mechanisms but instead a measure of how much agency a player has over his own objectives. A novice Texas Hold'em Poker player will have less agency over his ability to succeed than a pro will despite having the same random distribution of cards.

In Mate and Stranger Danger, players have different amounts of agency over their play. In Mate, despite having a random assortment of cards from which to play, a skilled player can beat a novice in most instances. Upsets rarely happen in the lowest-randomness games and sports. There are few upsets in Olympic weightlifting, for example.

Sports with more uncertain outcomes foster great underdog stories. In soccer, an unpredictable awkward bounce near the goal can be the difference between victory and defeat.

---

1. I want to avoid a discussion of what it means to be truly random here. For our purposes, we will use randomness as shorthand for uncertainty generated by the system and vice versa, even though this is an inartful shorthand.

Leicester City's 2016 Premier League victory was one of the greatest underdog stories in sports history as the team was given 5,000-to-1 odds by British bookmakers at the start of the season. It is difficult to speak of counterfactuals and say that Leicester City's victory was due to the inherent luck in an uncertain sport and that a repeat under the same conditions would turn out differently. However, Leicester City finished in the middle of the 20-team league the following year, with fewer than half of the wins of the top team. Sometimes luck smiles; other times it does not.

Consider Figure 2.4, which compares a game's level of uncertainty over the game's outcome (which may or may not be due to randomness) with the degree of player agency over that outcome.

	High Uncertainty	**Low Uncertainty**
High Agency (Players Play Games)	Games of adaptation	Games of measurement
Low Agency (Games Play Players)	Games of fortune	Games of determinism based on outside forces

Figure 2.4 Game types by uncertainty and agency

In high-agency, high-uncertainty games, players win by best adapting to uncertain changing conditions in addition to adapting to the actions of opponents. A less-skilled opponent may benefit from the uncertainty in the activity to squeak out a win. These games are often the best spectator activities because the outcome is in question. Most popular sports fit this category.

Texas Hold'em fits this category well and, as an example, it helps to demystify the tension between luck and skill. Any hand of Texas Hold'em suffers from the variability inherent in the card draws, but in the long run, skill will triumph. Doubters of this should view the performance of the Carnegie Mellon University's Libratus AI in a 2017 competition against a number of poker pros in heads-up play. Libratus would not be able to beat professional poker players just by playing the odds of the cards. That would be too predictable and could be exploited by skilled players. Random deviations would lead to more random outcomes. Instead, Libratus learns from its opponent's play and tries to exploit its weaknesses.[2] Consistent victories could only be possible if the game was one of skill, even if any individual hand was greatly uncertain. After 120,000 hands, Libratus beat all four poker pros handily. The margin of victory was such that it had only a 0.02% likelihood of the victory being due to chance.

---

2. I'll forgive you if you think this sounds more sinister than the AI applications in the previous chapter.

High-agency, low-uncertainty games act as measuring sticks to gauge a player's virtue at whatever the game measures. In these, the outcome of the game is entirely in the player's hands but there should be little change as to the likeliness of the outcome from the beginning of the match to the end. The strongest arm should win an arm-wrestling match, all else being equal. The contest itself is measuring that metric. These are less interesting in terms of who will win because the outcome should be understood before the contest begins. What makes these interesting is *how* a player wins. The contest is more about the players than the play. Watching a powerlifting competition is not interesting because you want to know who will win; rather, it is largely based on spectacle of the feats of the competitors.

In low-agency, high-uncertainty games, players have less control over who wins. This isn't a normative statement. It simply defines who is in control of the winner of the game. Low-agency games need not be boring. Millions play lotteries, slot machines, and roulette—all of which leave very little to player agency.

A low-agency, low-uncertainty game is harder to imagine. In this case, the winner is deterministic, but out of the player's control. It could be argued that these kinds of games cannot be interactive by definition because the interactions are meaningless to the outcome. Perhaps "fixed" or unfair games meet this category; games based on criteria that are unexploitable by the players, like a beauty contest, may also qualify. Another candidate here is the solved game in which both players are aware of the solution, such as Tic-tac-toe played by adults.

It is important to think of these not as a 2×2 discrete set of conditions but as a gradient. The four categories above simply serve as an example to understand the parameters.

Types of Uncertainty in Mechanics

In the above analysis, luck and skill do not exist on a simple spectrum where the decrease in one corresponds to the increase in another. Instead, elements of luck and skill exist in two separate dimensions that matter to the player: Will adapting my play during the game affect the game result? And how likely is it that we know who is going to win in advance? It is also important to understand that uncertainty that stems from the unpredictability of players is different from the uncertainty that stems from random systems.

One perspective that has been helpful to me in my design work is considering the *directionality* of randomness. The directionality of randomness in a mechanic refers to the chronological effect of a random event.

Output randomness refers to a player's action mediated by a range of possible random results. An example would be the result of a die roll in Monopoly giving the player the option to buy a particular property. If I want to buy Illinois Avenue, the only way I am going to get to is with the help of a random event. If I need a full house in Texas Hold'em, I'd better hope the cards come up. If I need brick in The Settlers of Catan, I'd better hope I roll a number that produces it since my opponents won't trade with me. In output randomness, the player action (roll the dice, refuse to fold) comes before the random event. I make the decision and hope the game cooperates. In LCR or Baccarat, I make the decision to play and the game decides whether I have won.

Input randomness refers to a random event's result framing a player's action. In this type, the player can act based on the randomly generated information. An example is getting to see the next piece in Dr. Mario or Tetris. Although that piece may be determined randomly, seeing it informs the decision I make with my current piece. In a game of The Settlers of Catan, the board is set up randomly, but players do not make decisions until they see that board setup. In input randomness, the random event happens and then the players use the randomized result to make a decision.

One of the most abused theoretical animals in the history of rhetoric is Schrödinger's cat. In the classic thought experiment, physicist Erwin Schrödinger places a cat in a box with a device that holds a radioactive atom. If that radioactive atom decays, then it releases a poison and the cat dies. In Schrödinger's model of physics, we cannot know whether the atom has decayed or not until we open the box and observe it. His cat is both alive and dead until we make the observation.

In a case of output randomness, we have a Schrödinger's cat situation before we make our action. The cat could be alive or dead with some probability of each. In an input randomness situation, we open the box and get the information. We know whether the cat is alive or dead before we make our decision.

A good example of this is in the classic 1995 board game The Settlers of Catan.[3] The initial placement of settlements is very important to success because it gives players their early supply of resources.[4] The island's resource-generating land types and their resource-generating frequency are randomly distributed before players make their decision. Because of this, their decision is informed by making tradeoffs between odds of production, production breadth (will I have access to brick?), and spatial desirability. If this information was not provided and is instead generated randomly after players placed their initial settlements, players would only have the spatial desirability on which to base their placement, and starting positions

---

3. Newer versions call the game simply *Catan*, but most still refer to it by the original name.

4. Game awareness survey results indicate that The Settlers of Catan has a surprisingly high awareness among those surveyed, so I will not go deep into rules here. If you are unfamiliar with the game, you absolutely must play it for both its historical and creative value.

would likely be the same in every game—the only difference being that the random distribution may give some players a vast resource advantage over others. Since players do in fact know this information before making their decisions, the relative values of starting positions are as close to even as possible. This is a satisfying instance of input randomness.

The Settlers of Catan also has output randomness. The pips on the individual tiles correspond only to the probability that the tile will produce. Say your only settlement abutting a brick tile is on a 5. 5s are a fairly common result to roll, appearing around 11% of the time. But 11% is no guarantee that a 5 will be rolled. If you need that brick to proceed, you may be in for a long wait and there is very little you can do if the dice do not cooperate. You may need brick to start your building engine, and your stingy opponents may not want to trade. The odds are close to 31% that you will go at least 10 turns without rolling a 5. The odds are close to 9.5% that you will go 20 turns without that tile producing. You are at the mercy of the dice. This is output randomness.

Some Settlers of Catan players prefer to smooth out the output randomness by replacing the die roll with a 36-card deck of cards that has the die roll results in the proportions expected by chance. This way, you can ensure that a 5 will be "rolled" by roll #33 as there will be four "5" cards in the deck. You can also be sure that 5 will be rolled exactly 4 times every 36 rolls. While you don't know when that tile will produce, you have some insurance against the dice always rolling in favor of your opponent and never in favor of you.

It is tempting to say that input randomness is better for a strategic game because that information informs our decisions and thus gives players a clearer basis on which to make their decisions. I am lukewarm on that approach. Input randomness allows for clearer player agency, which can be a value that game designers wish to reflect in their work. You likely can cite examples of frustrating events in games where a random result killed your motivation to keep playing. But we will see examples in this text that are great strategic games that have a good deal of output randomness. Classics like Poker and Backgammon and modern games played at a high level such as Magic: The Gathering and League of Legends are full of output randomness.

Even if you discount the actions of millions of lottery and slot machine players, there clearly can be a level of excitement in a purely random outcome even if the stakes are higher than the few minutes or hours invested in games. In 2016, a Pittsburgh-based entrepreneur started Pack Up + Go, a company that sells travel packages in which the customer doesn't know where they are going until they reach the airport.

A common criticism of the concept of randomness directionality is that output randomness is just input randomness *for the next turn.* That is, I may need to need a lucky card draw in Hearthstone but then that card is in my hand and becomes one of my options for strategic play in the future. I think this is a fair criticism, but that it somewhat misses the point. A turn may not be the best delineation of time for the focus of a mechanic. A turn may consist of many decision points and many random events. Some events may happen simultaneously. The unit of observation is most likely a player action or decision, not an artificial timescale like a turn. Output randomness could certainly be input randomness for the next turn, but what matters is the decision at the time the player is making it and what information is available to that player to make that decision.

We are doing philosophy here, and as such we can neither be proven right nor wrong. Instead, we can just have convincing or unconvincing arguments. Randomness directionality is a tool, and if you find it convincing, it can help you understand the impact of randomness on a system.

Randomness and Perceptions of Fairness

"The game is cheating!"

We have all said this before. You don't have to deny it—I'm just a book; I can't tell anyone. Some random event happens in a single-player game that shouldn't have happened by chance alone. The opponent magically draws the right card, rolls the right number, or gets the perfect counter-item to ruin your day and you get upset because you believe that since the random number generator and the game rules are controlled by the same entity that they must be in collusion, unfairly teaming up to take you down.

Part of what makes randomness in games so unpalatable for some players is the feeling that randomness isn't "true" and is instead weighed against the player, making his task more difficult than it is displayed to be. This effect is compounded by our propensity to vastly overestimate our grasp of probability and randomness.

One problem is that we are prone to *apophenia.* Apophenia is the deriving of unrelated patterns from otherwise random data. Most of us have seen shapes in clouds or the man in the moon. A Toledo woman saw the shape of Jesus in a pierogi and sold it on eBay in 2005 for over $1,700, just as the scriptures instruct us to do. Perhaps you have tried to sync up Pink Floyd's *Dark Side of the Moon* with *The Wizard of Oz* to look for similarities. Some of us think that a certain number "is due" in the lottery or that our dreams can affect the future. We seem to be hardwired to believe that meaningful patterns exist within structures unaffected by whatever made that pattern.

Numerous psychology studies have repeated our inability to identify what patterns are truly random and what are human generated. For instance, look at the three sequences in Figure 2.5 that represent ten flips of a fair coin. Which sequence was generated randomly?

	1	2	3	4	5	6	7	8	9	10
Seq. A	H	H	H	T	H	H	T	T	T	T
Seq. B	H	T	T	H	T	H	T	T	H	H
Seq. C	H	H	H	H	H	H	T	H	H	T

Figure 2.5 Three coin-flip sequences

Studies have shown that the average person finds A and B plausibly random while C does not look random. And yet, all three sequences have the exact same probability of occurring.

Game designers are sometimes flummoxed by player perception of randomness. In the development of later Civilization games, the game's developer Firaxis would get complaints from players that they were losing battles too often—that the game was mis-representing probability. When a player's 1-power army went up against an opponent's 9-power army, the game assigned the weaker army 9-1 odds. When the player was lucky and won 10% of matches, they praised their own luckiness. However, when players were on the other side, having their 9-power army lose to a 1-power army the expected 10% of the time, the game seemed broken and unfair. Firaxis changed the mechanics of their game in a couple ways. First, they used their standard probability system for close matches: A 3-vs.-2 match would have the 3 win 60% of the time. But in lopsided matches, they rounded up the stronger player's army to 100%. Also, if a player had 2 losses where they should have a 1-in-3 chance of winning against the AI (like in the example above), they cheated in the player's favor so that the player would automatically win the third.

Other games cheat in the player's favor to help cushion our perceptions of randomness. In Peggle, players shoot balls in a Pachinko-like level that carom wildly and whose trajectories are difficult to project after the second bounce. Using this gap in our knowledge, Peggle's designers can cheat in situations by subtly changing a ball's bounce angle a few degrees to avoid a pit. It looks natural to the player and makes them feel lucky and skilled.

Many of Blizzard's games implement what is colloquially referred to as a "pity timer." The best cards in Hearthstone are of "legendary" rarity and are very rare. Player statistics across 27,000 pack openings have shown that a pack has around a 1.1% chance of contain-ing a legendary card. At this rate, someone opening 40 packs would have only a 35.8% chance of getting at least 1 legendary. If you buy 40 packs, Blizzard will tweak the odds and make sure that you have at least 1 legendary in those 40 packs. This allows players to feel lucky, even though there is a good chance that they were actually unlucky.

Streaming music service Spotify fields a regular complaint from its users that its playlists aren't actually random. Some users go as far as to say that Spotify has secret deals with record companies so that their songs come up more than others. Spotify, Apple, and other services have had to change their random music playlist algorithm to be less random. Imagine a playlist with 100 songs, 10 of which are from Radiohead. There is around a 64% chance that there will be two Radiohead songs back to back in that list. That usually doesn't bother us. There is around a 7% chance, however, that there will be three Radiohead songs back to back. That just doesn't feel random. These services change the distribution to be less random, ensuring that there is a sufficient enough distance between Radiohead songs that the distribution "feels" random.

Summary

Before 2010, Americans were warned to avoid butter, beef, and eggs because the dietary cholesterol they contained would increase their likelihood to develop heart disease. The guideline limit was for a diet to be under 300 milligrams/day. Now scientists have done a 180 and believe that the amount of cholesterol consumed has little effect on the likelihood of heart disease for most people. In fact, earlier efforts to reduce cholesterol consumption may have led to higher rates of Alzheimer's disease and depression. Nonetheless, the public relations damage has been done, and most still believe that consuming cholesterol is a bad thing. This, of course, isn't a signal to eat 30 eggs a day, just that cholesterol levels shouldn't be what is stopping you.

Game designers have a similar problem with randomness. Many have a knee-jerk reaction against randomness in all cases, limiting it wherever it could possibly show up, thinking that the removal of random elements will necessarily increase player agency. This is an overcorrection that keeps designers from fully experimenting with the possibilities in a design space. Most of the top games on BoardGameGeek.com, for instance, make use of some input and output randomness.

By understanding the uses of random elements in terms of player agency, designers can create an uncertain experience that still matches the level of agency they are looking for from players.

GAMES COVERED

Playlist Game #2: LCR

Designer: Uncredited

Why: As a highly successful game of pure luck, LCR allows designers to appreciate what decision making brings to the play experience, both mechanically and aesthetically.

Playlist Game #3: Mate

Designer: G. Castellan, translated by Sid Sackson

Why: Mate is a somewhat-simple card game of pure skill after an initial random distribution. Randomness of card drawing is ameliorated by immediately playing a mirror-match and comparing scores. Mate shows how a medium that easily affords randomness does not need it to support a compelling game.

Playlist Game #4: The Settlers of Catan

Designer: Klaus Teuber

Why: Besides the historical significance of ushering in German strategy board games as a hobby with global import, Catan is a great example of many design principles. Most relevant to this chapter is its use of input randomness to determine the island's locations combined with the output randomness in resource distribution.

CHAPTER 3

PUSHING ONE'S LUCK

"Nothing is as obnoxious as other people's luck."

—F. Scott Fitzgerald

It is hard to imagine now, but in the early 1980s, television game shows rarely used technology to mediate the game. Results in game shows like "Jeopardy" or "The $10,000 Pyramid" were based entirely on the contestant's ability to answer questions. After a quiz show scandal in the 1950s, many game shows introduced random elements. Shows like "Card Sharks" were focused on random processes mediated by a giant deck of cards—hardly high tech. So when "Press Your Luck" debuted in 1983, it was fairly unique.

Press Your Luck or Press Your Skill?

In "Press Your Luck," contestants earned "spins" that could be deployed on the "big board." The big board was a panel of squares that would light up in an unpredictable sequence. When the contestant yelled "Stop!" and hit her button, the sequence would stop and the player would win whatever prize was currently illuminated. Players could keep doing this until they ran out of spins. What would stop them is the potential to hit a "whammy." Whammies were illustrated by little cartoon monsters. Hitting a whammy would immediately end your turn and reduce all of your current winnings to zero. Therefore, players had to "press their luck," deciding to risk their current winnings in the hopes of winning more or banking what they already had to be safe.

In "Press Your Luck," players see a board of 18 spaces that cycle among three different results (see Figure 3.1). One of the spaces is highlighted, and that highlight jumps around making it hard to reliably stop on a particular location.

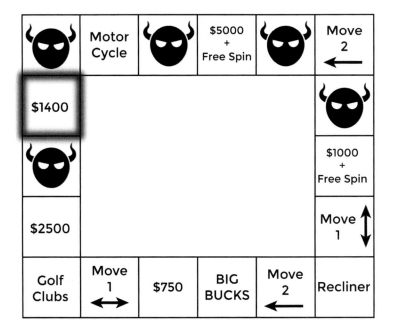

Figure 3.1 Example of a "Press Your Luck" board

"Press Your Luck" was a compelling game show. In trivia-based shows, you either know the answer or do not—there is little drama. But most spins in "Press Your Luck" were loaded with tension. Should the player keep playing? What's on the board? Stop now! No! Wait!

One of the mechanics in "Press Your Luck" was that some spaces awarded the player money and an additional spin. Theoretically, if a player could reliably hit these spaces, he could play forever. The odds of this, however, were fairly astronomical. While the odds changed from season to season, in mid-1984 players had a 16.67% chance of hitting a whammy on any individual spin and they had a roughly 26% chance of getting a prize plus a spin.

Using simple Monte Carlo simulation with some assumptions, we can model what is likely to happen in the game. For one model, we assume that a player has seven spins, an average space is worth $1,000,[1] and the player will bank his money if he reaches $5,000. In that case, the player walks away with money 40% of the time and hits a whammy 60% of the time for mean winnings of around $2,000. The average player who wins a non-zero figure will take home $5,000.

If a player is brave and always plays out all of her spins no matter what, then she will successfully navigate the whammies approximately 13% of the time and whammy out 86% of the time for a mean winning of $1,500. But the non-zero winner does a lot better, taking home over a little over $10,000 on average. The odds for "Press Your Luck" are shown in Figure 3.2.

	$4k	$6k	$8k	$10k	$12k	$14k	$16k	$18k	∞
5	40%	34%	26%	22%	22%	22%	22%	22%	22%
6	40%	34%	24%	19%	17%	17%	17%	17%	17%
7	40%	34%	23%	17%	15%	13%	13%	13%	13%
8	40%	34%	23%	16%	12%	11%	11%	10%	10%
9	40%	34%	23%	16%	11%	9%	8%	8%	8%
10	40%	34%	23%	16%	11%	8%	6%	6%	6%
11	40%	34%	23%	16%	11%	8%	6%	5%	5%
12	40%	34%	23%	16%	11%	7%	6%	4%	4%

Figure 3.2 "Press Your Luck" simulation results

Odds of winning any money are based on number of spins (rows) and a "walk-away" amount (columns). For small amounts of walk-away money, it doesn't matter how many spins you have because you generally walk away first.

---

1. This is not the average payout of a "Press Your Luck" board. However, it is arbitrary because whatever you set this to, you can make your walk-away values multiples of it. For instance, if the average board payout was instead $2,000 (doubled), then the same probabilities would hold by doubling the walk-away amounts.

You should notice that the riskier strategy pays the winners better for taking on that risk but does so at the cost of lower odds. You see this pattern in many games of chance. In lottery scratch-offs your chance of winning is higher, but the purse lower. In lottery drawings, the jackpots are large, but the odds are much smaller and the expected payouts much lower. And the more spins you start off with makes the potential payoff higher and the chance of using all of your spins successfully less.

This tension drives the show, even if the audience and the players do not realize it. Banking your money is the mathematically best thing to do, but doing so gives you less money if you turn out to be a winner. Thus, do I do the safe thing for small money or the risky thing for large money? It's a real decision. And it differs from the television game shows of the past because what might be the right decision for you at home may be different from the right decision for the player on the show.

No Whammy

What is better than luck? Not needing it. The May 19, 1984, episode of "Press Your Luck" was filmed in front of a live TV audience. Michael Larson, introduced as an ice cream truck driver from Ohio, was one of the contestants. In the second and final round, Larson would stun the audience, the host, and the CBS executives by spinning 43 times in a row without hitting a whammy, racking up $110,237 in winnings. Remember that this was long before "Survivor" and "Who Wants to Be a Millionaire." Results like this on game shows were unheard of.

The odds of not hitting a whammy in 43 spins by chance alone is less than 1 in 3,000. But what makes this more astronomical is that he entered the round with 7 spins and so had to continually hit spaces with a bonus spin. The odds of this happening by chance alone was 1 in 250 hextillion. What happened couldn't have happened by chance alone.

Indeed, it didn't. Larson, reportedly obsessed with get-rich-quick schemes, found one that worked. He recorded "Press Your Luck" reruns on a home VCR, meticulously pausing and recording the supposedly random patterns. He found that two of the squares on the board always showed a bonus spin. This narrowed Larson's search to figuring out when that square would be highlighted. It turned out that the board's pattern looped five different sequences, which he deduced through meticulous study of the tapes. Once those were memorized, Larson would just have to wait long enough to identify which of the sequences he was seeing and then hit the buzzer as it was switching to the two guaranteed bonus squares.

With practice, Larson turned the purported game of fortune into a game of measuring Larson's ability to match the patterns. CBS responded by changing the number of patterns to 32, making it harder to identify which pattern the board was currently displaying. Despite CBS's argument, what Larson did wasn't cheating. It was certainly against the spirit of the game, but producers can only design the rules of the game. If the spirit is not reflected in the rules, it is the design that is incorrect, not the play of the players. The lesson for game designers here is clear: Most players will want to play to the spirit, but if you have a system that can be gamed, just one bad actor can throw a wrench in the system.

It's in the Name

From a system's design standpoint, "Press Your Luck" shows a good example of what Jesse Schell in *The Art of Game Design* calls *triangulation.* In triangulation, a player is faced with two or more options where each option is a tradeoff between risk and expected value. The higher the expected value, the higher the risk. A decision between any other pair is dominated: Low risk/high expected reward vs. low risk/low expected reward is obvious and high risk/high expected reward vs. high risk/low expected reward is obvious.

One game that provides a pure example of this is Blackjack. In a hand of Blackjack, players are dealt cards with the goal of getting a sum of values as close to 21 as possible without going over. As an example, imagine you are dealt a king and a 7 for a hand value of 17 and the dealer has one hidden card and one jack. A hand of 17 is okay, but not great. You can choose to stand and keep the 17 or hit and risk going bust. If you choose to hit, there are only 4 of the possible 13 cards that can be dealt without you busting: ace (1), 2, 3, or 4. You have a 69% chance of going bust.[2] However, if you don't, you will have a stronger hand and a higher likelihood of winning. There is, in this instance, a "right" move to do in the long run, but each individual hand still offers that choice between the safe, low-probability bet and the risky but rewarding-if-right option.

Blackjack is minimally interesting in the long run because it is easy to memorize the table of when it is probabilistically in your favor to hit or stand. This makes these decisions rote and takes the agency away from the player if followed. There are other games that handle the decision of pushing one's luck in a more strategically interesting way.

We mentioned Sid Sackson when we covered Mate in an earlier chapter. Sackson rediscovered Mate, but it was not a design of his own. One of his finest designs was a 1980 board game succinctly called Can't Stop. In this game, players try to be the first to have three of their pawns reach the top of the game board. On a player's turn, he takes three temporary white pawns and rolls 4 six-sided dice. The player can then combine the four dice into two sets of two. For instance, if I rolled a 1-2-3-6, I could make a 3 (1+2) and a 9 (3+6), a 5 (2+3) and a 7 (1+6), or a 4 (1+3) and an 8 (2+6). Players can then place and/or move their temporary pawns up a step from the corresponding column on the board.

---

2. This is inexact as the odds change depending on what cards are visible from the dealer or other players and how many decks the game is using.

What makes Can't Stop more than a simple exercise in probability is the following rule that suggests the title: You can have as many rolls and movements in a row as you like. However, if you ever make a roll and cannot place or move a pawn, you lose all the movement you gained that turn and have to pass the dice to the next player.

If my temporary pawns are on 2, 7, and 10 for this turn, then on each subsequent roll I have to be able to make a 2, a 7, or a 10 with the dice I roll.

Use the diagram in Figure 3.3 as an example of a two-player game between you (with your pieces as diamonds) and me (with my pieces as moon icons). We've already played a turn each, and our pieces are on the locations shown in the figure. It is your turn.

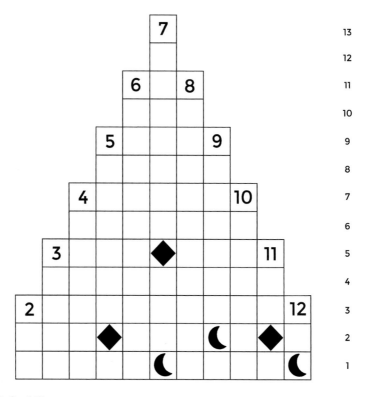

Figure 3.3 Can't Stop

You roll 1-1-3-3. You can make 2/6 or a pair of 4s. Neither of these help with the columns you started on the last turn. Two moves on the 4 column is nice, but the 2 column only takes 3 moves to reach the top so you decide to use 2 and 6. You place two temporary markers on the first row of 2 and 6. You may quit here and pass, but there is no reason to do so because you still have one temporary marker left. You choose to roll again.

This time you roll 2-2-4-5. You can make 4/9 or 6/7. If you chose 4/9 you would only be able to move one of them since you have only one temporary pawn left. So you choose 6/7. You move the temporary pawn you placed last roll in the 6 column up to the second row and, since you are already at row 4 in the 7 column, you place the temporary marker at row 5. You may quit here and pass to me. You have placed all of your temporary pawns, so on your next roll you will have to make a 2, 6, or 7. Since 7s are the most common result to get, you feel pretty confident and push on.

You roll 1-1-1-2. Yikes! You can only move the 2, so you do, moving it to the second row. You are one row away from scoring. If you roll again, you will have to roll a 2, 6, and 7 or lose all of your progress from the turn. Now what do you do? The odds are not so easy to calculate in your head. You decide to pass to me. You replace your temporary pawns with your diamonds as shown in Figure 3.4.

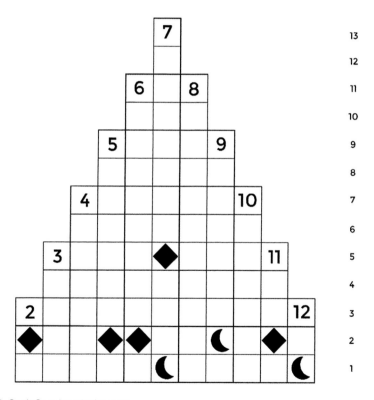

Figure 3.4 Can't Stop later in the game

It is my turn, I'm really itching to move that 12 up and lock up the 12 column. I roll 1-4-6-6. Excellent! I pair this into 5/12 and roll again. I get 2-2-2-6. That doesn't help either of my previous results, so I can choose either 4 or 8 for my last temporary pawn. Although 4 requires fewer rolls to reach the top, 8 occurs more often. I decide since I am trying to get 12s that I need something with a higher probability in order to not bust. All my temporary pawns are out: 5, 8, and 12. I roll again: 2-4-5-5. That makes 6/10 or 7/9. No! I bust! I can't move a pawn up, so I remove all the temporary pawns from the board. I get no movement this turn.

Play continues like this until someone captures three columns by moving their pawn to the top of a column. Once a column is captured, it is off limits. No player can move in that column for the rest of the game. Because of this, you may end up busting on your second (or first!) roll. This changes player calculations significantly.

Can't Stop is a simple game that could have been designed hundreds of years ago. As I continue to roll, I am increasing the expected reward of my turn in terms of number of moves but also increasing my risk. The triangulated decision happens dozens of times in a game of Can't Stop and is a distilled version of more complicated triangulation decisions that occur in other games. In Halo, do I attack with an assault rifle (high chance to hit, low damage per hit) or a sniper rifle (low chance to hit, high damage per hit)? In League of Legends, do I want to use a low-damage targeted ability that guarantees a hit, or a high-damage skill-shot that has a chance of a complete miss?

Greed and Risk

Another game that represents this dynamic well is Bruno Faidutti's Diamant (renamed "Incan Gold" in the United States). In Diamant, players represent treasure hunters delving into ancient ruins to recover gems and artifacts. Each turn a new card is revealed. If it is treasure, it will have a number of gems on the card that the players split as evenly as possible, leaving any remainder on the card. After every card is turned, players may choose to leave. In that case, all leaving players split the remainder gems and they bank all of their gems from the round. They are tempted to do this both because of the bonus of the remainder gems and because there are also hazard cards in the deck. If two of the same hazards appear, then all players still in the ruin lose all of their gems collected on this trip.

As a round progresses, more and more hazards appear, making it more and more likely that the next card turned will bust every player still in the round. But because fewer players remain in the round the deeper you go, players who stick it out are rewarded by splitting their gems among fewer players. Cards are drawn until all players leave or lose due to hazards.

In the round illustrated in Figure 3.5, there are three players. The first card is an 8. Eight gems can be split among three players by giving two to each and leaving two gems behind. The next card is a bomb hazard. No gems are awarded and players can start to feel nervous that a second bomb will ruin their round. The next card is a 5, which is split by giving one gem to each player and leaving two behind.

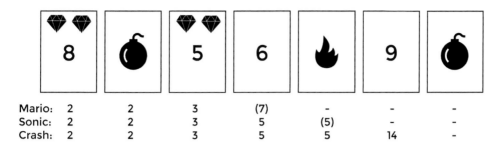

Mario: 2	2	3	(7)	-	-	-
Sonic: 2	2	3	5	(5)	-	-
Crash: 2	2	3	5	5	14	-

Figure 3.5 Diamant

Now that there are four gems left behind, it is tempting to leave. Players have to weigh their possible future gems and also if other players are likely to leave. If two players leave at this point, they would each only get two additional gems, which isn't a high payout. Mario looks at the board and decides it is so early in the round that no one else will want to leave. He leaves and is the only one leaving, so he gets four additional gems and is locked in at seven for the round.

The remaining two players push on. A 6 is drawn, which can be split evenly between two players at three each. The next card is a fire hazard. Now if a bomb or a fire is drawn, players will bust. Sonic looks at the situation and decides to leave. He will receive no additional gems, but he will lock in his five gems for the round.

Crash is now by himself as he decides to push ahead. The next card is a 9, which he doesn't have to share with anyone. His total is 14 gems. He doesn't know when he will be the only player left again so he decides to press on for at least one more card. The next card is a bomb. Since it is the second bomb, it is a bust. Crash has to leave his 14 gems behind.

In this example, you can see the richness of the decision making given a simple setup. Players have to consider not only their likelihood to bust on the next card, but weigh their stay or leave decision against the remainder gems on the board and their opponent's likelihood of taking those gems. Each player makes only one decision with only two options per card turn, yet that decision has numerous contingencies to consider.

Let Them Eat Cake

It is very important to game players that games they play be perceived as fair. What "fair" means often varies wildly from player to player. Is a fair game one that is easy to beat? Dark Souls is a game with brutal difficulty. Some players see its many instant-kill situations as unfair, while others see it as a worthy challenge. Fairness cannot simply be an even distribution of events. Dark Souls is weighted heavily against the player. According to statistics on

Steam,[3] only 30.5% of players have beaten Dark Souls 3. Even a short, comparatively easy game like Portal has only a 65.3% completion rate.

Uneven distribution of resources is one of the triggers of player issues of fairness. If one player randomly draws a card that gets her ten resources and another draws a card that gets him two resources, the random draw seems unfair.

One technique to mitigate feelings of unfairness is to leave distributions in the hands of players. A mechanic that uses this is called the *cake-cutting* algorithm and can be seen in many multiplayer games. In it, there is some bundle of resources that needs to be distributed to players. One player decides on the distribution amounts, and every other player gets to choose before the player making the distribution. Imagine a cake that is 20 square inches in area that needs to be split between two people. One person would split the cake. If he splits it into one part that is 18 in^2 and one that is 2 in^2, then the other person will choose the 18 in^2 piece. He is incentivized to cut as evenly as possible because the largest possible smaller piece is half the size of the cake.

Cake-cutting becomes really interesting in situations where players have to split resources that have unequal values. Say that one was faced with a game of Monopoly where two players had to decide the distribution of a Boardwalk property, a Pennsylvania Avenue property, $1,000, and three random Community Chest cards. One player may value Pennsylvania Avenue more because they are in position to make a green monopoly. You could value each at their mortgage value, but what do you do about the random cards?

The problem gets more interesting when you split among more than two players or situations where the values of the things being split are different among different players. With three players (let's call them Leon, Jill, and Rebecca), one player (Leon) cuts the cake into three pieces. Then Jill and Rebecca point to the pieces they want. If they point to different pieces, then they take those pieces and the cutter (Leon) gets the third. If not (as in Figure 3.6), one of the other players, this time Jill, cuts a piece off her favorite slice so that it is equal to her second-favorite slice. That fraction is set aside. Rebecca now gets to decide whether she wants the newly trimmed piece or one of the other two pieces. Then Jill gets to choose, but if Rebecca didn't choose the slice she trimmed, Jill has to take it.

Leon sorts the collected loot into three piles in a way that he would be happy with any of the three. Jill and Rebecca simultaneously point to their favorite pile. Had they picked different piles, they could each take their favorite pile and Leon could be satisfied with the remaining one.

---

3. These completion rates were calculated by dividing the players who triggered the "completed the game" achievement by the players who have triggered the earliest possible achievement, in order to try to weed out players who didn't actually try to play the game.

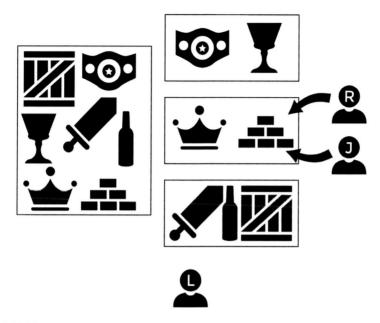

Figure 3.6 Multiple players want the same pile.

Jill trims off two bricks from Jill and Rebecca's favorite pile (see Figure 3.7). By choosing two bricks, she says that, to her, the middle pile is now equal in value to the second-best pile. Thus, if Rebecca chooses either the middle pile or her second-best pile, she will have no regrets.

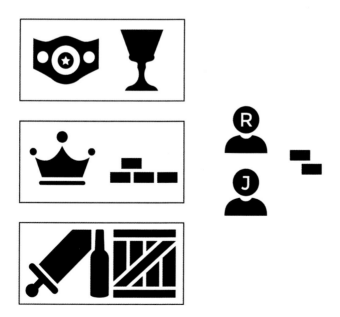

Figure 3.7 Two players choose from the piles that the third split.

All three players should be happy at that point. Leon got one of his original three pieces, which he cut thinking it was a fair distribution. Jill got one of the pieces that she trimmed into what she thought was a fair distribution. Rebecca got to choose from all three pieces, so she has what she thinks is the best piece.

What about the trimmed bit? This starts a new problem where the trimmed bit is a new cake to divide among the three. Leon shouldn't care about the trimmed bits since his original distribution thought that the slice that included the trimmed bits was already fair. So he can be removed from consideration of receiving the trimmings. Jill and Rebecca have a standard I-split-you-choose cake-cutting problem (Figure 3.8).

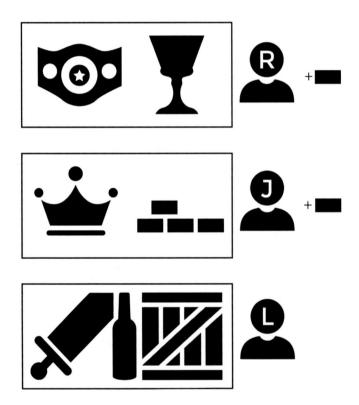

Figure 3.8 Splitting the trimmed bits

Rebecca chooses the top pile after the trim, meaning it must be of greater value to her post-trim than the middle pile. Jill gets the middle pile, which was just as good as the top to her, so she has no regrets. Leon gets the bottom pile, which he created as to have no regrets. The two trimmed bricks get evenly split between Rebecca and Jill. Leon has no regrets because it doesn't affect his original split, and Rebecca and Jill already chose piles without extra bricks, so those are a bonus. Everyone wins.

If that seems like a complicated way to split something into three evenly-valued pieces, that is because it is. In 2016, researchers at Carnegie Mellon developed an algorithm to solve a n-person cake-cutting problem with a finite number of steps. Unfortunately, their algorithm can require up to $n^{n^{n^{n^{n^n}}}}$ steps, meaning that even a four-person cake-cutting problem could require astronomical computing power. It is simply not applicable to games. Researchers believe that it could theoretically be reduced to n^2 steps, which would be a great advance.

Equity

Whether it appears via player decision making or by random processes, inequitable outcomes trigger changes in our behavior. When we are frustrated at another player's lucky results, it may be more than just a character flaw. That desire for equitable treatment may have an evolutionary basis. In a 2003 study, researchers trained capuchin monkeys to trade a rock for a reward. At first, all of the monkeys received cucumbers when they traded, which they enjoyed. Then, some of the monkeys received grapes when they traded, an even better reward. When the cucumber-rewarded monkeys saw that the other monkeys received grapes, they stopped eating the cucumbers, and in some cases, threw the cucumbers back at the researchers. What was once a nice reward became distasteful simply because some other monkey had it better.

In the 1980s, economists engaged in a series of experiments of what would be called *The Ultimatum Game.* It begins similar to the cake-cutting problem. There are two players. One player receives a stack of cash and must divvy it up into two piles, one specifically designated for him and one for the other player. The other player then can accept the distribution, in which both players get what was assigned, or reject it *in which case both players get nothing.* Simple game theory would tell us that since $1 is greater than $0, a player who is faced with a $99-to-$1 split would still take the $1. What researchers have repeatedly found is that players will harm themselves if they can harm another for being unfair. In one experiment, half of offers at 30% or lower were rejected. That means half of people would give up $30 to make sure their opponent didn't have $70 instead of a more fair $50-$50 split.

Considerations of equity are important even in games in which inequities are largely determined randomly. Recent research has suggested that participants are likely to reject the ultimatum at the same levels if the offer was generated randomly or by an impartial algorithm. Thus, it may be not that we want to punish any particular bad actor, but that we reject entire systems that we see as unfair. As designers of systems, this should be a salient consideration.

Summary

Luck is an ingredient. It is neither good nor bad on its own, but just as in the case of base cooking ingredients like salt or sugar, it is contingent on the recipe and the palates of the consumers to determine what is an appropriate quantity and technique to include. For example, players of dense European-style strategy board games tend to say that they want no luck in their games. What they are saying is that they want to be in control of the outcomes of their decisions. A spectrum between skill and luck is a meaningless construct. Instead, consider how luck affects the appearance and effectiveness of a game's decision making. What appeared to be luck in "Press Your Luck" was not at all, creating an inequity that nearly ended the show. Similarly, games that appear to be purely skill based can still be influenced by random factors, and those random factors will be discounted by players as long as they are seen as fair.

GAMES COVERED

Playlist Game #5: Can't Stop

Designer: Sid Sackson

Why: While every turn of Can't Stop is deeply random, players generally feel like the results of the game are within their control.

Playlist Game #6: Diamant/Incan Gold

Designers: Bruno Faidutti and Alan Moon

Why: Diamant is an elegant push-your-luck game that packs levels of tactical evaluation into simple decisions.

CHAPTER 4

PIECEMEAL PERSPECTIVES

"Artists are people driven by the tension
between the desire to communicate and the
desire to hide."

—D.W. Winnicott

A common inspiration for fledgling designers is the desire to tell stories. Of course, stories were told long before video games were invented. What is the deeper inspiration is the desire to tell stories in a new way—a way that is highly dependent on the reader for discovery and interpretation. These kinds of stories are written not simply to be enjoyed in a vacuum but to be discussed and dissected.

> **warning**
>
> **SPOILER ALERT**   This chapter will contain descriptions of the games Aisle, Her Story, Orwell, and Event[0] that may contain spoilers. If you wish to play those games without foreknowledge of their systems, then please do so before reading this chapter. The author will attempt to avoid spoilers where possible.

Interactive Fictions

Interactive fiction (IF) is a niche genre, having peaked in market share in the mid-1980s. IF games present the player with a text prompt and the player types in what he wants the player character to do. In most IF games, the interaction is limited to a small number of verbs that the game is programmed to understand. In most games you can "move [direction]" or "take [item]" because these are common verbs that most game authors would anticipate. But sometimes, an IF player's experience is struggling with how to express their action in a way the game understands rather than struggling with a puzzle that the game presents as its enjoyable challenge. For instance, if I need to light a candle and I type "light match," the game might not understand that phrase, only understanding "strike match." The more situations a game has, the less likely that every possible permutation of actions will be covered.

Designer Sam Barlow released the IF game Aisle in 1999 (see Figure 4.1). What made Aisle different from most IF games to that point is that it was designed to be replayed a large number of times, with each play being a single action described by the player. This allowed the designer to prepare many responses to the one situation. Each playthrough reveals more and more about the character in the world, leading the player to more ideas of possible interactions to try.

> Late Thursday night. You've had a *hard* day and the last thing you need is this: shopping. Luckily, the place is pretty empty and you're progressing rapidly.
>
> On to the next aisle.
>
> **Interesting... fresh Gnocchi--you haven't had any of that since... *Rome*.**
>
> The aisle stretches to the north, and back to the south. The shelves on either side of you block your view of the rest of the supermarket, with only the brightly coloured aisle markers visible.
>
> You have stopped your trolley next to the pasta section, bright plastic bags full of pale skin-tone shapes.
>
> There is a brunette woman a few metres ahead, filling her trolley with sauces.
>
> >|

Figure 4.1 Aisle

Figure 4.2 is an example of an entire playthrough of Aisle.

```
>look at woman
You stare at the woman. She is about your height, maybe even a little taller. And beautiful too, with superb
hair. Strange; you haven't thought that about a woman for a while. Not since Rome.

You continue to stare at her. You wonder if she is called Clare.

Then she moves on to the next aisle. You grab a bag of pasta--penne--and carry on with your shopping.

                              ----------

                    One more story over. Then again...
```

Figure 4.2 The simplest playthrough of Aisle

By looking at the woman, you are given a memory of a name (Clare) and a place (Rome). That's something you can use in further playthroughs.

By figuring out what the player should be interested in, the decision space of the game opens up. What is at first a simple setup of a man buying pasta at a supermarket gains more and more context as the game is explored. By modern standards, Aisle is clunky as the limits of the interpreter still stymie players in revealing the gulf between what they want to know and what they are allowed to know.

Barlow would go on to work on commercial games for over a decade, but to understand what is likely his most important work so far, we need to take an aside into two largely unrelated histories.

Actors and Interactions

Full-motion video in video games has had a troubled past. The first uses of actual actors in games was hampered by the high cost and unreliability of laserdisc technology. Full-motion video was largely panned as a gimmick in search of a use, rather than a pioneering technology.

Mad Dog McCree was released in arcades in 1990 and was largely an exception to the prevailing quality of full-motion video games. In it, a player played as a wild west gunslinger, playing through pulp western set pieces with a light gun. Players had to shoot bandits, stop a lit fuse leading to dynamite with a precise shot(!), and save the mayor's daughter from the titular "Mad Dog." While the acting and writing were both poor, the game played smoothly. The campiness of the sound effects and production were acceptable in such a novel play setting. Mad Dog McCree is memorable less for bringing innovations in design to market than for being a small success in a market of full-motion video game failures.

Night Trap was released for the Sega CD in 1992. In it, players played as special agents monitoring a house party of teenage girls (as they do?) and remotely triggering traps to protect them from invading limping vampire things. Again, the acting and writing were quite poor and the interactions were limited. The game received mixed reviews at release. Its future would have been a footnote, if not for an unlikely source of attention.

In 1993, future vice-presidential candidate Senator Joe Lieberman and Senator Herbert Kohl would hold a senate hearing into violent video games. Lieberman used Mortal Kombat and Night Trap as his go-to examples of video games that should be banned from purchase. Lieberman confessed during the hearing that he had not played Night Trap. Senator Byron Dorgan called Night Trap "a sick, disgusting video game" that is "an effort to trap and kill women," despite the game's goal being exactly the opposite. In the hearing, it was repeatedly stressed that the danger was clear and present because the graphics had become so realistic in comparison to something like Space Invaders.

The controversy over video game violence made Night Trap more popular. Despite being pulled from large retail chains, it went on to sell over a million copies. The controversy around it was one of the driving factors behind the establishment of the Entertainment Software Ratings Board. In 2017, Night Trap was rereleased in a "remastered form."

There are numerous reasons not to use full-motion video in games. Digital video takes a lot of storage. Compressed video needs to be decompressed, which takes computing power. While it is easy to edit a game's sprite, reshooting video is expensive and cumbersome. As technology has evolved, "realistic" presentation became possible without the use of full-motion video. If a game designer needs to add a character to a scene, a digital character can just be dropped in whereas a physical actor would require a reshoot.

Thus, full-motion video has fallen into disuse. Some cases have been made for the use of video as a small portion of the interface, such as in the Command & Conquer: Red Alert games.[1] Remedy Entertainment's Quantum Break interspersed in-engine play with live-action, full-motion video cutscenes, but interactive elements were not present during the cutscenes.

Armchair Jurors

"Public radio projects" and "cultural phenomenon" are rarely found in the same sentence. From the producers of "This American Life," "Serial" was released in podcast form in late 2014. "Serial" told the real-life story of Adnan Syed, a high school student convicted of

---

1. The avowed campiness of this series may make the use of full-motion video palatable. If players expect melodrama when seeing full-motion video and the design delivers the melodramatic, it may be a good match.

murdering his ex-girlfriend in 2000. Syed's story had all the drama of the best crime fiction: sketchy alibis, conflicting witnesses, ambiguous evidence open to interpretation, cultural tensions, layered motives, and a lawyer who may not have had her client's best interests at heart. It was a compelling production and audiences agreed; in the first season, at least 80 million "Serial" episodes have been downloaded. And audiences were split. Many think that Syed is innocent—or at the very least, there isn't enough evidence to convict him. Others argue that the preponderance of the evidence is enough and the system worked. A network of websites and podcasts sprung up from "Serial" listeners, collecting evidence and making their cases.

As a true crime story, Syed's story is intriguing and entertaining. But there are many true crime stories out there just as wild and just as controversial. Truman Capote's 1966 *In Cold Blood*, despite questions of its veracity, is often cited as one of the key works in the history of true crime. *Helter Skelter*, a 1974 book about the Charles Manson murders, sold over 7 million copies. In the 1980s, crime shows like "Crimewatch" and "Unsolved Mysteries" further asked viewers to participate in the stories described. In the 1990s and 2000s, news organizations started to pull on audiences' love of the true crime story, dedicating endless hours to the O.J. Simpson trial,[2] the JonBenét Ramsey investigation, and the Casey Anthony murder trial. In 2015, Netflix released their "Making a Murderer" documentary series, which took the "Serial" format to video.

One element that separated "Serial" from the others was its delivery. "Serial" was released as a free podcast, with new episodes appearing every week. In a culture lately obsessed with binging on media, the pause between weeks allowed for fans to spend time between episodes theorizing and conversing about the episode's contents. Its podcast format allowed for its audience to consume it while engaged in other activities, as opposed to a television show that would require largely undivided attention.

A compelling true crime separates itself from fictionalized crime in one particular way—the audience feels that the truth is out there for them to capture, not concealed by a narrative device. This makes true crime ultimately more participatory than fictionalized crime and may be why it seems to trigger some of the same elements that make interactive stories so compelling.

Her Story

After a successful career in commercial studio games, Aisle's developer Sam Barlow returned to the independent scene in 2015 with Her Story. Her Story combines the interpretive and voyeuristic elements that drive the popularity of true crime stories with the nonlinear slowly

---

2. More people watched the O.J. Simpson verdict live (which occurred in the middle of the day on a weekday) than watched the Super Bowl that year.

revealing narrative structure that he used in Aisle. Instead of presenting information textually as he did in Aisle, Barlow chose to present the story as a series of police interviews as seen on aforementioned true crime shows and as heard on the "Serial" podcast.

Players start in Her Story seeing a '90s-style graphical user interface for a computer. A simulated reflection and bend in the edges of the screen make it look like you are using an old cathode ray tube monitor. In a window is a search box, already keyed in with the term "MURDER." A number of results are listed in Figure 4.3. Watching the results makes it clear that the various videos are from different recording sessions; they don't particularly make sense together without context. Players can add or remove tags from the videos to mark them for a later search.

Figure 4.3 Her Story

All that players have to go on from the initial search are things that they can glean from those early videos. What names were said? What places? If "Murder" provides results, what related terms might, like "Victim," "Weapon," or "Police"? From these, players can make an ever-expanding web of videos, each one filling in the story bit by bit. But some videos contain information that is contradictory to other videos and some lead to narrative dead ends. It is the player's job to reconcile these elements, but the game itself never really tells the player if they are right or even on the right track. The game also tests the player's comprehension skills. They aren't just waiting for a code word; instead, they have to deduce important elements from subtext and nonverbal cues.

The videos are cut in such a way as to eliminate the detective's prompting question. A real police interrogation record would never leave this out, but it serves to further muddy the waters as to the context of the answer. Since answers will necessarily be viewed out of order, players have to work backward to understand the line of questioning that spawned a particular answer. Sometimes the background in the interview location can be a clue as to which clips go together. Since events happen in the game's timeline between recordings, this can sometimes be informative.

While there is a "winning" state of Her Story, there isn't the traditional cycle of feedback. It is positive feedback to see a new video unlocked, but that video may not provide clues to further player understanding of the narrative. That winning state also doesn't put a neat bow on the story; there are plenty of items left to interpretation. This allows for the game to exist outside the context on an individual play—something that helped push "Serial" to more viral engagement.

But Her Story takes the participatory nature of "Serial" one step farther. Whereas "Serial" listeners were subject to host Sarah Koenig's juxtaposition and editing of events, Her Story allows clever participants to gain more information than other players by finding additional clues and piecing them together in a more consistent narrative. It is as if "Serial" theorists could squeeze more blood from the podcast stone by force of will.

The congruity of the interface also serves as a point of participatory immersion. You, the human playing the game, sit at a computer terminal typing in commands to direct you, the avatar, to sit at a computer terminal typing in commands. You, playing in the present day, are at a temporal distance to the recordings set in 1994.[3] The avatar you represent is also at a temporal distance to the events recorded. That avatar is never shown. You don't exist in a 3D space in Her Story. You have no sense of place. You only have what you can find in your searching.

Everything within Her Story has to be assembled from a distance. Like Plato's Allegory of the Cave, we have to deduce the nature of objects from only their shadows. One of Barlow's inspirations for Her Story was an experimental piece by J. G. Ballard called "The Index." "The Index" is a story (of sorts) of a character told only through the index of his supposed autobiography. Instead of directly receiving a narrative account of the subject's life, the reader instead is left to infer events from the inclusion of various topics in the index. The narrative then doesn't appear in chronological order, but in alphabetical order. Likewise, in Her Story, players have to piece together the events that happen off camera based on the limited information presented. Narrative elements don't appear in chronological order here either; they instead appear in a pattern guided by player actions.

---

3. A great aesthetic choice was that Barlow filmed all of the segments using a standard HD camera, output the recording, and saved it to a vintage VHS tape and then reimported it back into digital form to preserve the artifacts and color limitations of the simulated media.

Orwell

Another game to try this expanding narrative technique is Osmotic's 2016 game Orwell. In Orwell, players also play as an avatarless individual manipulating a computer interface (see Figure 4.4). In this case, the player is using a government surveillance suite called Orwell to read people's phones and emails in order to snoop out possible terrorist activity. Players get documents and can highlight areas of interest to find in further documents. When elements of a document or artifact can open new areas of interest for the Orwell engine,[4] the player can drag them into a dossier for later use.

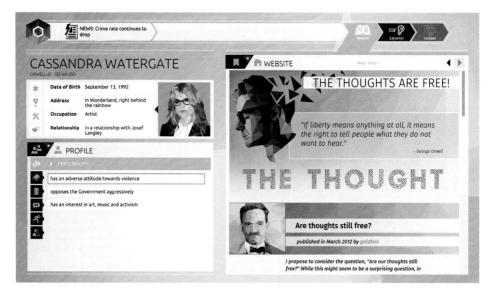

Figure 4.4 Orwell

This is a bit less effective in a design sense than in Her Story, particularly because the game highlights the important information as possible hooks for the Orwell engine. Where in Her Story you must decide for yourself whether the character's mention of a particular place is important, in Orwell the game literally highlights the place name and gives you immediate feedback as to whether that element leads to further information. This takes the process of narrative discovery out of the hands of players and puts it in a more straightforward semi-linear narrative model.

Although there is much room for improvement in Orwell from both a design and narrative perspective, the contrast with Her Story in both areas helps a designer to understand the

---

4. One would think a government wouldn't call their snooping system "Orwell," but the U.S. Defense Advanced Research Projects Agency's Information Awareness Office had as its logo the masonic-influenced Eye of Providence casting its gaze from space over the entire world. We probably shouldn't underestimate the willingness of governments to be that audacious.

potential methods, structures, and most importantly, challenges in a narrative design that gives the player freedom in determining his or her spigot of information.

The Eye Above

As we have seen in an early chapter, early computer scientists like Turing were concerned with what would happen when computers could approximate real intelligence. Perhaps it is the above-average neuroticism of authors and game designers, but the trope of the insane and malicious AI has been in deep use since at least Arthur C. Clarke and Stanley Kubrick's 1968 book and film *2001: A Space Odyssey.*

Ocelot Society's 2016 game Event[0] follows in that tradition. In Event[0], the narrative starts with the player character having to evacuate her spaceship and dock with a derelict ship of unknown origin. The game takes place in an alternate history where commercial space travel was common in the 1980s, so player interaction with computers is all done in a command-line interface (as in Aisle).

The player interacts with the ship's AI, "Kaizen," by typing in commands at numerous terminals (see Figure 4.5) scattered on the inside and outside of the ship. Kaizen is a fairly responsive AI, and its ability to react to numerous player questions and comments both directly and indirectly leads to the game's penchant for narrative tension. Kaizen is up to something, and it is up to the player to figure out what.

Figure 4.5 Event[0]

In Event[0], the player is immediately faced with the mysteries of what happened on this ship and why it is so far from Earth. Kaizen's reactions to player questions spoons out information in a piecemeal manner. Depending on what the player asks, how "nicely" the player treats Kaizen, and other factors, the information given to the player will differ. Thus, players will finish the game with different perspectives on the same events, depending on what information they are able to glean in the playthrough.

Summary

Differences in audience reaction in other media are often caused by differences in literacy of the form being considered. For example, the 2016 television series "Stranger Things" can be enjoyed as a sci-fi/horror pastiche. But aficionados of 1980s culture can appreciate how the show constantly alludes to popular culture of the era, from *Altered States* to *E.T.* Two viewers may take different things from the viewing experience based on their literacy of the form.

The interactivity of games offers the ability to fracture that experience further. Two Her Story players may have vastly different interpretations of events based not just on their literacy of the form but on the actual events observed. Two Event[0] players may have different theories on what happened on Kaizen's ship, not because one player paid better attention than the other, but because their interactions with Kaizen revealed different information. This difference is not valuable in itself. It can be easy to confuse players by adding random narrative elements; that isn't the point. The point is to extend the depth of the experience by allowing players to engage in different perspectives that leverage player interaction with the narrative rather than forcing a strict set of events on players and hoping that their literacy allows them to recognize that depth.

GAMES COVERED

Playlist Game #7: Night Trap

Designers: James Riley and Rob Fulop

Why: Besides the historical significance of the game, Night Trap shows a good example of working within technical constraints. Each intervention that the player enables needs to have its own videos recorded for each permutation. The design contingencies stemming from this lead the design to balance between a simple production that is dynamically uninteresting or an interesting decision space that is very difficult to produce. Night Trap doesn't do a particularly good job at straddling that dichotomy, but it reveals the tensions in doing so.

Playlist Game #8: Her Story

Designer: Sam Barlow

Why: The ending of the game is available from the start of the game; you only need to know what search term to enter. This puts the unfolding of the narrative entirely within the player's control instead of being on rails as the player moves from one narrative event to the next.

Playlist Game #9: Orwell

Creators: Osmotic

Why: Orwell provides another example of a narrative that is revealed by player actions. Although it is more linear than the other examples in this chapter, it shows that this technique is not limited to the experimental.

Playlist Game #10: Event[0]

Creators: Ocelot Society

Why: A clever language interpreter (or at the very least, a hand-waving facsimile of one) is at the heart of this adventure game that combines the command-line interactions of the IF era with the 3D exploration of the "walking simulator" era. The interactions the player engages in directly affect what information is revealed to the player.

CHAPTER 5

PERMANENCE

"When you stir your rice pudding, Septimus,
the spoonful of jam spreads itself round making
red trails like the picture of a meteor in my
astronomical atlas. But if you stir backwards, the
jam will not come together again."

—Tom Stoppard, *Arcadia*

Decisions are only interesting if they have consequences. Of course, most consequences evaporate when the magic circle of the game itself collapses. But within, what can we do to make the stakes of decisions meaningful?

Interactive Fictions

The Legend of Zelda is considered by many to be the predecessor to the modern role-playing video game. Zelda was developed at the same time as Nintendo's Super Mario Bros. and the two were designed to be quite different. Whereas Mario was designed to be linear, Zelda was designed to be open. The goal was explicit in Mario, but the goal was a bit more implicit and challenging to understand in Zelda. Early playtesters were frustrated with the openness of the latter game. Designer Shigeru Miyamoto responded by taking away the player's sword at the beginning of the game, forcing players to communicate with others to figure out how to proceed—a skill that would be necessary for uncovering the game's secrets.

One other innovation pushed by Zelda was an internal game save. Many games used passwords at this point. But a password could be easily transferred; if my buddy gives me his string of characters (or worse, I get them from a magazine), then I can start my game where he left off without earning it. Instead, the cartridges in the American version of Zelda contained a small battery with a memory chip that allowed for the game to be saved. This innovation was new for console games. Computer games, even more of an enthusiast hobby, had used this since Zork since most computers had some sort of internal memory they could leverage.

Being able to save one's game greatly changed the play dynamic for players. No longer were they forced to complete a game in a single sitting. This achieved more than respite for players. Now they could alter time itself for the characters in their worlds. Choosing to make a risky jump in a run of Donkey Kong had real consequences. The player only had so many lives; once those were up, he had to start over. Now, to some degree, players could base their risk assessments on how far away from the save point they were. If the player was able to save right before that "risky" jump, the possible penalty was erased. If the player failed, he could jump back to the save point like the failed jump never happened. This adds another level to the decision making, similar to the "Press Your Luck"–style mechanics described in Chapter 3, "Pushing One's Luck." What was a tough but relatively unmemorable battle in Persona 5 becomes a harrowing, nail-biting experience when the player has played for an hour without saving. One unlucky roll of the dice could lead to a game over and that hour of play would need to be repeated.

Fiero

Many designers found game saving to be a necessary evil to be designed around, begrudgingly cursing players for their ability to change the stakes of their carefully designed systems. But as with most innovations, game designers also found a way to make lemonade from lemons. One particularly sadistic train of thought went, "If players can save at any point, then we can make our games excruciatingly difficult. Then every decision point will be tense." This philosophy was exemplified in the 2010 platform game Super Meat Boy.

In Super Meat Boy, players play the titular character as he tries to traverse one-screen levels that have an absurd degree of difficulty. Players are expected to die dozens of times on each screen. Dying has very little consequences as a player immediately restarts the level with no loading or waiting. Super Meat Boy's world is filled with giant buzz saws, spikes, fire, and endless pits that require pixel-perfect movement and jumping abilities. According to Steam achievement numbers, only 5% of players ever beat the game.[1] There are no online records of numbers of deaths, but thread counts asking to compare death counts in online forums often have death counts in the tens of thousands. Super Meat Boy would be essentially impossible without the save points as only a few players have ever completed the game in a "no death" run. Despite its brutal difficulty, Super Meat Boy has sold well over a million copies.

Some players critical of the game ask why anyone would subject themselves to a game with such a frustrating level of difficulty. The answer is that it is only frustrating until it is conquered, and the rush of victory is that much greater for the high level of challenge. In her book *Reality is Broken,* author Jane McGonigal writes about the concept of "fiero":

> Fiero is the Italian word for, "pride," and it has been adopted by game designers to describe an emotional high we don't have a good word for in English. Fiero is what we feel after we triumph over adversity. You know it when you feel it—and when you see it. That's because we almost all express fiero in exactly the same way: we throw our arms over our head and yell. The fact that virtually all humans physically express fiero in the same way is a sure sign that it's related to some of our most primal emotions.... Fiero, according to researchers at the Center for Interdisciplinary Brain Sciences Research at Stanford, is the emotion that first created a desire to leave the cave and conquer the world. It's a craving for challenges that we can overcome, battles we can win, and dangers we can vanquish.

Fiero is relative. Some people get it when they run with the bulls in Pamplona, some get it when they fight mixed-martial arts in a cage, some get it when they play Super Meat Boy, and others get it when they play Monopoly. The bull-runners aren't likely to achieve fiero from Monopoly nor vice-versa.

Super Meat Boy, for many, is the top of the scale for challenging fiero in games. The Dark Souls games are also popular for this. But there are games that make Super Meat Boy look tame in comparison and predate its popularity in making the quick save-reload loop the core of gameplay.

Kaizo Mario World is a homemade hack of Super Mario World for the Super Nintendo/Super Famicom systems. *Kaizo* refers to the hacking of existing commercial games but has become shorthand for hacks of excruciating challenge. In Kaizo Mario World, players play what looks like Super Mario World, except the levels are remixed to be completely unfair. Invisible blocks are placed in areas players are likely to jump, instant-kill elements like munchers are placed in copious amount in unlikely areas, and players can die on the introduction screen or even

---

1. I can attest to being in the 95%.

after successfully completing a level. A 2007 video of a player playing it has been viewed over 5 million times on YouTube. It is more fun to watch for the schadenfreude than it is to play.

Also in 2007 was The Big Adventure of Owata's Life. It is a freeware game that deals in the same kind of frustrating platforming as Kaizo Mario World. You play as an ASCII-art stick man trying to traverse single-screen levels. In Figure 5.1, the player character is on the right. A moving platform above a spiked pit stands between the player and the signpost on the left. In any other game, the moving platform would make the jump tricky, but not tough.

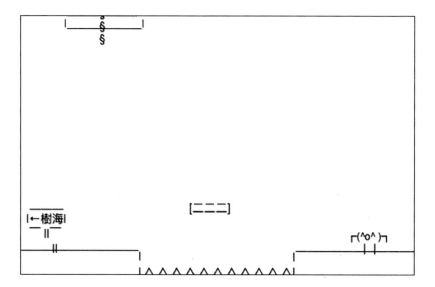

Figure 5.1 The Big Adventure of Owata's Life. Owata is about to have a bad time.

When the player lands on the platform though, the spikes immediately rise up and destroy the player (see Figure 5.2).

The first time the player makes the jump, he is almost guaranteed to be killed by the spikes rising up. Since he immediately is reset, this is a quick lesson. He has to time it so that he is only on the moving platform for a split second, far enough to the left that he can bounce off and land on the ledge to the left. When he lands on the ledge, the slab at the top of the screen immediately drops and kills him.

So the player has to jump onto the moving platform as far left as possible, jump immediately without pause to the ledge to the left and land far enough to the left that he has time to continue moving left to reach the end of the screen safely. Or so he thinks. You actually do not have the time to make it to the sign post to the left no matter how far to the left you start your jump (see Figure 5.3). Instead, you have to trigger the initial spikes, jump back, jump on the moving platform as the spikes are moving down, land on the left ledge to trigger the slab, jump back to the moving platform and then jump on top of the slab. Needless to say, this is very difficult—and this is only the first screen.

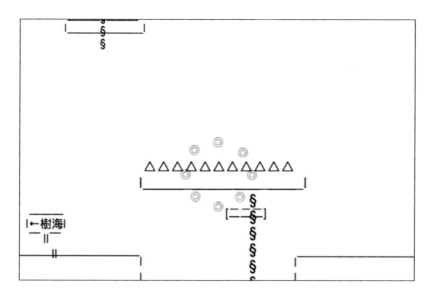

Figure 5.2 Owata had a bad time.

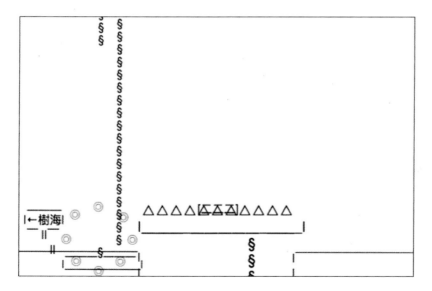

Figure 5.3 No matter how far you jump, if you haven't already triggered the left platform of spikes, it will crush you.

Owata's Life inspired what would be a more popular, if still niche, title in the same year called I Wanna Be the Guy: The Movie: The Game. I Wanna Be the Guy outdoes the difficulty of Owata's Life by introducing additional elements that are deceptive and can only be conquered by trial and error. For example: Fruit, commonly a health item in most platform games, instantly kills you. Sometimes fruit will stay put, sometimes it will fall when you get near, other times it will fly straight up or to the side when you approach. At one point, a convincing error message appears that then falls on the player and kills him. There is a save point that can kill the player.[2] Only brute force memorization can get you through. The key to the design of these games is not to be impossible, but to provide just enough progress that the player thinks success is possible. The designer of I Wanna Be the Guy, Mike O'Reilly, sums up the design tension: "[H]ow much can I piss [the player] off, and have him still play the game?"

A game that leverages this in a less abusive way is the Souls franchise of games by FromSoftware. The Souls games are notoriously difficult 3D action-adventure games. But they are not difficult just for the sake of difficulty. Demon's Souls game director Hidetaka Miyazaki has said that "[h]aving the game be 'difficult' was never the goal. What we set out to do was strictly to provide a sense of accomplishment. We understood that 'difficulty' is just one way to offer an intense sense of accomplishment through forming strategies, overcoming obstacles, and discovering new things." In other words, fiero.

Memories of Places That Have Never Been

In Chapter 2, "Randomness and Cholesterol," we referenced Erwin Schrödinger and his cat-based thought experiment. Schrödinger may be the earliest source of the "many worlds" interpretation of quantum mechanics. While put forward more explicitly by others, a vastly simplified explanation of the theory is that every possible universe exists simultaneously and every branching point splits off a new set of universes from all possibilities at that point. For example, there is a universe that is exactly like your own except that when you read the previous sentence, you put this book away and never read this sentence about you putting the book away. There is also a universe in which you read this sentence and immediately the phone rings.[3]

By saving and reloading, we fork the possibilities in a game character's world until we see the one we desire. At the end of Fallout 3, the player is given an option to use or refuse to use a weapon given to her by another character. What the player chooses causes a particular cutscene to play. If the player refuses, she sees the appropriate cutscene but may still wonder what would happen if she did the opposite. By saving and reloading, she can easily see what would happen with no permanent change in the game world. Which is the "true" ending? Both—every possible world exists. That, however, feels unsatisfying. What good is it to make a decision about the fate of the world if it can easily be rolled back as if it never occurred?

The concept of *permadeath* has been around at least since 1980s. Rogue made the concept core to the experience. In Rogue, the player is an adventurer in a procedurally generated Dungeons and Dragons–style dungeon, where he meets monsters, gains powers and items, explores, and dies. But unlike the standard role-playing game (RPG) model we are used to, in

---

2. Which may be a nod to Chrono Trigger (1995).

3. I'm banking on that happening to at least one reader so that I can look like a wizard.

Rogue (and in the many similar games inspired by it, such as those NetHack called "rogue-likes"), once the player dies all progress is erased. There are no takebacks. If you turn a corner and find a murderous grue, tough luck. This makes every step in a roguelike potentially meaningful. One of the original designers of Rogue, Glenn Richman, explains: "[P]ermadeath is [just] an example of 'consequence persistence.' Do I read this scroll, do I drink this potion? I don't know. It might be good. It might be bad. If I can save the game and then drink the potion and—oh, it's bad—then I restore the game and I don't drink the potion. That entire game mechanic just completely goes away. So that was a whole reason why, once you have taken an action and a consequence has happened, there's no way to undo it."

Some games have tried to preserve the narrative power of in-game decisions by manipulating a player's ability to save and reload. In the aptly named 2009 game You Only Live Once, the player plays a Mario-esque platform game with a similar save-the-princess narrative wrapping. The only difference is that when the player dies, the game is truly over. Reloading the game makes no difference. Even playing the game on another site does not bring the character back to life. The only way to retry the game is to delete your browser's Flash cache (which would also delete every other saved game in the cache). Needless to say, the fact that players cannot easily circumvent this design element makes some incredibly frustrated, as evidenced by the players who searched out the author's personal website to complain (see Figure 5.4).

This game sucks. What game has multiple cutscenes for your death depending on how you die and doesn't let you play it ever again? Games are supposed to be enjoyed multiple times, not just once. That is why I give it a 1 star other than the fact that I can't give a 0 out of 5.

Comment by Vaeth — August 6, 2009 @ 2:13 pm

its not nice is you plzy it once and you die then you have to play it on another website this sucks

Comment by hadi — August 9, 2009 @ 5:23 am

Well since I'm not a member on kongregate, I'm leaving my comment here.

Lots of people on kong are complaining about how yo only live once. The people defending you are saying that the point of the game is to teach you about whats gonna happen to you. Now screw this stupid game. Do people seriously think that a giant pink lizard is going to kidnap your girlfriend. You're game gets a -11/100. Screw this game, add, a restart option or only let people once every hour or day.

Comment by Pissed Off — August 10, 2009 @ 5:15 am

this game sucks

Comment by hadi — August 10, 2009 @ 8:57 am

Figure 5.4 Breaking expectations sometimes leads to unhappy "fans." Never read the comments.

The 2015 indie hit Undertale has a number of clever design choices, but one worth noting here is how the game enforces permanence. Like many RPGs, Undertale has "good" and "bad" endings, and the player may save and replay the game to trigger different possible events. However, Undertale's save files are multi-tiered. Instead of just remembering the current state of the game, it also remembers the state of every other playthrough. Thus, if you get the "Genocide" ending to the game, subsequent playthroughs will reflect that and the best ending of the game will be permanently unavailable. Overwriting that game save or even deleting the game on Steam does not reset the game. In fact, certain methods of trying to avoid the consequences of in-game decisions are monitored by the game. If you try to reload after a particularly tough decision, one of the in-game characters will make fun of the player for trying to take the easy way out!

This is an interesting evolution of some permanence techniques used specifically to try to counter the problem of software piracy. 1988's Zak McKracken and the Alien Mindbenders required players to enter a code every time the player changed in-game locations. The code key was packed in the game's box with the manual.[4] If a player entered an incorrect code too many times, the player was put in an in-game jail and was forced to listen to a lecture on copyright infringement. 2014's The Talos Principle used a similar jailing technique, locking players in one of the game's elevators a few hours into the game if it detected a pirated copy. The 1994 game EarthBound contained a bit of copy protection that allowed players to play the near 30-hour game, then froze the game on the final boss and corrupted the player's save file if it detected a pirated copy. 2012's Game Dev Tycoon was a simulation about running a game studio that, when detecting a pirated copy, poetically had the player's studio lose more and more money to software pirates until the game could no longer be played. While these aren't directly related to using permanence to alter consequences of *in-game* decisions, they often use the same techniques.

Games that are designed to be franchises can leverage their lasting commitment to better enforce the permanence of in-game decisions. A popular example of this is Bioware's Mass Effect series. 2010's Mass Effect 2 would allow players to import saves from 2007's Mass Effect. This import preserves many of the player's decisions from the first version, including which characters the player decided to sacrifice in the first game. Those characters are completely unavailable in later entries in the series, leading to different mechanic and narrative setups. Although Mass Effect doesn't require a player to stick with their decisions from a previous game, having the option of a kind of permanence helps create the illusion of a persistent world. This kind of transfer is not unique to Mass Effect. The Wizardry series has allowed players to transfer characters from game to game in the series since at least 1990.

---

4. Remember manuals?

Summary

Games, by their nature as simulations, have the freedom to play with the player's causal expectations. By understanding the player's relationship with the permanence of their decisions, designers can create decision points that are both meaningful and memorable. Without this permanence, decisions become arbitrary.

GAMES COVERED

Playlist Game #11: Super Meat Boy

Designers: Edward McMullen and Tommy Refenes

Why: Super Meat Boy was one of the first commercially successful "pixel perfect" platformers. The play loop consists of copious dying and restarting. While the game is brutally difficult, the feelings of success when beating a tough level are commensurate.

Playlist Game #12: I Wanna Be the Guy: The Movie: The Game

Designer: Mike O'Reilly

Why: "Masocore" games are a subgenre of interest when it comes to understanding challenge in games. These games, of which I Wanna Be the Guy: The Movie: The Game is a popular entry, routinely engage in what would be terrible design decisions in any other genre by explicitly putting players in positions where they do not have the information to succeed. That players can succeed anyway is part of the spectacle of these games and makes them popular as spectator events as in streaming marathons.

Playlist Game #13: Dark Souls

Designer: FromSoftware

Why: Fiero is the feeling of victory in overcoming a difficult challenge. Dark Souls is a surprising commercial success partially because of its unforgiving difficulty. A setup that would be rote and uninteresting in another 3D action game becomes tense and strategic in a game that does not allow for an easier difficulty. The fiero generated by beating even an early boss is not worth the effort for some, but is the primary driving force behind an entire demographic of game players.

Playlist Game #14: NetHack

Designer: Various (Open Source)

Why: NetHack is one of the most popular successors to Rogue. It features permadeath as a core mechanic but has a much richer encyclopedia of possible character actions. For instance, one of the enemies in the game is an eel that can drag you under the water to kill you. Writer John Harris explains the possible ways a player can deal with the creature in NetHack:

> "He can just use a means of taking care of the eel from afar, and since they can't leave the water that's not too difficult.
>
> Or he might grease his armor, making it difficult for the eel to gain hold.
>
> Or he might wear an oilskin cloak, which is similarly slippery.
>
> Or he might wear an amulet of magical breathing, making drowning impossible.
>
> Or he might polymorph into a monster that doesn't need to breathe.
>
> Or he might bridge the water with ice using a wand of cold, since eels are harmless out of the water.
>
> Or he might teleport the eel with a wand, hopefully onto dry land.
>
> Or he might trap the eel in a small pool by pushing boulders into the spaces around him, creating land.
>
> Or, if he's levitating, he can stop, surprising the eel and making him lose his grip.
>
> Or he could just wear an amulet of life saving."

Playlist Game #15: Undertale

Designer: Toby Fox

Why: Toby Fox's hit Undertale was recently voted as the "Best Game Ever" on a GameFAQs contest. While the hyperbole is strong with this one, Undertale certainly is a remarkable game for many reasons. This chapter mentioned the permanence of its narrative choices, but it also has clever design in its conflict mechanics and offers so many mechanical and narrative sleights of hand that simply playing it is preferable to explaining it further.

CHAPTER 6

MECHANICS AS MESSAGE

"All play means something."

—Johan Huizinga, *Homo Ludens*

What is a game about? Is Super Mario Bros. a game about Italian plumbers? Or is it a game about jumping? Or is there a deeper subtext? Or is it a combination of all of these things? Or are games essentially meaningless pastimes? In this chapter, we discuss some games that have a design that leads us to ask further questions about the medium and the world outside the medium.

> warning
>
> **SPOILER ALERT!**   This chapter contains descriptions of the games Passage,
> The Marriage, and Bioshock that may contain spoilers. The Bioshock section
> in particular contains major spoilers in both play and story. If you wish to play
> those games without foreknowledge of their systems, then please do so
> before reading this chapter. The author will attempt to avoid spoilers where
> possible.

Where Meaning Exists

Compare playing a commercial video game to the playing of an album of music. We use
the same word for both actions, yet the meanings are far removed. We acquire this media
in the same way (largely through downloading these days) and take a similar posture when
experiencing it. When we play a game, we are acting on the game. When we listen to music,
we are passive; the music is acting on us. The language we use reflects this. When we speak
of the play of an individual in a sport, we talk about the athlete's *performance,* the same term
we use for the expression of a musician in a concert. The audience at that concert is independent of the expression of the performance. Thus, the game player is much more like the
musician than the audience.

Consider the following three pieces of music: Frederic Chopin's "Nocturne Op. 9 No. 2," an
instrumental; Franz Schubert's "Der Leiermann," sung in German; and Don McLean's
"American Pie," a popular song sung in English. The English song is the most clearly expressive to English speakers. We understand the words and convert them into meaning. But the
other two convey the same or similar emotions of loss quite clearly. This is done without the
literal description of events. The ability for music to convey emotion is different from simply
using elements that directly signify those notions. Even if it is the case that our meaning
comes from cultural norms outside the works of music themselves, then those outside forces
can still possibly act on us in other forms. Performance is expressive. We have no issue saying that a skilled violinist's particular performance is expressive, yet we balk when saying
someone's League of Legends play is expressive. Philosophers have dealt with this question
for centuries in the realm of music. How can a series of individual sounds express anything
at all beyond the noises themselves? A full examination of the history of this argument is well
beyond the scope of what we wish to achieve here. What is it about the play of games that
makes it seem like the act itself lacks expressiveness?

First, there is a cultural sense of authorship that is divorced from many games. Whereas the
authorship of the experience of viewing a painting is clear and the meaning of the work can
be directly observed and interpreted, the author of a game is not as philosophically simple.

Is the author of the experience of a game the person or persons who came up with the rules, those who host the physical space of the game experience, or those who interpret the rules via in-game actions? We don't speak of the author of American Football because it is a game that has been slowly changed by hundreds of different actors from its origins over innumerable iterations. In the first versions of the game, players could not pick up or carry the ball, similar to the rules of soccer. Now, however, through years of changes, carrying the ball is the core activity of the game. If the origin of the author of the experience is unclear, and if thousands have changed the core experience piecemeal over decades, what could it possibly have to say?

Second is the evolution to games as solitary experiences. A game player sitting alone in his room playing Metal Gear Solid seems to be taking in what the game is offering, not expressing anything himself. If he was being expressive, who is he expressing to? Play is ephemeral if not saved in some form. If there is no audience, can there be an expression worth discussing?

Perhaps this is missing the point. In "The Ontology of Play," philosopher Eugen Fink writes that "we must distinguish between the intrinsic meaning of play—the meaningful bond between things, actions, and played relations—and the external meaning, the meaning of play for those who initiate it and take part in it, as well as the meaning it is supposed to have for the spectators." Using this perspective, we can separate the performative aspects of play from the authorial aspects of the game itself.

The element that separates games from other art forms is its requirement of audience participation. No game exists in a bubble distinct from its consumption by players. Although more traditional media need to consider the social and cultural framework in which the media will be consumed and interpreted, game authors also have to consider how the consumers will interact with the media itself. Authors generally are not concerned with how quickly the reader reads; musicians don't generally concern themselves with the specs of the listener's stereo. But game designers need to consider the actual act of playing as an element of their art. It is in the act of playing itself that games are uniquely qualified to deliver meaning.

Some prefer to use tools and methods appropriated from other media to establish the meaning of a game. Cinema has a longer history of artistic acceptance than games, and the vocabulary and customs have long been adopted into a sense of general media literacy. The use of dramatic camera angles in Resident Evil, for example, has more to do with the cinema legacy of Alfred Hitchcock than it does with any interactive purpose. This media literacy makes it easy to talk about games in terms of other media: the characters, the plot, the story, etc. That is, of course, where these easy segues from other media exist. Where they do not, explanations tend to stretch based on the semiotics of what is on screen or on the game board (i.e., Chess is about medieval class structure, Super Mario Bros. is about rescuing a princess) rather than dip one's toe into the language of the interactive.

When you take the approach that we should use the same process to evaluate games as we do films, it is no wonder that games come up so short when it comes to meaning. For every film, filmmakers don't have to reinvent the camera; they don't have to worry about the decisions their characters could make; they don't have to worry about the hardware that will project the film. Filmmakers can spend more of their creative energy focusing on the meaning of their art. We can laugh at the stilted delivery of the original Resident Evil's voice actors because their delivery is legitimately poor. But the game innovated in so many ways unrelated to its story that it is clear where the developers spent their time. And by the commercial success and legacy of the game, it is clear that the market is rewarding something other than the game's film-like elements.

Games that focus on story are common. Most, however, treat the story as something that happens largely without the player's involvement. Either the player is on rails, watching the story unfold around him as on a ride at a theme park, or the player's agency is taken away during moments where key story events take place. When Sephiroth kills Aeris in Final Fantasy VII, there is literally nothing the player can do to change it. He has no control; nothing learned or experienced in the game itself can affect that story element. The story happens around the player. The interactive elements are largely unrelated to the story elements.

Marriage of Theme and Interaction

In some games, however, the story and the interactive elements are highly coupled, either thematically, mechanically, or both. In 2006, former Electronic Arts executive Rod Humble released a small freeware game called The Marriage. Humble urges people to play the game before reading too much about it, so I will stress the same. Play the game before reading the following paragraphs. Humble's goal was artistic in nature—to create a game in which the meaning was derived from the interaction of the elements of the name, not the representation of those elements. Thus, the game is abstract in presentation: There is a blue square, a pink square, and a number of small spheres. The background also changes colors over the course of the game.

The game starts with the blue square and the pink square coming towards each other. By hovering your mouse cursor over the squares, you can get them to move toward each other, but the blue square shrinks. When they collide, the blue square shrinks and the pink square grows. Hovering your mouse cursor over the circles destroys them and gives size to the blue square. When the squares collide with non-black spheres, they grow. Black spheres make them shrink. If either square shrinks to nothing, the game ends. Quickly players realize that the game is about keeping the blue and pink squares in balance for as long as possible.

The Marriage betrays Humble's aversion to representational elements in a number of ways. First, the name itself provides a framework for the interactions. Indeed, it would be difficult to tie the in-game actions to anything discrete without it. Second, the two main elements in the game are colored blue and pink (see Figure 6.1). These have gender-based connotations, especially given the title.

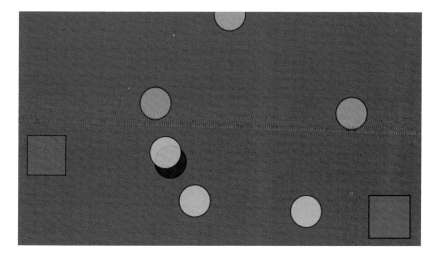

Figure 6.1 The Marriage

With those small touches, the meaning of game mechanics become a little clearer. One interpretation is that the marriage is a tradeoff between outside interests (the circles) and the need to be intimate (the collisions). What it says about gender roles in that the male color is diminished by coming in contact with the female color seems a bit cynical. What seems a bit more elegant is that trying to micromanage by constant intervention usually leads to a game over; trying to force a marriage into harmony just doesn't work. The game never outright says this, but it is clear when trying to glean a message from the nearly abstract play space.

September 12th

In the buildup to the United States' 2003 war in Iraq, newspapers were full of op-ed pieces with opinions on the increasingly likely conflict. Millions of words were written on the topic, printed in newspapers or increasingly influential online sources. There was little shortage of opinions on what the world should do about the possible threat of Saddam Hussein.

In that climate, Gonzalo Frasca created the game September 12th. When it starts, players are presented with an isometric view of a middle-eastern city. Non-player characters scurry around the town. Eventually characters holding what appear to be AK-47 rifles will appear. Your mouse acts as a reticle. By clicking, you can send a missile to blow up the rifle-wielding terrorists. There is a small delay between launching and the missile reaching its target, so often you will blow up innocent bystanders or buildings. In that case, neutral non-player characters will mourn at the sight and some of them will turn into terrorists. There is no way to win September 12th. You cannot eliminate all of the terrorists. You can only hope to minimize damage and the spread of the terrorists.

September 12th's message is simplistic, even by the standard of op-ed pieces. Frasca himself doesn't wholly agree with the game's message, instead crediting it as a tool to facilitate discussion. September 12th is credited as one of the first "news games," games that use interaction with elements of current events to comment on the systems behind those events. September 12th was so novel in its austere mechanics that it continues to be used as an exemplary persuasive game.

Passage

Although empirical research is mixed on the topic, in some instances creativity can be enhanced under constraints. A great example of this is Jason Rohrer's 2007 game Passage (see Figure 6.2). Rohrer made the game for a contest where a game could be played in no more than 5 minutes and have no larger a resolution than 256 pixels by 256 pixels, although strange aspect ratios were encouraged. That small pixel space and time constraint meant relaying anything meaningful would be difficult. To Rohrer, an advocate of games as an expressive art form, these constraints would combine to allow for a game about a complex subject: the passage of time.

Figure 6.2 Passage

In Passage, a player can move an avatar up, down, left, or right. As the game starts, the player cannot see far in the up-down direction but can clearly see the elements on the left side of the screen. As the player steps right, he gains points as shown in the upper right. The player can also walk into treasure chests that dramatically increase the score.

Early in the game, the player sees a female character. If he approaches the female character, the two become married and move in lockstep (a bit different metaphor than The Marriage). This has a tradeoff: The player earns twice as many points when married, but because the two move in lockstep, the player cannot move into areas where only one character can fit. These areas often have treasure chests.

As the game progresses, the player moves farther to the right of the screen. The weird compressed bits on the right decompress and the bits passed to the left start to compress. Eventually, the player grows old. The further he moves to the right, the older he gets, graying and moving more slowly.

If the player married, eventually his companion dies. As I use Passage as an example in my teaching, I've watched hundreds of students play the game for the first time live in class. Nearly every player reacts with shock when the companion dies. They stop movement. They stop trying to get more points. They walk in a circle. They try to figure out a way to bring her back. But there is no way back. Eventually, the player too dies and turns into a gravestone. While there are many keen metaphors in Passage, I find the death of the wife character to be the most illustrative. It interrupts the player's life—He stops moving forward, stops caring about the things he had cared about up to that point, and instead fruitlessly rages against the rules. He feels sorrow for the 8-pixel-tall wife he met 2 minutes prior. It is certainly not novel to feel real emotions when characters we know to be fictional die. However, this is usually due to the severing of a long-built attachment based on the character. Passage's wife character has no lines, exhibits no personality, and exists for a less than a few minutes of interactive time.

Dissonance

For some reason, we get really excited over the prospect of global civilizational collapse. Wikipedia lists over a hundred articles detailing "end of the world" dates that have come and gone.

Dorothy Martin, a Chicago housewife, convinced followers that aliens told her that the world would end in flood in December 1954, but her believers would be rescued by UFOs. Believers gave up their possessions and even spouses to wait out the end of the world with Martin. 1955 came without the alien intervention. Her cult survived the mistaken prophecy.

Jim Jones preached that the world would end in nuclear holocaust on July 15, 1967. Even after that prophecy turned out to be less than accurate, he still convinced over a thousand adherents to move to Guyana and drink poison.

Christian radio personality Harold Camping spent $100 million of his radio business's money advertising that the end of the world would happen in 2011. Followers donated their worldly savings to Camping only to end up disappointed in their own continued existence.

Whether it is aliens, nuclear war, or the second coming, when a prophecy fails to be fulfilled, believers generally don't slap their knee and say, "Shucks, guess I was wrong about that." Instead, they double down.

Psychologists have called the discomfort that comes with holding contradictory beliefs "cognitive dissonance." Since we rarely can change the facts of the real world, when we feel cognitive dissonance we change our cognition of the facts in order to resolve the contradictory beliefs as seen in Table 6.1. For Martin's UFO cult, they decided that their publicity had saved the world from destruction. Thus, the fact that the world wasn't destroyed wasn't relevant.

Table 6.1   Cognitive Dissonance Examples

"The world will end on December 20, 1954." "The world did not end on December 20, 1954." $\perp$	"The world will end on December 20, 1954 *if we are not pious enough.*" "The world did not end on December 20, 1954." $\therefore$, we must be pious.
Together, these facts are dissonant.	By changing the cognition, the facts are no longer dissonant.

Dissonance is a stressful event, and we work to get rid of it. But the work we put in is often not a conscious effort. Sometimes instead of trying to resolve the dissonant environment, we walk away. We don't really need to understand why we are walking away; we still try to avoid or play down the dissonance. Have you ever disliked a person for no clear reason? You may be subconsciously reacting to something about that person that you find dissonant. Dislike is a way to distance yourself from some dissonant feature or behavior that you want to avoid.

Bioshock and Dissonance

2007's Bioshock won a slew of awards including the British Academy of Film and Television Arts (BAFTA) "Best Game" award and an Academy of Interactive Arts & Sciences (AIAS) award for "Outstanding Achievement in Game Design." It is in the top five PC games of all time as determined by Metacritic scores. That critical acclaim was well rewarded at the register as the game has sold over 4 million copies.

Bioshock is a first-person shooter (FPS), meaning that the game largely is concerned with traversing an environment and killing things that mean to kill you. In most FPS games, that is all there is. There is usually some kind of world-building involved, but that serves as a garnish to the main course of tactical killing. No one cares about the world of a game like Duke Nukem 3D—why would they? There is something with aliens and Duke has to kill 'em. Although Halo provides a world in which the action can happen, it still largely consists of "something with aliens and Master Chief has to kill 'em." Call of Duty? Something with Nazis and someone has to kill 'em.

Bioshock took an approach different from the norm. While Bioshock wasn't the first mainstream FPS to treat the context of the game's actions as important in comparison to the baseline action (see also Thief, Deus Ex, or Bioshock's spiritual predecessor System Shock 2), Bioshock was able to appeal to a more mature medium and parlay it into commercial success.

In Bioshock, you play as a silent, amnesiac protagonist (double trope points here) who survives an airplane crash only to find a portal to an underwater city. The city is wrecked and in disrepair and patrolled both by insane drug-addled residents called *Splicers* and hulking monstrosities called *Big Daddies*. The player has to sneak, set traps, and kill to traverse the environments and find out what happened in the city.

Early on, the player finds messages from the creator of the city, Andrew Ryan, that sets up the city's philosophy—a kind of Randian work-as-salvation self-interest. This philosophy should be largely compatible with FPS players. After all, most games treat every other story character in the game as interesting only insofar as they are able to help or harm the player character.

Bioshock tries to subvert this philosophy in an interesting way. The Big Daddies are paired with *Little Sisters,* small female children that help the Big Daddies harvest what is essentially magical mana from the dead. When a player defeats a Big Daddy, she is faced with a choice: She can "harvest" the Little Sister, killing it to gain power, or "rescue" the character to cure her of her insane ties to the Big Daddies. The Little Sisters are not abstract blobs—your decision to rescue them or not is proposed to be a tradeoff between in-game power and releasing a little (innocent?) girl from pain. This is your standard good-versus-evil tradeoff, ham-fistedly offering you a choice between saint and madman. But in the context of the city's eat-or-be-eaten Hobbesian state of nature, it is a philosophical versus strictly numeric evaluation.

Or at least it should be. If the player harvests Little Sisters, she gets power (measured by an in-game currency called *ADAM*) right away. But if she rescues, while she does get a small amount of ADAM she also later receives presents from her rescued Little Sisters. These presents largely even out the ADAM differential between harvesting and rescuing, making the decision meaningless from a resource perspective.

By the end of the game, the player realizes that the overriding theme of the game is that of the illusion of individual control. Players in games rarely have true freedom of control. They are led from one set piece to another, and their decisions are funneled down into a small handful of acceptable endings. The best games give players meaningful decisions to make. But because that is hard to do, in lieu of that many games try to dress decisions up to make them look like the player had agency. Bioshock both dresses up decisions to make players look like they have agency and actively points out how the player is lacking agency. While interviews with the developers have indicated that the decision to make the resource differences trivial between harvesting and rescuing was an external decision made by the publishers, it seems like it fits well in the theme of lack of choice, even if it is less satisfying to players.

Designer Clint Hocking called the tension between what the game systems are asking you to do (be self-interested) and what the game narrative is asking you to do (help non-player characters) *ludonarrative dissonance.* This term seems highfalutin' to those who don't study games deeply, but the concept is really core to the artistic merit of games. Ludonarrative dissonance is a conflict between the actions of players in a game and the narrative applying to those characters. In Elder Scrolls V: Skyrim, you have freedom of movement of your character while non-player characters talk to you. While a monk tells me the secret of the Dragonborn, I can be jumping in place, swinging an axe, or dropping pottery on the floor. In a movie, the director would cut and make the actor react appropriately. In a game, giving the player freedom allows these moments of dissonance to distract from either the thematic story elements (by letting me jump around like a fool) or the interactive elements (by holding me in place during a cutscene).

In the end, Bioshock doesn't end up being the critique of Rand's objectivism that the developers seem to have been aiming for. From a purely narrative context, the city of Rapture fell not because of the creator's self-interest, but because people started using drugs that turned them into superhuman psychopaths. It is hard to imagine some sort of collectivist safety net keeping society together when a single person can take a pyrokinesis drug and wreck the world. It is a critique of superpowers more than it is a critique of self-interest. From a game systems context, the game still embraces self-interest even beyond the issue of the ADAM harvested from Little Sisters. There are few if any characters in the game that you can sacrifice to leave the world better off. An end cutscene that is given when you save enough Little Sisters suggests this, but that is still in the realm of narrative, not gameplay systems. Every system is designed to funnel back into the uncritical expanse of player power, hence the dissonance.

Systems as Politics

In 2010, at the Game Developers Choice Awards, an annual event at the largest game developer gathering in the world, a producer for a new game that was taking the world by storm came onto the stage to accept an award. His company was roughly 2 years old but in that time had helped to popularize an entirely new business model for the games industry. In his on-stage remarks, he said that his company had openings and that he wanted folks to come and join him. In an industry where open positions are usually distributed among those already in one's personal network, that kind of call is remarkably open.

The audience, game developers who were otherwise quite well behaved, responded with boos.

The award was for Farmville, and the company with openings was Zynga. Zynga had a popular reputation at the time for stealing ideas, suing their competitors, abusing privacy and social network norms, and, most damningly, making tepid money-extracting Skinner boxes instead of games. Nonetheless, in early 2010 Farmville was seen as a real threat. It had 83 million monthly active users. Competitors were scrambling to release their own titles to meet the market demand. It was widely seen that resources were being diverted from the design and production of traditional games to these new "social" products that held questionable appeal to those used to the traditional titles. Zynga would have a $7 billion initial public offering the next year.

Needless to say, this is a period in which Zynga and Zynga-style games were on everyone's minds.

Two months after the Game Developers Choice Awards, Ian Bogost would release Cow Clicker on Facebook as a "social" game. A noted critic of Zynga's practices, Cow Clicker was a companion piece to a panel discussion that would discuss the most abusive practices of Zynga-style game design.

In Cow Clicker, players have a virtual field with a 2D representation of a cow. If the player clicks the cow, he is awarded one "mooney" (the game's currency) and the cow will make a mooing sound. The player would see a timer that would count down from six hours. Once the time expired, the player could click on the cow again, get additional mooney and restart the timer. There were eight spaces on the field where players could see their friend's cows. By adding friends, players could get additional clicks and mooney when their friends participated. Each action was paired with a prompt to post to the player's wall to boast of their "accomplishments." Players could use their mooney to accelerate the timers or buy "premium" cow designs. Players could also spend real money for virtual mooney.

The game, designed to be perfunctory rather than fun,[1] was intended to be a satire of the weaponized inanity of Farmville. Farmville made its money by encouraging players to spend it in order to avoid its own countdown timers and repetitive tasks. For a percentage of players large enough to be profitable, paying money was preferable to simply walking away. Cow Clicker would emulate that. You could pay money to avoid the game timer, but to what end? It only allowed you to click a cow, see a score increment by one, and hear a ridiculous stock sound effect.

To Bogost's horror, the game—intended only to be an example at a conference—gained a niche foothold. In a few months, it had over 50,000 active players. Bogost responded by adding additional "features." You could get clicks for clicking on friends' news feed posts about how they had just clicked. Cheaters began to "hack" the game by using automated clicking scripts.

---

1. I'm reserving "We put the 'fun' in perfunctory" as a slogan right here.

After the game took up more and more of Bogost's time, he decided to drastically alter the game. He added a "Cowpocalypse" timer to the game that would count down the time until some major event. Players could donate money to extend the timer, of course. He collected $700 from fearful players. But eventually the countdown hit zero and the cows were removed from the game. You can still click every six hours in the space formerly occupied by a cow and get clicks, but no rewarding moo sound happens. Nine months after the cows disappeared, Cow Clicker still had 3,000 active players. Even after Facebook disabled a number of the technical foundations that were used to support the game, Cow Clicker is still playable with a reduced feature set on Facebook. It has about 500 daily users, seven years after release.

Cow Clicker was a victim of its own success. Bogost made an inane Facebook game and while many players played the game ironically (author included), some played it in earnest. Cow Clicker never had to hang up a sign that said, "Cowville" or that the game was by "Zyngo" for the satire to hit home for all but the most aloof players. The message was entirely in the mechanics of the game and the dynamics generated by players. The thematic message required literacy of the politics of game development in 2010. Players who played the game with a sense of irony found a harmonious consonance between these thematic elements and the game's mechanical rapacity.

It suggests an interesting dynamic with the concept of the sincerity of play. In *Homo Ludens*, cultural theorist Johan Huizinga speaks of the person who interacts with a game in an insincere way: "The player who trespasses against the rules or ignores them is a 'spoil-sport.' The spoil-sport is not the same as the false player, the cheat; for the latter pretends to be playing the game [...] It is curious to note how much more lenient society is to the cheat than to the spoil-sport. [...] By withdrawing from the game he reveals the relativity and fragility of the play-world in which he had temporarily shut himself with others." In Cow Clicker, being a spoil-sport is part of the fun.

Parable of the Polygons

While Bogost received significant media coverage for Cow Clicker, he was previously known for his philosophical work on games and criticism. One of his most widely disseminated concepts is the concept of *procedural rhetoric.* Procedural rhetoric as defined by Bogost is "the art of persuasion through rule-based representations and interactions, rather than the spoken word, writing, images, or moving pictures." That is, games and other interactive media can persuade in a unique way that more traditional forms cannot.

Cow Clicker was a form of procedural rhetoric. The author wanted to convey how shallow and exploitative these kinds of games were, so he didn't just give interviews and write articles about how social games are "troubling specimens of human tragedy"—he made his argument in the form of a game.

Writing is comparatively easy compared to making games. I should know. So why try to convince anyone using interactive media when text is easy, doesn't require specialized hardware, and can be much more opaque in meaning?

As a case study, let's turn to the topic of racial segregation. It is easy here in the 21st century to dismiss racial segregation as an antiquated concept. Dustin Cable, a researcher at the University of Virginia used 2010 US Census data to create visualizations of racial segregation in America. You can find it at https://demographics.virginia.edu/DotMap/. Zoom into any large city in the United States and you can easily see how people of the same race cluster together when they decide where they are going to live. Zoom into Detroit and one can clearly see areas delineated by race. There are blue "white areas," green "black areas," orange "Hispanic areas," and red "Asian areas." Detroit's "Eight Mile Road" clearly delineates a racial boundary. North of the road is mostly white while south of the road is mostly black. By some metrics, Detroit is America's most racially segregated city. Other cities show more integration between races.

An easy explanation would just to be to throw up one's hands and count everyone as insidiously racist. While that tactic is a handy shortcut in politics, it is unsatisfactory as an explanation. Economist Robert Schelling wrote in the 1970s about this very topic. Using graph paper and coins, he created an agent-based explanation that discounted any sort of systemic animus. Schelling used coins as agents for families and graph paper to represent where those coins would live.

Schelling then applied some rules to the agents. They wanted to be in a diverse neighborhood. However, if they are too far in the minority, they would get unhappy and move. He would then apply the preferences to each coin-agent individually, moving them to an open spot if they were unhappy until the maximum number of coin-people were happy.

This preference to be in a diverse neighborhood where at least some of the folks there share some surface characteristics with you seems rational and intuitive and not at all racist. But in practice, these kinds of preferences lead to the kind of segregation seen in American cities.

Figure 6.3 presents an example of the kind Schelling used. A coin is unhappy if one third or fewer of his neighbors are like himself. The dime at D5 would be unhappy. Of his eight neighboring spaces, three have pennies, one is a dime, and four are empty. Only one of his four neighbors are like him, so he will want to move. He won't move to a place where he will also be unhappy, so that rules out locations like E4.

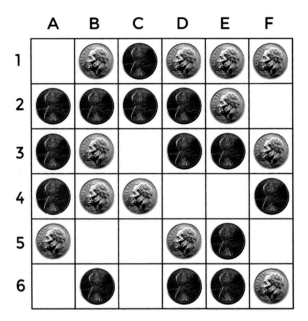

Figure 6.3 A Schelling-style example

Say he moves down the road to A6. It is a diverse neighborhood: 50% of his neighbors will be pennies and 50% will be dimes. But once he moves in, B6 is unhappy. All of his neighbors are dimes. He looks to move to a diverse neighborhood, so he moves to C3 where he will have three dime neighbors and four penny neighbors. Once he moves in, now B3 becomes unhappy because he is now overrun by pennies. And so on.

Through many iterations, the neighborhood becomes more and more segregated based on the execution of a seemingly innocuous preference.

This is unintuitive, so it was largely only understood by economists and policy wonks and hasn't been a part of the cultural or political consciousness. However, in 2014, game developer Nicky Case and math blogger Vi Hart released Parable of the Polygons (Figure 6.4) that repackages Schelling's work in a procedural form. Parable of the Polygons imagines a world of triangles and squares that exhibit various states of happiness if near some proportion of triangles and squares.

Case and Hart start by letting the player drag the shapes around in order to make them happy. This is slow and somewhat hard to do efficiently, much like Schelling's experiment with the coins. But since computers are really good at quickly running through iterative tasks like Schelling's pennies and dimes example, Parable of the Polygons becomes much more illustrative than Schelling's static example.

Because players can run through the simulation many times while changing the input parameters, players can see what rule changes enable or prevent the city's segregation from increasing. This is an apolitical example that ends up providing real political rhetoric.

The master stroke of Parable of the Polygons is in how it guides the player toward a conclusion favored by the authors by slowly setting up evidence. First, they set up the problem. Then, they allow players to explore the problem. Then they offer a solution *as if it was just another parameter in the simulation.*

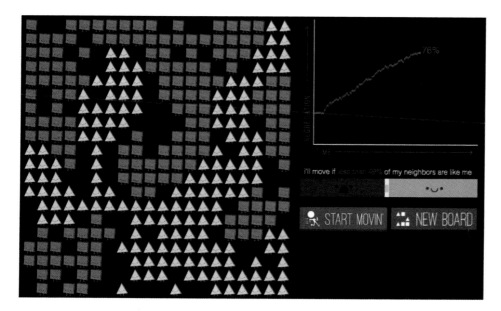

Figure 6.4 Parable of the Polygons

Late in the experience of Parable of the Polygons, the authors allow the player to make a shape unhappy not only if its neighbors are not like himself, but if his neighbors are *too much* like himself. By adjusting this metric, segregation decreases over time. This is the only metric presented that does this. The message is clear: Choosing diversity when it is presented isn't enough if you do not demand it in situations where you are already in a comfortable homogeneity.

What players choose to do with the information they gain playing Parable of the Polygons is up to them. Perhaps they think that the model is too simplified to be a useful parallel to real life, perhaps it makes them consider supporting diversity efforts that they previously had not considered, or maybe their world view can deepen beyond simple dichotomies of good and evil and look at the subtle forces that shape larger dynamics. One can hope. Regardless, Parable of the Polygons provides a real argument using rules, not words. If this is possible in a simple web page, what is possible in more robust simulations? What is possible in games that mix the thousands of years of developed rhetoric in written and spoken forms with the new possibility of procedural rhetoric?

Summary

Games have a unique ability to address the world around the player because they are driven by the actions of the players themselves. Being in a car accident is more memorable and evocative than witnessing strangers in a similarly sized accident. Experiencing something as the agent that caused that change is immensely powerful and underutilized in games as a whole. While it is largely experimental games that ask larger questions about the world and society, there is no reason this cannot become a more mainstream thematic shift.

GAMES COVERED

Playlist Game #16: The Marriage

Designer: Rod Humble

Why: Humble's art game is a simple example of how a game's meaning can be largely outside what is represented directly in the game. It is the interaction of these abstract pieces combined with the framing of the title that gives the game its thematic interest.

Playlist Game #17: September 12th

Designer: Gonzalo Frasca

Why: September 12th uses a system to deliver a message about blowback that seems fundamentally different from reading or hearing about the topic.

Playlist Game #18: Passage

Designer: Jason Rohrer

Why: Rohrer's Passage is one of the best examples of meaning through mechanics. It is a small, self-contained art game, but every element and interaction is packed with thematic meaning.

Playlist Game #19: Bioshock

Creators: Irrational Games

Why: Bioshock was one of 2007's most acclaimed games. It showed a willingness to blend the straightforward action expected in mainstream commercial titles with the philosophical inquiry of more literate forms. Its success is debatable, but it remains an essential experience for designers looking for deeper integration between theme and mechanics.

Playlist Game #20: Cow Clicker

Designer: Ian Bogost

Why: Angst towards social game developers was high around the time of Cow Clicker's release. But you do not have to commiserate with that angst to appreciate how the mechanics of the game worked both as a coherent game and a satire of the industry in which it was a participant. That it worked as a game both sincerely and ironically, depending on the audience, is a testament to the flexibility of delivering one's message through mechanical means.

Playlist Game #21: Parable of the Polygons

Creators: Vi Hart and Nicky Case

Why: Parable of the Polygons is a procedural explanation of a social issue. It is a kind of pamphlet in game form. This game form gives it a unique rhetorical context that can be emulated by designers to some degree in larger and more complex projects.

CHAPTER 7

REQUIEM FOR A PEWTER SHOE

"I think it's wrong that only one company makes
the game Monopoly."

—Steven Wright

Games like Marbles or even Pogs generate more attention for the
aesthetics of the game pieces than the function of the pieces in the
context of the game's magic circle. Although a golfer may put more
focus on the particular clubs he uses for superstitious purposes,
generally golfers expect to choose their clubs based on the efficacy, not
their aesthetics. Except insofar as they are used within the rules of golf,
the look of a golfer's clubs has little to do with the play of the game.
A particularly interesting category of games is the one in which the rules
themselves become the game pieces.

Pieces and Meaning

The physical pieces of a game are often considered with outsized importance. Consider the tokens in Monopoly. It hardly matters whether one is a car, a dog, or a thimble, yet players assign outsized importance to getting their preferred piece. When Hasbro decides to change the included tokens, it makes the news. In 2013, the iron was removed. In 2017, the thimble, wheelbarrow, and shoe were relegated. Clearly, players felt the new penguin, Tyrannosaurus rex, and rubber duck tokens had better cultural significance. Those three topped a survey with over 4.3 million responses. Your token in Monopoly has no special powers, doesn't have much of an aesthetic presence on the board, and isn't customizable in any way. Monopoly still plays the same way as it did when you were little, even if you can no longer be represented by a cannon. Players could be represented by differently colored glass beads with no change in game dynamics.

As we discussed in the previous chapter, one of the features of games that positions them in a different space from its more static media brethren is that the interactive nature of games opens the doors to new rhetorical and aesthetic effects stemming from that interactivity. A game can be beautiful aesthetically, but it can also be beautiful in how its systems function. Subjectively, I can say that a game like Go has both types of beauty. Soccer is colloquially called "the beautiful game"—the meaning of that colloquialism is that the systems in place in soccer result in beauty. When we speak of systems beauty, the pieces of the game become subservient to how they serve what the game as a whole represents.

The Buddha Nature

We humans have a hard time with logic. A few examples of this are covered in my book *Players Making Decisions,* but I would like to bring back this example from psychologist Peter Wason:

> You have the following four cards as shown in Figure 7.1. Each card has one letter and one number on opposite sides. Which of the cards must you turn over in order to test the truth of this rule: "If a card has a vowel on one side, then it has an odd number on the other"?

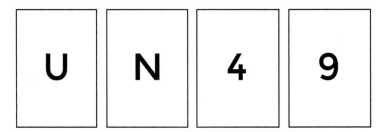

Figure 7.1 Wason test

Wason found that only 10% of respondents could answer correctly. Most people understand that you have to turn over the "U" card. If you do so and there is an even number, then you have disproven the rule. However, many choose to flip the "9" card. If there is a vowel on the other side, great. But if there is a consonant on the other side, that doesn't disprove the rule because the rule *says nothing about what should be on the other side of consonants.* The second card you need to turn over is actually the "4" card. If you turn it over and there is a vowel there, then that also disproves the rule. Table 7.1 summarizes the outcomes.

Table 7.1 Wason Test Example Outcomes

If you turn over the:	And there is a(n):	Then:
U	Odd number	Matches the rule
	Even number	**Rule is disproven**
N	Odd number	Irrelevant to rule
	Even number	Irrelevant to rule
4	Consonant	Irrelevant to rule
	Vowel	**Rule is disproven**
9	Consonant	Irrelevant to rule
	Vowel	Matches the rule

There have been a number of games to weaponize this difficulty in the form of a game. Eleusis is a game of inductive logic that uses a normal deck of cards. A much clearer game (based on Eleusis) is Kory Heath's Zendo. Zendo uses colored plastic pyramids from Looney Lab's Icehouse line and glass beads, but Zendo could be played with any agreed-upon components.

In Zendo, one player plays as a "master" and the others are "students."[1] The master starts the game by coming up with a rule that students need to guess. The master then sets up two *koans.* Koans are arrangements of game pieces that either reflect the rule or do not reflect the rule. For example, let's say my rule is "There are an even number of squares and an odd number of triangles." I then provide my students the two koans shown in Figure 7.2.

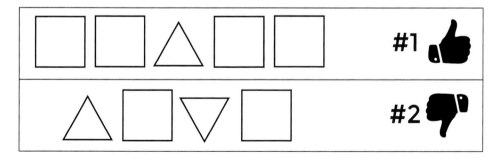

Figure 7.2 Evaluating the secret rule

---

1. A 2017 reprint of Zendo removed the Buddhist theming, so if you are looking to play the game, you may find different nomenclature in the rules.

Students know that koan #1 reflects my rule (the game says this koan "has the Buddha nature") and koan #2 does not. But there are countless rules that satisfy both of these koan results:

There are five shapes present.

There is no more than one triangle.

All triangles face upwards.

There are squares on both ends.

A square is never next to two triangles.

There are more squares than triangles.

The number of total corners is prime.

The number of each shape is a perfect square.

The display is horizontally symmetric.

In order for students to deduce the rules, they build a koan and then say one of two things: they may say, "Master" or "Mondo." If they say, "Master," then the master indicates whether the koan made by the student follows the rule. For instance, a student may state Triangle-Triangle-Square-Triangle-Triangle (Figure 7.3). The master would mark that koan as not following the rule. Thus, the student can eliminate the possibilities that "there are five shapes present" or "the display is horizontally symmetric" as the rule.

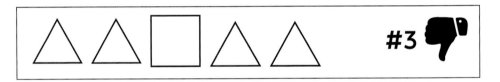

Figure 7.3 The master marks the koan as not following the rule.

The other option is to say "Mondo." In this case, every student guesses whether the student's koan matches the rule. The master then reveals whether it follows as he would if the student said "Master." Students who are correct gain a guessing stone.

With a guessing stone, the student may propose that he or she knows the rule. That player spends the stone and guesses the rule. If incorrect, the master must create a koan that either matches the proposed rule and not the true rule or vice versa. For instance, you spend a guessing stone to say, "Master, the number of total corners is prime." Since that is not the rule, I as master need to come up with a counterexample.

In Koan #4 shown in Figure 7.4, I show a display with 25 sides (not prime), but it meets the rule (odd number of triangles and even number of squares). I could have also offered a koan that was prime and did not meet the rule, such as Triangle-Square.

Figure 7.4 A counterexample played by the master

The student that first guesses the master's rule (or makes a guess that the master cannot figure out how to refute) wins and becomes the new master. There are some rules on koans that keep the game from being too combinatorially impossible. Koans cannot refer to other koans. They have to refer to only the pieces and the table themselves—no references to pointing at people, outside objects, timing, etc. are allowed.

Overall, the game is very challenging with a limited piece set. But what makes the game interesting is not the piece set. The pieces are just physical manifestations of the rules that created their order.

Nomic

Another game where the rules themselves are the game pieces is in the game Nomic by philosopher Peter Suber. Nomic is a game in which the rules are meant to be changed in creative ways. The original goal of the game is to score 100 points, although that can be changed. Players take turns proposing rule changes. A rule change may be something like "Players named Zack get to roll twice for points at the end of the turn." Then players vote on the rule change. Unless there are a large number of other Zacks, they will vote the rule down and I will lose points. If I can get rule changes to pass, I gain points. In any case, unless the rules change, I get to roll a die at the end of a turn. The next player may propose a rule that anyone who refers to himself in the first person loses 10 points. If that is voted on, it becomes codified in the rules.

Since nearly any rule change is possible, the breadth of possibility in a game of Nomic is immense. The "magic circle" of the game can even come into question because players can ratify rules that may trigger outside the context of the game. Of particular interest to game designers is the ability of players to change the design of the very framework of the game.

Sure, there are mutable and immutable rules, but what other categories can we come up with? What happens when rules are in conflict? How do we break ties? Does assigning a die roll to points seem unfair? Change it to points based on number of votes. Did that devolve into a popularity contest? Change rule submissions to secret proposals chosen at random.

Nomic provides the essential form of a game in which rules are themselves the game pieces. It is chaotic and often hard to handle but offers an intriguing canvas on which to test your rule-making abilities.

Eying Basic Grammars

Douglas Hofstadter's *Gödel, Escher, Bach* won the 1979 Pulitzer Prize for nonfiction and ranks among the most intriguing books of all time for game designers. In this book, Hofstadter wrote about an idea for self-manipulating games where every essential piece of the game was mutable. After all, the 20th and early 21st centuries have been dominated by the transition of slow, manual labor into algorithms that could be manipulated by machines. Algorithms are just collections of rules in a specific order. What happens when those rules can be changed by the very rules that define its nature? It is an interesting concept. Hofstadter would go on to write about Nomic for *Scientific American*.

In *Gödel, Escher, Bach*, Hofstadter would also discuss Bongard problems. These are logic problems in which 12 shapes would be separated into 2 groups of 6. One group of 6 would conform to a specific rule and the other would not. These problems would be at the heart of automated cognition. Can a computer figure out what the rule is based on only knowing 6 shapes that conform and 6 that do not? This problem would be the basis for Zendo.

Mu is a logical state discussed in *Gödel, Escher, Bach* that represents no answer as an answer doesn't apply to the question being asked. Mu rejects the categorical nature of the question. Mu comes from Buddhist teaching as a negative signifier. It is considered the "gate to enlightenment" in some texts. It neither "is" nor "is not."

With that lack of structure in mind, consider Titouan Millet's game Mu Cartographer. In Mu Cartographer, players are given an abstract set of interface controls with a small display of terrain that changes when those controls are manipulated (see Figure 7.5). The game gives no tutorial or helpful labels that would guide the player in her exploration. Instead, the manipulation towards useful ends is the game itself.

Figure 7.5 Mu Cartographer

At first, players will move around without purpose, as in early koans in a game of Zendo. But with careful experimentation and lucky accidents, they may figure out the cause and effect between various game widgets. Patient players will make real discoveries, and every user interface element will gain some sort of meaning. But much like the concept of Mu, you can make progress, but the question of an end is unanswerable. The elements you end up finding in this strange exercise echo the theme of being neither here nor there.

It is the slow unfolding of understanding your control systems and goals that is the essential core of Mu Cartographer. A game that immediately told you "this widget saves your location as a bookmark" would not only make the game trivially simple but would betray both the theme of Mu and the dynamic concept of the uncertainty surrounding your goals and tools. Much like good play of Nomic and Zendo is playful and creative but based on a complete internal logic, Mu Cartographer embraces creativity in your most basic actions to define a unique order of success that would be impossible in any other media.

Summary

Rules, to some degree, are a necessary component for games. Yet despite their ubiquity, few games treat them as anything but immutable axioms. Considering the immense variety in play states games can reach with immutable rules, games that treat rules themselves with a different consideration show a fertile area for interesting game designs.

GAMES COVERED

Playlist Game #22: Zendo

Designer: Kory Heath

Why: Zendo tests a player's ability to manipulate a vast possibility space not of positions or pieces, but of rules. The satisfying deductive aspects of the game often are more important than the win-lose end result for many players.

Playlist Game #23: Nomic

Designer: Peter Suber

Why: Nomic is an interesting case study for the malleability of rules. More of a role-playing exercise than a strategic game, Nomic tests the boundaries of player creativity vis-à-vis game design.

Playlist Game #24: Mu Cartographer

Designer: Titouan Millet

Why: What would be a user interface/user experience disaster in any other game, Mu Cartographer leverages to be the core puzzle experience. It raises questions about the playfulness of the basic experiences in digital games. Can a game be compelling if the rules are hidden or unclear? What makes for a tutorial design when that tutorial must be obscured? What are the differences between player assumptions about rules and actual rules? Mu Cartographer is not the first experimental game to raise these questions but is an excellent example in its class.

CHAPTER 8

THE SECOND CHANCE PHENOMENON

"I get irritated by designers who are so hung up on the 'art' that they are inflexible and unwilling to learn. [I]f your engineers recommend you change your design you had better know what you are doing when you ignore them."

—Richard Garfield

Often, if you ask a game designer about his or her influences, almost assuredly you will hear Dungeons & Dragons somewhere in that list. Rightfully so; Dungeons & Dragons has spawned innumerable mechanical and thematic tropes. And while most designers (especially those born in the 1980s and later) have some familiarity with Magic: The Gathering, often understated are the wide-reaching effects that game has had on the game design culture.

Flexibility

I often attend gaming conventions with prototypes that I hope to pitch to publishers. Every designer knows that this can be a stressful endeavor. You get to lay out your work in front of a stranger or acquaintance, and most of the time they will be able to find an excuse why they will not publish it. I never blame a publisher for this; they have to be excited enough to invest their time and money to make it a success. When a publisher says "yes," I expect them to be as enthusiastic about my game as I am. If it isn't a mutual effort, then it probably isn't worthwhile. Nonetheless, it can be heartbreaking to let down your guard with someone just for them to tell you your ideas don't work for them. It doesn't matter how many games you work on or sell, that anticipation of disappointment is still stressful.

I handle it by trying to be prepared. I've playtested my games thoroughly. I've done preliminary market research. I know what the publisher is and is not interested in from a genre and audience perspective. And I try to be flexible. If something needs to be changed to make it work, then I try to work within those bounds. And I always remember the story of Richard Garfield.

Richard Garfield was a mathematics PhD candidate at a prestigious university. But instead of worrying primarily about being published in academic journals, he wanted to be a published game designer. He'd been making his own games as a hobby for over a decade. He had a board game about programming robots to move around a factory floor that he and his colleagues thought was pretty exciting (it is the kind of thing math PhDs get excited over), and he really wanted to get it published.

Through a friend, Richard acquired a meeting with a newly formed publisher. He sent the publisher a prototype of the robot game. On meeting, the publisher told Richard that they weren't seeking to produce a board game—those required too much capital for their newly formed business.

At this point, Richard could have had a number of responses. He could have packed up and waited to find a publisher who would be as enthusiastic as he was about his robot game. He could have tried to convince the publisher that the robot game would be a good investment. But what he asked instead would forever change the business of hobbyist games. He asked what the publisher was interested in publishing and promised to deliver them something he would want to back. The representatives from the publisher said that they were looking to make a card game with fantasy artwork that would be quick to play between longer games at conventions.

Richard went back to the drawing board. He had been making prototypes of card games for over a decade. He combined concepts from two of his old, unpublished prototypes: a card game in which players could add or remove unique cards to or from their deck so that every game would be different called Safecracker, and a game called Five Magics that tried to distill the sprawling Cosmic Encounter alien battling board game down to a small card game form.

The publisher was interested in this new idea. It was risky, though. There were a lot of design unknowns. Two years of prototyping and playtesting followed. It was released at the Origins Game Fair in 1993 as Magic: The Gathering. It was a hit. Magic: The Gathering (or sometimes just "Magic") combined the fun and discovery of baseball card collecting with a competitive and challenging game. Magic is now a $300 million a year business and has a professional scene with cash prize pools upwards of $250,000. There are new Magic expansions released like clockwork quarterly—more than 50 exist currently.

In Magic, players assemble a deck of cards from their collection and battle against another player's deck. Thus, the game has two phases.

In one phase, the player has to construct a deck. The player must not only pick cards that synergize together but also must try and predict the types of decks an opponent might play. Magic is balanced in an attempt to be truly transitive—no one card or deck type should be unbeatable on its own. Instead, a rock-paper-scissors relationship exists during that deck-building phase. You could make a deck with a few big creatures, but a control deck would have tools to remove them. That control deck would be overwhelmed by a deck with a bunch of small creatures. But the small creature deck wouldn't be able to handle the sustained damage from the big creature deck.

The second phase of the game is the actual play of the game. Just because that big creature deck *should* lose against the control deck doesn't mean it will. Skillful play and good old luck can carry a game.

The combination of these two phases gives Magic a strategic shelf-life that approaches the best sports. Sports commentators can talk about the individual performances of players on the field, but what dominates discussions are the strategies of team and player building. Magic takes that into cardboard form: You need to think about the game even when you aren't playing.

We can consider Magic on its own as a great success that happened at the right place at the right time. Under that lens, Magic is a great story of financial success. But Magic is so much more with regard to design impact. A slew of also-ran customizable card games (CCGs) followed in the mid-1990s to attempt to capitalize on the format to largely middling success, exceptions being CCGs based on Pokémon and Yu-Gi-Oh!. Only recently, as teenagers weaned on Magic have become professional designers in their own right, are we seeing an impact on the larger games market.

Garfield finally got that robot-programming game published well after Magic shipped. It is called RoboRally and has been reprinted multiple times. It has won numerous awards.

Hearthstone

Blizzard Entertainment is one of the 600-lb. gorillas of the games industry. Their Warcraft, Diablo, StarCraft, World of Warcraft, Heroes of the Storm, and Overwatch franchises are hugely successful financially and critically. In 2006, Blizzard licensed their characters from World of Warcraft to Upper Deck for a CCG. Many Blizzard staffers were huge CCG fans (and in almost all cases, that meant huge Magic: The Gathering fans), so when it came time to propose a smaller, more agile project they proposed what would become Hearthstone.

Hearthstone is a purely digital CCG. This allows Blizzard to both save on the costs of printing and distributing physical cards but also allows them to wholly control the secondary market. In Magic, hobbyist stores and websites provide liquidity and arbitrage to what would normally be a fairly illiquid market. A single card once sold on the secondary market for more than $27,000. Magic's publisher sees no part of that transaction.[1] But in a digital setting, the publisher can always have control over all elements of each player's collection, thus deciding what exactly the secondary market will look like and taking a cut if necessary.

Magic already had an online, digital version. While it was profitable, it suffered from numerous usability and functionality issues. One of the issues was with the design of Magic itself. In Magic, almost any game effect can be interrupted with another game effect. This means in an online game of Magic, nearly every action has to be verified by the opponent in case the opponent wants to interrupt. For example, if I want to attack you with my Goblin, I can tell the game that the Goblin will attack. Now, flow of the game transfers to you as the game asks whether you want to interrupt this action. You have an Unsummon card in your hand that removes a creature. You choose to not use it. Control passes back to me. I have a Giant Growth card in my hand that makes my creature bigger. I choose to use it. Control passes back to you. Now you can decide to actually use the Unsummon given what I've done to the creature. You choose to do so. This exchange can happen fairly quickly in real life, but in a digital setting, switching focus back and forth requires many interactions with the game from each player where the opponent must wait for input. If each interaction above takes 10 seconds while a player notices he is on turn and then manipulates the user interface, then a simple attack has taken almost a minute. It greatly changes the feel of the game.

Hearthstone was able to ameliorate that problem by ensuring that no rules or particular cards require the opponent's input. Instead, you take your entire turn and then the opponent takes his entire turn. Instead of dozens of periods of waiting during a turn, you only wait for the opponent's turn to play out. The strategic density is preserved by allowing for cards to be triggered on certain conditions instead of waiting for user input. It makes for a faster and smoother play session.

---

1. Many estimate that the secondary market sales volume is larger than the sales between the publisher and retailers.

Hearthstone started as an experimental project for Blizzard but now is one of their tentpole franchises. Hearthstone now makes more money than Magic: The Gathering. Whether that is sustainable into the future is anyone's guess. At the very least, Magic has had an impressive nearly quarter century of design impact.

Dominion

But Hearthstone's story is only of limited interest from a design perspective. Every megahit ends in two ways: Either the hit dies off itself and is remembered as a fad,[2] or something improves upon it and supplants it. The story of Magic and Hearthstone is the latter and has been played out many times before in the games industry and will play out many times hence. What is truly interesting are the mutations that a megahit inspires in the DNA of designs that aren't directly tackling the same problems.

Donald X. Vaccarino (often called "Donald X.") is a long-time Magic fan. Beyond being a fan, he was highly active in the Magic community. He would design fan sets and even has a credit in the *Comprehensive Rules of Magic.* In an interview, he credits Magic with inspiring his design career: "It introduced me to the concept of interacting rules on cards—I had never seen Cosmic Encounter or Wiz-War. It made me a bunch of friends who showed me gamer's games and Euros. It inspired me to make my own games, with many of the early ones pursuing the 'game where the rules change' idea to various extremes."

Unlike Richard Garfield, Donald was mostly making games as a fun activity for himself and his friends. He had a game that he called Spirit Warriors that he really liked. As he was making an update to it for an upcoming play group, he realized the game was far too big and complicated to finish in time. In earlier tests, players couldn't understand the complex interactions for calculating game effects.

So Donald scrapped it down to its most basic elements in order to have a game ready for testing. His play group loved it. They loved it so much that they stopped playing most other games. Eventually, the game was pitched to Rio Grande Games and would be published in 2008 as Dominion. It would go on to sell over 2.5 million copies and win the Spiel des Jahres and Deutscher Spielepreis, the first game since 1996 to win both of Germany's prestigious board game awards.

If you recall from above, Magic had two phases: deckbuilding and play. Dominion distills Magic down to just the deckbuilding without the collectible elements. In Dominion, deckbuilding *is* play. Players start with access to a market of approximately 20 cards that may be in their deck over the course of the game, but that market is different from game to game.

---

2. Pogs went from an unstoppable cultural phenomenon that every tween kid played in 1993 to completely irrelevant by the end of 1995.

They each start with the same boring deck of some weak money and victory point cards. On a turn, players draw the top five cards of their deck, play any actions and money they have in their hand, and then buy new cards for their deck. This becomes an engine: You buy cards that allow you to buy better cards that allow you to buy better cards. This might be a rote activity if not for the decision regarding when to start buying the victory point cards that you need to win the game but do nothing to help your deckbuilding engine.

Dominion fixes problems that many players had with Magic. Cards come in complete sets. Players don't have to buy packs and hope for lucky random results. Since all players are playing with the same sets, a rich kid that can afford the "best" cards doesn't have an advantage over anyone else as he does in Magic. Additionally, many players love the deckbuilding aspects of Magic but find the play of the game itself to be less interesting. Dominion completely removes this aspect while keeping the rich problem space of the vast number of card combinations.

Dominion spawned an entire genre of deckbuilding games such as Ascension, Star Realms, and Legendary. But Dominion's legacy is felt far beyond the genre it created as games in other genres have adopted deckbuilding as a mechanic in a larger game. But for designers looking for inspiration, very little matches the initial power of possibility in the original Dominion. It is difficult to play it and not immediately imagine other possible cards or different strategies you could pursue. The design space is very rich.

7 Wonders

The deckbuilding aspects of Magic, I feel, are what has kept the game in the gaming consciousness for more than 20 years. The game itself is fine but ends when a player reaches zero health. The deckbuilding aspects of Magic never end. There is endless online debate about deck composition and about mechanical combination, and when a new set is announced or leaked, players excitedly search their collections for the best juxtapositions of new cards with old.

The fun of deckbuilding carried over to variants for Magic. An early variant was called *sealed deck*. In this variant, a player got a set number of sealed packs of cards from the store and had to build a deck around whatever was there and play against opponents with a similar restriction. This was a fun deckbuilding exercise, but it was hard to make truly interesting combinations with such a limited set of cards. You never knew what the other player may have received, so there was an aura of mystery.

A group of early Magic playtesters combined their love of Strat-O-Matic Baseball and Magic and created what is called a *rotisserie draft*. In it, all the players in a tournament open packs together and choose from the displayed cards to make a deck, much like a professional sports team drafts players out of college. This, much like its real-world analogue, had a lot of interesting strategy but took a lot of time. And since every pick was by design public, you knew the contents of everyone else's decks.

This has evolved into what is called a *booster draft.* In a booster draft, players open a whole pack of cards (15 cards in this case) and choose one, passing the rest to the player on their left. You would then receive 14 cards from the player on your right, from which you would pick the best card remaining and continue passing. By the end of 3 packs, you would have 45 cards to play with, each card having been picked based on its ability to work with each other card you have chosen. Much like sealed deck, this kept the mystery of not knowing what opponents may have but played faster, while preserving the interesting decision making involved in a draft.

A problem with booster drafts (and all of the variants I have mentioned above) is cost. Drafts are a lot of fun, but they take a lot of time. And since every pack needs to be sealed, each draft has a significant cost to each player. Players were already trying to apply drafting variants to board games like Race for the Galaxy to solve this cost issue, but there were limitations to doing this for constrained games in which drafting wasn't considered in the original design.

Antoine Bauza was working on a game about the seven wonders of the ancient world that could be played by seven players. He tried numerous mechanics in combination with the theme but was having trouble settling on something as every new attempt sprouted new problems. Eventually, he tried drafting as a mechanic. That was the mechanic the game needed. It would be published in 2010 as 7 Wonders and would go on to win the Kennerspiel des Jahres (a subcategory of the Spiel des Jahres mentioned above particularly for more complex games) and the Deutscher Spielepreis.

In 7 Wonders, each player represents a civilization. And much like a Magic draft often has three packs of cards, there are three decks representing three ages of development from which players do a booster draft. Those cards represent buildings, military power, scientific discovery, and other effects that players use to make their civilization more powerful than their neighbors'.

Just as Dominion took the deckbuilding aspect of Magic and made it a self-contained game, so did 7 Wonders take the popular drafting variant and isolated the activity that made it fun by developing it into its own game.

Summary

Magic: The Gathering has a deep legacy. Beyond the games it has directly inspired, which I detail above, most designers here in the 2010s came of age being inspired by two games: Magic: The Gathering and Dungeons & Dragons. We will discuss the latter later. But what both games have in common is a robust structure that welcomes players to ask, "What if...?" and change the game experimentally. What if I had a card that pulled random cards out of the opponent's deck? You could make this card on paper, slip it in a card sleeve, and try it out.

These games invite creativity far more than even more popular games within the zeitgeist. Mario is a great design and almost universally known, but until Super Mario Maker, it didn't do much to allow players to participate in the design process. Games that are interesting on their own merits and also set to inspire future designers by allowing them into a participatory community are rare and should serve as a baseline literacy for current and future designers.

GAMES COVERED

Playlist Game #25: Magic: The Gathering

Designer: Richard Garfield

Why: Most game designers are familiar with Magic: The Gathering. If they aren't, they should make it a priority to become familiar with it. But beyond the game itself, Magic created multiple entire genres. CCG design lessons would be adopted in many card, board, and video games. CCGs have an entirely new set of design challenges since it is impossible to know what cards a player may own or combine.

Playlist Game #26: Hearthstone

Creators: Blizzard Entertainment

Why: Blizzard stole a good deal of the market share from Magic while creating a product that couldn't be traded or sold on the secondary market. They did it through leveraging the company's ability to make polished and sought-after games. The differences between Hearthstone and Magic are the most interesting to compare because they share many of the same problems but have different strategies for addressing them, both in terms of game design and product design.

Playlist Game #27: Dominion

Designer: Donald X. Vaccarino

Why: Dominion, like The Settlers of Catan before it, broke through a highly insular board gamer culture to reach a level of mainstream success. This success was based on taking a mechanic from a rich game and exploring it in isolation. Many have attempted this technique with other games, but few have preserved a level of design possibility as has Dominion.

Playlist Game #28: 7 Wonders

Designer: Antoine Bauza

Why: Just as Dominion lifted the deckbuilding aspect of Magic to make a self-contained game, 7 Wonders explores the concept of drafting as a self-contained game. 7 Wonders was not the first to do this but serves as a rich example of the flexibility of exploring one mechanic in depth.

CHAPTER 9

CHALLENGING COMPLEXITY

> "Any fool can make something complicated. It
> takes a genius to make it simple."
>
> —Woody Guthrie

Marketing and design are often in conflict. When I listen to novice designers pitching their ideas for games, it is never more obvious. We learn by modeling the behaviors that we see in the world. Marketing is meant to be memorable, whereas design tends to be invisible. Thus, it becomes hard for novice designers to create something unlike the flashy, big-budget experiences that they are used to consuming.

Retracing Your Steps

Most game designers start out as game consumers. They begin to make games because they have had such a fulfilling time consuming games. And so fledgling designers often model their behavior on what they think professional behavior would look like. Unfortunately, the sausage making of actual game production largely happens behind closed doors and under nondisclosure agreements. What is public facing are dog-and-pony show media events like the Electronic Entertainment Expo (E3). And the behavior that is modeled there is that vague, Big Idea-style promises are what get people excited about games. Perhaps that gets consumers eager to consume games, but this is largely worthless when it comes to making games.

Every year, the biggest video game developers and publishers set up shop in Los Angeles for E3. If you have never been, imagine the loudest casino floor you've ever been in multiplied by the human density of New York's 4-train at rush hour. The show floor houses hundreds of demos that try to impress potential retailers to stock their upcoming titles and has evolved into being a consumer media event as well.

The capstones of E3 are the publisher press conferences in which well-rehearsed sales pitches are made to the public at large for games that will be coming out in the next 6 months to a year. It is an arms race of hype where a video that shows only the name of an upcoming game can get riotous standing ovations. Longer segments detail new franchises in order to get the public at large interested. These segments usually have a demo of the game combined with numerous promises of what the game will be at launch. In Ubisoft's 2012 demo of the upcoming game Watch Dogs, their CEO said the game would "revolutionize the way players would interact with each other." They presented a game with an open-world version of Chicago where nearly everything could be hacked and used toward in-game goals. When the game actually came out, the scope was significantly reduced. While it performed well, it had been sold as so much more. Players were disappointed with what was overall still a pretty solid game.

Ubisoft and every other developer and publisher are incentivized to exaggerate at E3. With hundreds of games showcased each year, and with releases often many months in the future, only the most vociferous hype can survive until release. Consumers never learn though; they continue to soak up the promises every year. The allure that new games might be everything we imagine them to be is too compelling.

What developers and publishers do at E3 is marketing. They want you to be excited about buying a potential game from them, and they will do what they can to paint just enough of the potential game in your brain and let you fill in the rest. When done in an environment with many competitors, this becomes a large-player-count prisoner's dilemma where the equilibrium is that everyone tries to oversell their game to get just a little bit more mindshare than their competitor. Most of the games shown at E3 will be financial failures for their companies. The promises made about those games will be largely forgotten.

When making games, you must be explicit as to what you want to make. A promise of a real-life, open-world Chicago is no good to a team that wants to create it. At what level of fidelity will it be? Will every broken sidewalk and mailbox be implemented? Does every street need to be accurate? Or just the major landmarks? Which landmarks? Which ones should be left out? What happens when you reach the edge? Can you go into every building or just some? Which ones?

The problem with big promises is that they spawn questions that spawn questions until every possible ambiguity is made explicit. It's not enough to say that you will now add a flame flower to Mario. That might be enough for marketing folks to sell the idea of a flame flower to an audience, but the folks making the game now need to know how the flame interacts with every other object in the game. Complexity is exponential in that case; the bigger the game, the exponentially bigger the design ramifications.

But when you are trying to sell a game, small and elegant aren't particularly motivating sales points. You rarely see pitches at E3 that lean on elegance or parsimony. "This Mario game is 50% smaller than the last!" is never said, even if making a 50% smaller game makes the game better than the last. The cultural bias is ever toward bigger and more expansive promises for games. It is tough to get hyped over the small ones.

Small games with small scope are just as if not more important than large games. They drive a large part of the mobile market and provide for a more easily analyzed design space. For example, it would be fairly easy to fully describe the design behind a simple mobile game like Flappy Bird. Implementable design decisions make for observable game dynamics from which a designer can learn and emulate. The same technique is not as easily applied to a game with numerous nested systems like Civilization 6. Critiquing the design there would take an understanding of how every system relates to each other. While not impossible, it is much harder. Yet novice designers want to propose the next Civilization and ignore the next Flappy Bird.

This is why it is important to spend time examining games with smaller scopes that nonetheless leverage a clever design to create a worthwhile experience. The first we will examine came at its simplicity from an otherwise extremely complicated source.

Drop7

An alternate reality game (ARG) is a hard category to truly define. It is a concept that stretches what a game is until it blends with the real world by using real-world mechanisms as game mechanisms. One of the most popularly cited ARGs was called I Love Bees. In a trailer for Microsoft's Halo 2, there was a brief flash that included the URL for a beekeeping website. Visiting that website kicked off a narrative about a possibly rogue AI, and that narrative could be expanded upon by solving rich, crowd-sourced puzzles that often involved things well outside the bounds of traditional games, such as visiting a real pay phone at a certain time to hear a clue.

ARGs being hard to monetize (how can you pay someone for access when the game is open to all?) lead them to be used largely as a novel form of marketing some other monetizable media property. In the case of I Love Bees, that property was Microsoft's Halo franchise. New York-based studio Area/Code was hired to promote the CBS network's television drama "Numb3rs" in the form of an ARG. This ARG was called Chain Factor.

In Chain Factor, players played a simple puzzle game that was featured inside an episode of "Numb3rs." Players could play the game itself on the Chain Factor website. Player progress was not limited to a single player's achievements but instead to the community as a whole. For example, a new clue in the surrounding story about the evil, mad game designer[1] could be revealed only when the score of all players summed to a billion points. Then a small glitch would be unlocked that, when combined with the glitches of other players, unlocked a new power in the Chain Factor game itself. Chain Factor was a competent ARG[2]; it was certainly easier than other contemporary examples. But even after the 6-week campaign for the show ended, players kept coming back to the simple puzzle game inside Chain Factor.

After the Chain Factor ARG concluded, Area/Code decided to clean up the puzzle game that everyone clearly enjoyed by removing even more features from it. They released it as Drop7 in 2009.

Drop7 looks like many other abstract puzzle-style games in the vein of Tetris. Players have a 7 × 7 grid and must drop numbered circles onto the grid as in Connect 4 for as long as they can until they run out of room. A circle breaks and disappears if its number matches the number of circles in its row or column, omitting spaces. Periodically, a row of gray circles will appear from the bottom, pushing everything else up. Grey circles can only be broken by making a match adjacent to them twice, which turns them into a normal circle. The rate at which these gray rows appear gets shorter and shorter as the game goes on, converging the game to an end point.

In the example in Figure 9.1, the player has a 4 to drop. There are a number of good places to drop it. If the player drops it in the seventh column, then there will be a row with 1-7-7-4 and so the 4 would disappear. If the player drops it in the second column, there will be a column with 4-6-5-6-X. In that case, the 5 would disappear since it is a column of 5, leaving 4-6-6-X. Now that it is a 4-sized column, the 4 will disappear. So that's a pretty good drop because it gets rid of itself and one other.

---

1. How could they tell?

2. This is probably underselling the narrative of Chain Factor a great deal.

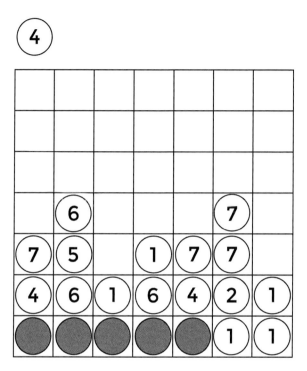

Figure 9.1 Drop7

But a better move may be to drop it in the first column. This would leave 4-7-4-X (Figure 9.2, top-left) and the 4s would disappear from being in a column of 4 and the grey on the bottom row would have a crack from being matched against once. That would drop the 7 down into the second row from the bottom (Figure 9.2, top-right), making a row of 7 (which would make the 7 disappear) and breaking the grey circle into a 2. Now the second row has 6 circles, so the 6s disappear (Figure 9.2, bottom-left). This single drop ended up removing 5 circles in total (Figure 9.2, bottom-right).

In most casual games of this type, the goal is to match like elements—say, candies in Candy Crush. The subtle difference that makes this much more interesting is that a disc's type changes in relation to how many are in its row or column, meaning that you are not only trying to move discs to favorable positions in relation to what they are next to but what they are near in the context of the rest of the game space. As such, there is rarely a move in Drop7 where you don't have an interesting decision to make about what you want the board to look like. As you reach the end of the game, your moves become more and more constrained. That tipping point where you no longer have any good moves is often due to your own poor play rather than the 1-to-7 random number generator (although that generator can be sadistic at times).

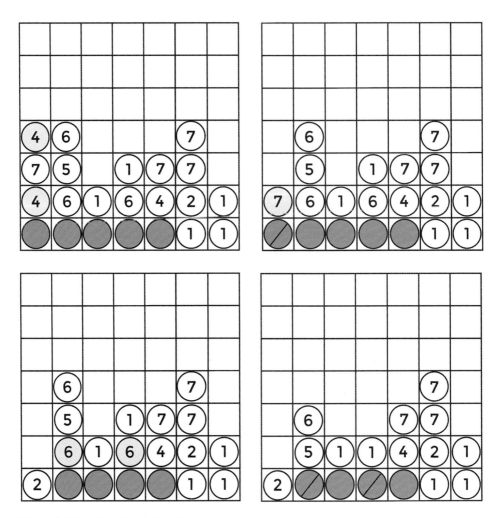

Figure 9.2 Breaking discs in Drop7

This depth, given very simple rules, makes Drop7 an interesting article of study for other game makers. The original version of the game within Chain Factor had a number of powerups: bomb discs, a power that raised the value of 1s, a power that destroyed prime numbers, and so on, but none of those carried over to Drop7. They weren't needed. The matching and chaining itself was compelling enough. It is tempting as a designer to try something and say, "What does it hurt to keep it?" We are very good at justifying what is a sunk cost. It takes fortitude and insight to remove something that is functional to have a simpler, more coherent core. Drop7 does this very well.

Triple Town

I carry my E-ink Kindle device with me everywhere. It is a device that does one thing (displaying books) incredibly well. When Amazon announced that the E-ink Kindles would also have games, I was pretty excited. What a convergence of my interests! This was during the short period between the burgeoning of independent mobile games and the ubiquity of tablets like the Kindle Fire and iPad. When the latter appeared, games were largely forgotten for the E-ink Kindles and they returned to their solemn duty as reading devices. But for a short time, there was a market for E-ink games and the best by far was created by Washington-based indie studio Spry Fox, called Triple Town.

Triple Town has been described as a match-3 game meets Civilization, and that is a pretty pithy description. The player is presented with a 6×6 board that represents the player's town. She is then given an item to place on any empty space in the town. If three of the same item touch, all three smash together at the position of the last-placed item to become the next higher valued object. Three grass tiles become a bush. Three bushes become a tree. Three trees become a hut. Three huts become a house. There are also bears that pop up to ruin your plans. They must be placed like a normal item, but when completely trapped, they die and turn into a tombstone. Of course, three tombstones can be matched to create a church, starting a new, different hierarchy of objects.

In the example in Figure 9.3, the player has grass to place. If he places it where the arrow is pointing in the top-left image, then those three grasses will merge into a bush.

Next, the player has another grass to place (Figure 9.3, top-right). If he places it where the arrow is pointing, those grasses will merge into a bush as well.

Now that three bushes are next to each other, they will merge into the next-higher object, a tree (Figure 9.3, bottom-left). Now the board is fairly clear for new placements.

Life in Triple Town is never as neat and predictable as in Figure 9.3. But with careful play, the randomness in your next item and in bear movement can be mitigated a great deal. For instance, to make a set of three houses, you must carefully make a set of three huts, making sure the last hut is in the right position to leave the house where you want it. That would be easy if huts were placeable objects, but most of the time you are placing lower-level objects. So to place a house effectively, you have to plan three huts effectively. But to place a hut effectively, you have to place three trees effectively so that they match at the right position. But to place a tree, you must place three bushes effectively. A house is made of 3^4 or 81 grass placements!

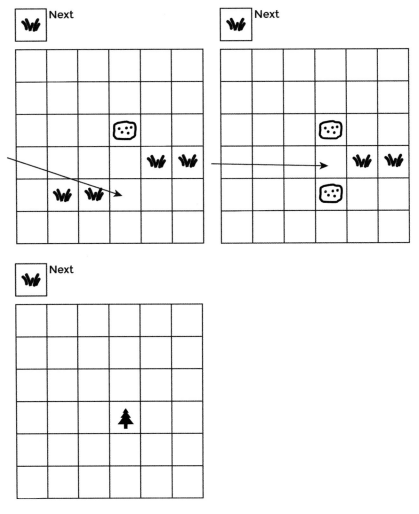

Figure 9.3 Play in Triple Town

Very skilled Triple Town players exist. Game designer Stephane Bura is one of the best. He has posted various tips and tricks online, culminating in a video showing a very efficient route to a flying castle (3^7 or 2,187 grasses, but achievable in 400 moves in his video due to some higher-level objects being placed and some use of wild crystals).

Stephane's technique requires deep planning. He calls his technique a recursive spiral (see Figure 9.4). His algorithm would be difficult to implement even if you knew what items you would receive to place or when the bears would show up and ruin your positioning. The recursive spiral requires a great deal of spatial awareness and flexibility to think the levels ahead needed for proper placement.

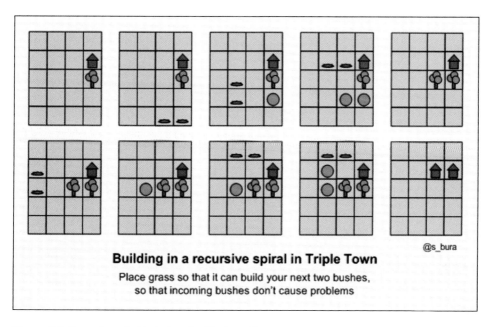

Figure 9.4 Recursive spiral technique by Stephane Bura

This is a great deal of complexity for success in a game where the core feature set is quite small. Novice game players can easily grasp the rules and play around with moderate success. But the depth easily exceeds the ability of most players to plan without significant technique and practice.

Game of Life

In a way, Triple Town shares a great deal with one of the early experimental uses of computers. In 1970, mathematician John Horton Conway published "The Game of Life" in a magazine article. The Game of Life is not a game in the traditional sense: It has no players, no win state, and no loss state. It is a theoretical model of life simplified down to a 2D grid with some straightforward rules.

In Figure 9.5, cell B2 has exactly three alive neighbors, so it is alive in the next step. Every other cell has less than two alive neighbors, so they are dead in the next step.

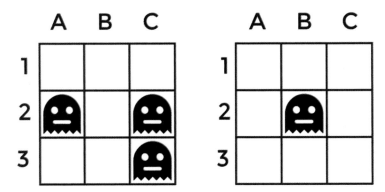

Figure 9.5 The Game of Life grids

These simple rules combine to create a wide variety of behaviors over turns from different starting patterns. While the computations for what goes into every cell is laborious to do by hand, it is easy for computers, which were gaining wider research popularity in the 1970s. The Game of Life has had extensive research interest since its inception because of the complexity of emergent behaviors that are able to be created from applications of these simple rules. In Figure 9.6, the pattern on the left steps into the pattern on the right, which steps back into the pattern on the left indefinitely.

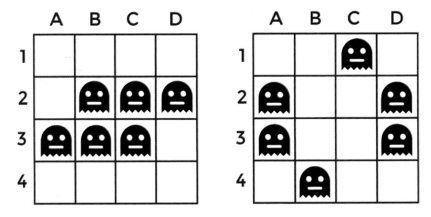

Figure 9.6 Patterns stepping into each other indefinitely

Where Conway's Game of Life gets interesting is in much larger and more complex patterns in larger or even infinite grids. *Gliders* are shapes that move across a large grid one step at a time. *Spaceships* are more complex shapes that move like Gliders. *Puffers* move across the grid but leave debris behind. *Rakes* are complex Puffers that leave behind debris in the form of Spaceships!

Then it gets weirder. Theoretically, a shape exists that can input any other shape and replicate it. Turing machines have been created within The Game of Life that make it theoretically possible to produce simulated computers within the game. One has been constructed already that can compute prime numbers. If this can be done, what is the upper bound of complexity that a Game of Life simulation can recreate? Can it create its own simulations? What would an AI look like in this schema? This grand amount of complexity comes from the simplest of rules.[3]

The Game of Life is interesting from a mathematical perspective, but "playing" The Game of Life is interesting even within the scope of understanding game design. Triple Town acts in a Life-like way. Instead of each cell being determined by an initial position until the end of time, the act of disrupting and drawing patterns continues throughout the game. Whereas a Game of Life enthusiast tinkers until finding the right combination of elements to make a Glider, Triple Town players like Stephane Bura tinker to find the right combination of steps to minimize the number of items on the board. The line of inquiry in high-level play is similar between The Game of Life and Triple Town and it is hard to deny the relationship, regardless of whether the Spry Fox Triple Town team was directly influenced by The Game of Life.

Pair Solitaire

The point of examining complex mathematical toys like The Game of Life is not to master them. Few designers, myself included, have a good theoretical handle on how they work at a deep dynamic level. Instead, the point is to appreciate what qualities give a system a depth well beyond the work required to make the system. There are many initial conditions for The Game of Life that do not result in all of the interesting emergence that we see. For instance, most of the starting positions end in uninteresting extinction. Where there is interest is in that narrow band of conditions that create entertaining dynamics.

The same is true for games. There are innumerable mechanics that can be randomly shoved together, but only a few show the depth of player dynamics that result in interesting and worthwhile games. Take a Klondike Solitaire game as an example.[4] The object of the game is to remove all of the cards. When you allow infinite shuffles and one-draw at a time, the game becomes almost trivially easy. When you allow no reshuffles and three draws at a time, the game becomes unsolvable at times. Somewhere is the middle is the intersection of rules and player behavior that creates a viable game.

---

3. In 2010, a Minecraft player created a functioning Game of Life simulation from redstone, leading us to ask how many levels of simulation can nest together? Can one theoretically create a Game of Life simulation inside Minecraft that itself simulates Minecraft?

4. This is the solitaire game repopularized when it became a pack-in application with Microsoft Windows.

In some spaces, that viable intersection is large. You can mess with the mechanics of World of Warcraft in a number of ways and it is robust enough that it won't fall apart. In a case like that, it can be hard to tell whether your design truly works because there are so many fail-safes built into its overarching complexity. A helpful skill for a designer is to be able to build something in a very small, elegant framework.

There have been hundreds of variations of Klondike Solitaire over the years. A novel approach came out on mobile devices in 2014 called Pair Solitaire. Pair Solitaire presents players with the deck of 52 cards distributed in a line. The goal is to remove as many cards as possible. All random elements are generated and visible before the game begins, unlike the random draws over the course of a normal Klondike Solitaire game. To remove a card, you need to have two cards of the same suit or rank separated by one other card. In the example in Figure 9.7, the only instance where there is a match of suit or rank separated by one card is with the first and third cards that are both spades.

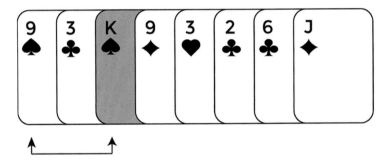

Figure 9.7 The first and third cards are both spades.

I've highlighted the king of spades because that is the correct card to remove. I can remove either the 9 of Spades or the king of spades. If I remove the 9 of spades, then there are no more possible matches and the game would be over. But if I remove the king of spades, then both the 9s at positions 1 and 3 are able to be matched and the 3s at positions 2 and 4 can be matched (see Figure 9.8).

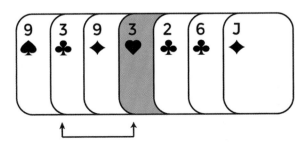

Figure 9.8 Two matches are now possible, the 9s and the 3s. Choosing the highlighted card gives more future options

I can remove any of the first four cards at this point. If I removed the 9 of diamonds, then I could start matching clubs, but I think it would be better to remove the 3 of hearts. In fact, I can get down to the best possible result of two remaining cards by doing so (see Figure 9.9).

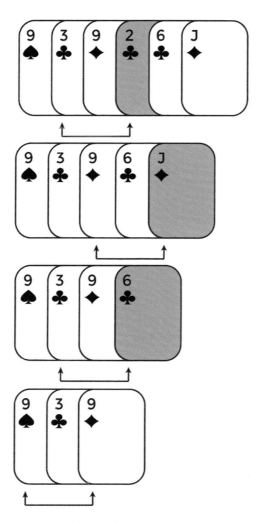

Figure 9.9 Getting down to two remaining cards

Pair Solitaire is interesting in that it is such a clever take on a century-old game form. It is possible that someone invented this game before Vitaliy Zlotskiy made an app out of it, but it wasn't documented or widely played. The fact that such a compelling simple game made with the most common of components could come out in 2014 suggests that the low-hanging fruit hasn't all been picked. If Pair Solitaire could lay dormant until just recently, what other clever, simple ideas are ready to be hatched?

Adding complexity to an already proven game mechanic is easy. Many software-as-a-service free-to-play games do this ad nauseam, complicating simple games with indecipherable reward schemes and tacked-on psychological hooks. Removing complexity and keeping a viable game underneath can be difficult, but is the only way toward more elegant game designs.

Love Letter

In digital games, a hefty, complex game takes up the same amount of physical space as an elegant, simple game. The same is not true for physical board and card games. A standard deck of cards is one of the most versatile compact-game collections, but it is hard to convey more complex mechanics with the abstract ranks and suits. Modern board and card game designs include many custom pieces to help relay a theme and make the player experience easier to learn.

Making custom cards and board game pieces can be expensive. That expense per-unit decreases as print runs increase in size. Thus, it is in the publisher's best interest to print as large a game as the market will allow to best leverage economies of scale and create customer visibility for a game on store shelves.

Board game forums on the internet often have threads where posters lament that they are out of room for games because they have bought too many and the box sizes have been getting larger and larger. The U.S. Census Bureau reports that the average size of a new home in 2016 was around 2,500 ft^2. In Japan, the average residence size is 1,310 ft^2. When you consider the amount of living space required for basic housing functions, the difference in space available for storing games is significant. This is one reason behind a movement of small form-factor hobbyist games from Japanese designers.

One of the most prolific and successful of the Japanese small-form designers is Seiji Kanai. While he had been publishing games in Japan since 2006, in 2012 AEG published his card game Love Letter to huge success in the West. Since then, re-themed versions of Love Letter have been released with Batman, The Hobbit, Archer, and Adventure Time themes. There is even a Wedding Edition that is to be used as wedding favors.

Love Letter is a game for up to 4 players that contains only 16 cards. While the thematic elements are fairly open to interpretation (and thus great fodder for easy re-themes), you play as someone hoping to win the affections of the princess. You do this by eliminating other courtiers (players). Being the only player left in a hand wins you a heart of affection,[5] four of which win you the game.

---

5. This was always kind of sad to me: "Oh, you are the only one left in court? I guess I like you the best by default then." Romantic.

Each player has a hand of only one card. On her turn, the player draws a second card and chooses one of the two to play. Each card has a rank-value and may have an additional effect when played. The *Guard* eliminates a player if you can correctly guess what card is in that player's hand. The *Baron* compares hands with another player, and the player with the lowest ranked card is eliminated. Play continues until there is only one player remaining in the hand or the deck runs out of cards. In the latter case, all non-eliminated players reveal their hands and the highest number wins.

Love Letter wrings a good deal of depth out of only 16 cards. There is the psychology of bluffing what you hold, the probabilistic risk-taking of guessing what an opponent may have, and the tactical maneuvering of getting others to gang up on someone when you are secretly the person with the power. It is quick and easy to teach while preserving a level of tactical nuance that makes the game replayable.

Love Letter spawned a short-lived market fascination with "microgames" that could deliver a worthwhile experience with a small number of components. Successful releases in this vein were Rikki Tahta's Coup, Masato Uesugi's Welcome to the Dungeon, and Adam P. McIver's Coin Age.

Summary

Many design challenges are run on board game designer forums that limit players to some small, arbitrary component limit such as 18 cards. These limitations help designers to work within constraints to create clever mechanics. Brett Gilbert's The Other Hat Trick is a particularly clever deduction game with only 17 cards that plays with exactly three players.

Restricting oneself to a small amount of components or mechanics means that every component needs to have a balanced purpose and be essential to the play experience. That exercise can cultivate a more careful, efficient practice of game design.

GAMES COVERED

Playlist Game #29: Drop7

Creators: Area/Code

Why: Drop7 feels timeless, as if it is a long-lost sibling of games like Tetris or Bejeweled that are meant to be endlessly sampled and remixed, except that Drop7 exists without the surrounding fandom. Its journey from Chain Factor to Drop7 shows a laudable amount of design restraint, removing functional elements from the former to make a stronger final game.

Playlist Game #30: Triple Town

Creators: Spry Fox

Why: Triple Town is a simple, experimental concept for a casual game that simultaneously delivers both a satisfying meditative experience for casual players and a brain-burning strategic puzzle for the enthusiast. While live free-to-play games tend to erode in their elegance over time as new concepts kruft up the original elegance, Triple Town's core remains a novel and elegant exercise for game designers to appreciate.

Playlist Game #31: Pair Solitaire

Designer: Vitaliy Zlotskiy

Why: Pair Solitaire is a digital port of a card game that would be playable with a standard deck of cards. There are thousands of these on App Stores. What separates it is a simple, novel mechanic that excludes any other possible interference from an excited designer. That novel mechanic and the restraint shown in making it as usable as possible at the exclusion of complexity make it a great example for designers to emulate.

Playlist Game #32: Love Letter

Designer: Seiji Kanai

Why: Seiji Kanai's Love Letter is a fine example of a design that can be expanded in innumerable ways but is published with very little unnecessary chaff. It served to inspire an entire crop of "micro" games within the board and card game community.

CHAPTER 10

LEARNING TO WALK

"Learning by doing, peer-to-peer teaching
and computer simulation are all part of the
same equation."

—Nicholas Negroponte

It is a widely known but likely apocryphal story that upon the first screening of *L'Arrivée d'un train en gare de La Ciotat* that moviegoers, unfamiliar with the capabilities and language of film, were so spooked seeing a train coming for the camera that they scrambled out of the theater in panic. Moviegoers today are more sophisticated, having been immersed in the form their entire lives. One does not need to have explained how a film works to appreciate it. Games, on the other hand, live or die by their ability for players to understand their unique characteristics.

The Price of Entry

It is hard to imagine now, but there was a time when you could walk into a bookstore (and there were a lot more bookstores then) and not find a prominent display of a genre called "young-adult paranormal romance." Stephenie Meyer's 2006 novel *Twilight* and its subsequent popular movie franchise kicked off a frenzy towards similar series like Cassandra Claire's *The Mortal Instruments* and Richelle Mead's *Vampire Academy.* An enthusiastic reader finishing *Twilight* had a variety of choices when looking for something else she also may enjoy. She could pick up *The Mortal Instruments* immediately and have no problem consuming the story.

A game player has a different set of problems from the story reader, and a game designer has a different set of problems from an author. A player of Dishonored cannot simply jump into Splinter Cell and immediately engage in the same experience, despite the genre similarities. It is expected in games that the first portion of the game is spent teaching the player how to interact with the game's systems. This portion in many cases can last hours of game time. Imagine if a *Twilight* reader had to go through a short boot camp of how to read, turn pages, and how to identify the point-of-view character before they could start the story of *The Mortal Instruments.* Few would take the time to jump from series to series.

Some game systems have become second-nature and rarely need to be retaught. Since Halo's popularity, movement of first-person characters in a 3D game space with a twin-stick controller has been standardized. Few games feel the need to explain that the left stick is directional movement and that the right stick is camera movement, or if they do, they do not belabor the point. But most mechanics need to be taught in every single game. Even if Dishonored and Splinter Cell have similar enemy vision systems, you can bet that each game will teach that mechanic before getting into the heart of the game. The game's designers cannot rely on the assumption that the player has played other similar games.

While learning about game systems can certainly be fun, it is rarely the primary reason players engage in play. Madden NFL players want to simulate the football games they watch on the weekend, not learn about how to switch to the "Gun Normal Y-Flex Tight" set or learn what the hell that even is. One site, Madden-School.com, offers a subscription service to help break down the minutiae that include six to ten ebooks per year on how to play the game.[1]

This isn't just a problem of overly complicated systems. Even simple, casual games are burdened with the need to teach their players despite the games themselves employing more straightforward mechanics. While a game like Threes! (see Chapter 12, "The Clone Wars") is simple and elegant, it would be difficult to enjoy without first understanding its rules.

---

1. While novels have CliffsNotes to help with the finer details as well, I am confident in saying that CliffsNotes generally aren't bought so that the end user can actually parse the original text successfully for purposes of enjoyment.

Building a Structure

When constructing a building, people generally do not assemble the pieces in a desultory, random way. Instead, there is a procedure based on the best practices of civilization's thousands of years of building. A contractor doesn't throw bricks up haphazardly and say that it is the building's job to make sure it doesn't fall over under its own weight. Yet this is often how we teach.

Everyone probably has an example or can at least recall the experience of a boring, frustrating tutorial in a game. Often a tutorial consists of the game giving users a haphazard series of facts about the game's mechanics, and they leave it up to the player not to fall over under the weight of the information.

Educators who, like builders, are part of a tradition lasting thousands of years, have their own methods for building knowledge from information in a practiced and careful way. Whereas builders hold up a wall with scaffolding until it can bear its own weight, the process of providing support while a subject learns is also called *scaffolding.* As a wall needs less and less support, scaffolding is removed until the wall stands on its own.

Great game tutorials often use the principle of scaffolding. Truly great game tutorials scaffold in a way where the scaffolding itself is invisible to the players. Older games had to do this out of necessity. An arcade cabinet in the 1980s could only fit so many instructions onto the cabinet itself and the games did not have the memory to support lots of text or special learning areas.

The quintessential example of this is the first world in Super Mario Bros. Now Super Mario Bros. is not by any means a hidden gem of a game. It ranked second only to Tetris in our Game Awareness Survey. However, it helps to examine this topic closely in games with which you are already very familiar because the learning mechanisms can be taken for granted.

Consider what a player may know when first playing Super Mario Bros. He may have played Mario Bros., but that is not necessarily true. Even so, the only mechanics that would carry over are movement, jumping, avoiding touching enemies, and hitting things with your head. Even very simple mechanics such as scrolling the screen by walking are not necessarily things the player has seen before. Without directly telling the player, "Walk to the right to continue the level," how does the designer let the player know this is the case?

Super Mario Bros.' first screen is a massive tutorial. First, there are no enemies on the screen, allowing the player to experiment safely. Second, the player character is not placed in the center of the screen—he is placed in the left third facing the right. Since he is facing the right, this implies to the player that is the direction to go. Finally, if the player doesn't heed this and instead goes to the left, there is a very small sacrifice in time as the player is already at the left edge of the screen. The player now knows quite a bit about the game before ever having to make a real decision.

As the player continues to the right, he sees some foreign objects (see Figure 10.1). A creature slowly sidles towards the player. Its slanted angry-looking eyebrows indicate that it is a threat. Moving left or right, the techniques learned on the previous screen will not save the player. Instead, he must experiment with the jump button. Luckily, because the monster moves slowly, the player has plenty of time to experiment.

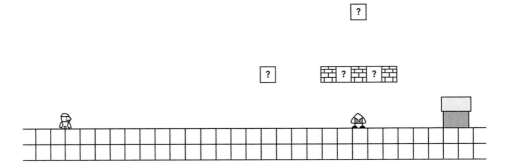

Figure 10.1 World 1-1 of Super Mario Bros., drawn by a master artist

On this screen are also question blocks. If the player rushes to the right and jumps to hit the question block, he is rewarded with a mushroom and the monster's movement is timed perfectly such that the player will stomp on the monster, eliminating it. If the player missed the stomp, he can still grab the mushroom, increasing his size, giving him an extra hit-point and giving him the ability to break brick blocks with his head. Because a pipe appears at the right of this screen, the player is blocked until he can prove that he understands jumping.

We are only a few seconds into the game and we have already learned a number of concepts. The game avoids overloading the player. Instead, the next few screens allow players to exercise what they have learned with a series of pipes and pits to jump over and Goomba monsters to stomp. There is very little else to learn in this level. The turtle makes his first appearance, there is an optional pipe you can descend into, and an invincibility star is available.

Except for the turtle, which will be essential knowledge later, everything else is optional. The true necessary mechanics have been taught in the first few screens. The rest of the level is making sure that the player clearly understands these mechanics before adding new things to learn. Slowly, Super Mario Bros. makes play more and more dangerous for the player as the scaffolding comes off. By the end, the player has chained together expertise against numerous enemy types, jumping, swimming, riding platforms, and dunking Bowser. Yet you hardly ever feel you are put into a teacher-student relationship.

The same approach was taken in 1993's Mega Man X.[2] Compared to older Mega Man games, Mega Man X is complex, so it may have been justified to slowly take a player back to basics and explain every mechanic in detail. But Mega Man X instead used simple level design cues to teach the mechanics. Players that already knew how the systems work flew through them and new players could use them as a testing ground. For instance, just as in Mario, the level design suggests the basic "go right" paradigm. It slowly introduces concepts and makes sure that the player masters them before continuing, not by providing explicit instruction and tests but by creating an environment where the player can do nothing but learn the necessary game elements. For instance, to teach the player that he can climb up walls, the game puts the player into a pit with a tiny gap on the right side. If the player falls into that tiny gap, Mega Man must attach to the wall. When the player sees Mega Man attaching to the wall, if he tries to jump (which he will because he has only seen two other mechanics so far), he will begin to climb the wall. This is done without any handholding or text prompts.

You may be tempted to think this was done of necessity in older games, but since newer games have a broader opportunity for audiovisual techniques, that a straight relaying of facts will be sufficient. For many game makers, it is sufficient simply because it tends to be the simplest technique to implement. Text tutorials are low cost and lack subtlety. Unfortunately, players tend to hate them as they take away the player's agency, immersion, and decision making. Many great modern games eschew explicit tutorials as much as possible.

Thinking with Portals

Portal is another game that is likely quite familiar to many game makers. It ranked in the top decile of the Game Awareness Survey. Yet Portal's tutorial is underappreciated. It lasts for almost half of the game, which would be an egregious tutorial length if handled in any other way. Portal introduces a mechanic and will not let you finish a room until the player has proven mastery with that mechanic. Portal requires a lot from players. Its non-Euclidean treatment of space was likely foreign to most players. It could not take anything for granted.

In the beginning of Portal, you are placed in a clear, glass cell. You are able to look around and have very limited movement. The camera is positioned by default at a digital clock that is ticking down from 60 seconds to zero. This both gives players the time to experiment with the controls in a safe environment (like the first screen of Super Mario Bros.) but also lets players know that something will happen at the end of that timer. Since it isn't blinking red or giving off any other known signals that it is a countdown timer to something bad, this provides a stress-free staging area while the worldbuilding begins. The voiceover counts down the 3-2-1 of the timer, redirecting focus back to that timer. The designers did not force the

---

2. Credit goes to YouTuber "egoraptor," whose video on the Mega Man series popularized how brilliant the tutorial level of the game is. Do watch it unless you are easily offended by foul language and the general noisiness of the classic YouTuber persona.

camera to look back; they trusted that their setup would have the player do the heavy lifting of control for them.

When the player looks at the timer, she can see the blue exit portal outside the cell and the orange entrance portal inside the cell. In both portals, the player can see a character. With some movement, the player will realize that she is the character she sees.

Now the player has more freedom. When she walks through the orange portal, she is facing the orange portal when she emerges, letting her know that it is where she came from even though it is discontinuous. If the designers had positioned the exit in another room, players might have assumed that the orange portal was just a hole in the wall.

That was only the first room. It involves around 90 seconds of play time; however, most of that is spent confined in the cell listening to the voiceover. Nevertheless, it teaches quite a bit without ever directly lecturing.

In the next room, the player sees a big red button. That big red button has a blue dotted line leading to a closed door. You do not need to know the video game trope that buttons on floors open doors when weighted to understand that the button and the door are related. Since this is the only way forward, the player is forced to experiment. When she stands on the button, the door opens and an X by the door changes to a checkmark. When she gets off the button, the door closes, but if the player is looking at the door at that time, she also sees a grey cube fall into the room. This leads to one of the few text prompts in the game. On the Xbox, this prompt has a picture of the RB button and the text "To Pickup an Object." Clearly, the player needs to pick up the object. It isn't much of a puzzle for the player to pick up the cube, place it on the button, and advance to the next area.

The player has to prove that she understands these concepts before moving on. It isn't a particularly challenging puzzle, but the action still feels like the player used her cognitive ability to progress rather than reading a text box that explained the concepts of blocks and switches and affirming that she understands.

Portal spoons out its lessons slowly. Look at the following list of concepts that are introduced and tested by room:

- Chamber 00, Room 1:

   Use the left stick to move.

   Use the right stick to look.

   Walking through a blue portal places you at the orange portal, and vice versa.

- Chamber 00, Room 2:

   Buttons can affect doors.

   You can pick up objects (use X).

   Cubes can weigh down buttons.

- Chamber 01:

  Portals can change their entrance/exit locations.

  You can carry things through portals.

- Chamber 02:

  The Portal Gun allows you to choose a portal entrance location, even if it is on the floor or ceiling.

  You can reach out-of-the-way areas by placing portals where you could not normally reach.

  Some surfaces won't take portals.

- Chamber 03:

  Portal exits are also portal entrances. (This was possible to learn in the very first room, but it wasn't tested until here.)

- Chamber 04:

  Mostly review! The knowledge gained in the first three chambers is reinforced (e.g., carrying objects through portals, weighing down buttons with items, portal exits being entrances).

- Chamber 05:

  Some triggers have multiple components. This is a minor lesson, so it continues the review.

- Chamber 06:

  Dark surfaces will not hold a portal.

  Energy balls will travel a straight path.

  Energy balls can be directed to receptacles to power elements (like weighted buttons).

  Energy balls cannot be touched.

- Chamber 07:

  Since many new concepts were introduced in the previous chamber, they are reiterated with a slight change in the challenge.

  You may have to drop through a portal onto a moving platform. Thus, peeking through a portal to see where you will end up is an essential skill. Look before you leap.

- Chamber 08:

  Again, the game must make sure you understand these concepts before adding more complexity, so it reiterates the challenges in different ways, including directing energy balls and dropping through portals onto moving platforms.

  You may be limited by acid pools on the floor that are instant death. (Another common video game trope.)

- Chamber 09:

  Energy fields will vaporize objects that you try to carry through them.

- Chamber 10:

  Momentum is conserved by portals. So if you fall a long way onto a ground-based portal and emerge from a wall-based portal, you will emerge with the speed that you entered, flinging you from the portal at a great speed.

- Chamber 11:

  Now you have the ability to place both the entrance and the exit of portals.

- Chambers 12–15:

  Old puzzles are combined with the freedom of being able to place both ends of the portal to combine all of the elements into a new toolbox from which to solve puzzles.

- Chamber 16:

  There are turrets that will kill you after a short delay when spotted.

  Turrets only see around the area of their laser.

  Turrets can be disabled by knocking them over with a cube or picking them up and throwing them.

- Chamber 17:

  Cubes and other objects can be held as a shield to block damage from energy balls.

- Chamber 18:

  There are some switches that are only active for a small amount of time. A ticking sound will indicate that a switch is active.

By this point, all of the mechanics have been taught and the story takes over. In Portal's case, this is about halfway through the game. Few players would tolerate 50% of the game being the tutorial before the "real game" starts, but very few have these complaints about Portal. Because the tutorial keeps players interested by retaining their own perceptions of agency and alternating between introducing a small number of new concepts and reinforcing the new concepts and how they relate to everything learned before, the section doesn't have the negative connotations that comes with being a tutorial.

Summary

Perhaps many players have poor experiences with education and that reflects their impatience with tutorials. Or perhaps players are simply frustrated with a game activity that doesn't adapt to their skill like other activities. Players have negative connotations associated with activities that may be seen as tutorials. Nonetheless, players need those tutorials to understand the basics of the interactive systems they are attempting to manipulate. A powerful technique is to "hide the vegetables"—let the main play experience act as effective tutorial using proven education tools and techniques.

GAMES COVERED

Playlist Game #33: Super Mario Bros.

Creators: Nintendo

Why: Obviously, most people know about Super Mario Bros. This entry is to emphasize focusing on how Super Mario Bros. slowly introduces concepts to players and then tests them on those concepts before allowing them to continue. Even what we take for granted, concepts like "move to the right to progress," have to be treated with care. It is easy to denigrate "dumb players" that cannot figure out our genius designs. But careful attention to how players learn our games ensures that we have enough players to appreciate our games.

Playlist Game #34: Mega Man X

Creators: Capcom

Why: In the vein of other examples in this chapter, Mega Man X's opening level provides players with all the tools they will need to begin their exploration of the game mechanics without feeling like a tutorial. This care is taken even though the game is the tenth in the series (counting handheld ports). It could be assumed that most players were already familiar with the majority of the systems; nonetheless, those expert players didn't feel like they were being slowed down for new players.

Playlist Game #35: Portal

Designer: Valve

Why: Again, most players know of Portal. But by examining it through the lens of the velocity of concepts introduced and evaluated, designers can see how much of the game actually is a tutorial versus how much of the game *feels* like a tutorial.

CHAPTER 11

MECHANICS IN MILIEU

"All one has to do is hit the right keys at the right
time and the instrument plays itself."

—Johann Sebastian Bach

Most game analysis tried to examine an experience as a hermetically
sealed object. Games are lists of rules, after all. Analyzing those rules
and how those rules work in conjunction seems to be a reasonable
approach. Leaving random number generation aside, a game should run
the same way given the same inputs for a player in 1987 Japan and 2017
United States. In this chapter, we will discuss some examples where an
examination of a game is meaningless outside the social and/or cultural
setting of its players.

Taste and Distaste

One of my favorite board game designers is Richard Breese. He largely makes worker placement games with very little conflict. In his games, you move workers around in an idyllic representation of medieval countrysides and win by being more efficient than your opponents rather than by denying them or beating them into submission. The art for most of his games is pastoral kitsch, and it would be tough to take offense to the worlds he creates.

In 2017, he launched his newest game, Keyper. In it, players have one of the Keyper ("keeper") figures shown in Figure 11.1. Like many of his fans, I was excited for the game enough to reach the dedicated message boards for it on BoardGameGeek.com. I was surprised to see a message from a German enthusiast who was concerned about playing the game. Why? Because of the low fidelity of the detail in the wooden figures, a figure that is waving (as the graphic is intended to be) looks a lot like a figure giving a straight-armed salute with its right hand. What is commonly called the "Nazi salute," the straight-armed right hand in the air is banned in Germany, with some exceptions, and is punishable by up to 3 years in prison.

Figure 11.1 A Keyper

Naturally, no one intended for the figure to conjure up that connotation. Certainly, very few people outside of Germany (Breese is British) would ever make that association. The point of bringing it up here is not whether the person who brought that up on the message board is right to be concerned or wrong, but to highlight that a component of how games are consumed must at some point take into consideration the social and cultural environment of its players. Nothing embedded in the construction of the rules or components is inherently designed to bring up negative connotations, but with a playgroup of a particular sensitivity, the play experience is changed.

More than 70 years after World War II, even trifling connections can make for some overt sensitivity. But the subject as a whole has not been taboo. In fact, there are enough games in both analog and digital form about World War II that they can be their own genre. The Medal of Honor and Call of Duty franchises often deal in revisionist history around the war to little or no fanfare.

Medal of Honor: Allied Assault was a 2002 PC release by Electronic Arts. In it, players interact using many of the verbs that are standard for the genre: walk, jump, crouch, switch weapons, run, reload, throw grenade, and of course, shoot. You shoot and kill a lot of people in Allied Assault. It is the only way to progress in the game.

The game had nearly universally positive reviews. It sold nearly a million copies. It received a 91% on Metacritic, a review aggregator. Of the 34 reviews listed on Metacritic, no one mentions the overt violence of the game as anything other than perfunctory. The blurb of the review from All Game Guide says, "Nazis are fun and rewarding to kill." That is such a normal sentiment among video game players that it goes without saying in most cases. Of course, the Medal of Honor Nazis are largely not shown committing the crimes that made them universal enemies in fiction in the entire modern era. We just take the game's word for it that the enemies the game puts in front of us are inhuman enough to deserve execution, and other means of progress need not apply.

Let's compare Medal of Honor: Allied Assault with one of its contemporaries. This game, released in the same year for the same platform, uses very similar verbs: walk, run, reload, shoot, etc. This game received almost universal scorn and was estimated to have only sold a few thousand copies. The game received the reception it did, not because the technical execution of the game was much worse than Medal of Honor: Allied Assault, although this game had poor execution no matter its competitors. The game received the reception it did because of its thematic content.

This game was called Ethnic Cleansing. In it, you complete the same verbs as you would in any other first-person shooter, but your enemies are racially stereotyped African Americans, Hispanics, and Jews. Whereas in Medal of Honor: Allied Assault, the hidden subtext is that most of these people you are using lethal force on are partners in atrocity, in Ethnic

Cleansing, you kill your enemies only because they are not white. The game is stupid and despicable and probably would have faded away with the tens of thousands of other moderately less stupid and despicable games if not for attention from media and advocacy groups like the Anti-Defamation League.

A purely rules-based examination of the two games would largely focus on differences in level design topology and secondary dynamics (such as AI behaviors). In these areas, Ethnic Cleansing is also atrocious. But no one hates Ethnic Cleansing because it is bad at being a game. They hate it because they live in a social and cultural environment where its thematic content is not acceptable.

Every game referenced in this book I have played and studied to some degree, except Ethnic Cleansing. I cannot motivate myself to find a mirror of the game hosted somewhere to try it. I've watched videos of people playing the game on YouTube. That's as close as I can get. Even though I would not be influenced by it (and don't see how anyone could actually change their opinion based on such a poor product) and can certainly separate the thematic content from the mechanical content, I nonetheless find it so distasteful that I cannot touch it. That is the power of the milieu in which the game exists.

Ethnic Cleansing is not the first nor will it be the last racist game. It isn't even particularly remarkable at being racist. In 1983, Custer's Revenge for the Atari 2600 tasked the player with committing a rape on a Native American woman. Another game of questionable-at-best sensitivity is a 2007 "educational" game for the Nintendo DS called Spanish for Everyone, which is full of derogatory innuendos about Hispanics.

Agency and Dilemma

Distasteful or even factually inaccurate thematic content is not enough to make a game void of value. What if distasteful content is used for an artistic purpose? Is that even possible? Many media personalities that do not care to become familiar with the form seem to think so. A media uproar surrounded 2005's independent art-game Super Columbine Massacre RPG! by Danny Ledonne. In it, players use the basic interface and verbs of 1990s-era Japanese RPGs to play through the final day of the mass-shooters in the Columbine High School shooting.

The game vacillates between documentary-style literal presentation and a farcical approach to the actual events of the incident. For instance, the entire second half of the game takes place in hell and is peppered with fictional characters and dead celebrities. Yet the end of the game features verbatim quotes from public figures the day of the massacre. There's art underneath the kitsch.

As with Ethnic Cleansing, Super Columbine Massacre RPG! only received popular attention because of media controversy. However, unlike the previously mentioned game, Super

Columbine Massacre RPG! actually contains a real, earnest reason for its distasteful content. As you play as killers Dylan Klebold and Eric Harris, you are first given the emotional framework that would motivate them and then you have the opportunity to make decisions as they may have. While the writing lacks subtlety and the decision making is nonetheless forced (and therefore mostly devoid of meaning), the agency given to the player provides a different perspective on the incident than any passive documentary could ever aspire to communicate. It is not a good game in the traditional sense, but it has something to say about a topic that few think the form of the video game should be allowed to address in a serious manner.

Media personalities that decried the game as glorifying Klebold and Harris miss the point entirely. The events of the Columbine High School massacre happen in Super Columbine Massacre RPG! at the player's pace. You *are* the killers. How you choose to continue in the game is a statement about the choices you make when consuming media. This choice does not exist in other media. Watching Gus Van Sant's film *Elephant* allows you to watch the same subject matter but from a distance because the audience can never have an effect on the events except only to turn it off. The statement of the audience's responsibility is much less direct when the audience has no impact. While the ability for the audience to enter a killer's mind and suss out their motivations may be more artfully handled in Van Sant's film, it is not nearly as direct as can be exercised in Ledonne's game.

Depression Quest and Indirect Representation

The ability to *be* the protagonist allows for a great deal of player empathy. Media personalities that do not play games yet decry their portrayal of charged subject matter see only the possibility for a player to become less empathic with their fellow person. What if the ability to be a protagonist could educate and create more empathy through a player's agency?

Depression Quest is a 2013 interactive fiction game by Zoe Quinn and Patrick Lindsey. In it, you play as a person suffering from depression and are faced with simple situations that may occur in a normal, everyday life. You choose how you react to those situations, but some options may be disabled or enabled because of the player's current emotional status and whether they are seeing a therapist or taking medication.

The interaction is fairly straightforward: Read a section of text and then choose one from a defined list of actions. What makes Depression Quest a particularly effective tool for showing a non-depressed person what depression is like is that the game shows the reasonable reactions that a healthy person might make and specifically marks them as off-limits, just as depression sufferers may know that their decisions are causing them further mental anguish but are stuck choosing them anyway. "Why don't you cheer up?" is a common category of responses to depressed people. Telling these people that it isn't an option is less compelling than showing them how it is not an option. It may not change their outlook, but what is ever guaranteed to?

Depression Quest isn't a fun game. The fact that one has to address that shows how far games need to come as an artistic medium. By noting that Depression Quest isn't a fun game, we are tacitly saying that the expectation is that games should be fun. The late president of Nintendo, Satoru Iwata, said as much: "Above all, video games are meant to just be one thing: Fun for everyone." That may work when you are the president of an entertainment company, focused on your own particular mission, but it is not a universal truth. Limiting a medium to one particular type of experience and then measuring it by the valence of that experience means that you are essentially ruling out other possible worthwhile experiences. Depression Quest cannot be measured as an experience by how fun it is like *Blackfish, The Hurt Locker,* or *Raging Bull* cannot be measured by the smiles on faces walking out of the theater.

It is worth noting that your experience with Depression Quest does not exist outside of your experience with depression. At its most technical level, Depression Quest is a big flowchart with some tracked variables. Riding from Node #1 to Node #14 to Node #72 without context is just a bland maze. Many "Choose Your Own Adventure" books can be said to have a near identical structure without any of the emotional touchstones.

Have you ever read a horror novel that is utterly nail-biting for the first two-thirds but falls apart when the author starts explaining the source of the terror in the final act? Or watched a mystery show that left you guessing at every turn but then felt unsatisfactory when the mystery was explained? You do not have to be an author, filmmaker, or game designer to have the necessary creativity to fill in the blanks of a mystery or horror story with the most compelling details imaginable. You likely never even nail those details down; they exist only as a subconscious set of possibilities. It is when those possibilities are extinguished by an authorial explanation that the man behind the curtain is revealed. And no matter how excellent that man is at pulling the levers, he will never be as good as the particular vector you imagined for the story. Directly telling or showing the audience something that fills in the blanks for them is necessary at times but can serve to limit the audience's imaginary version of events.

I believe that this is why Depression Quest works so well as an interactive fiction game. There are no characters modeled or drawn, so it is easier for the player to imagine himself as the protagonist. There is no dissonance that the player doesn't look like what the player imagines himself to be. There is no spoken dialogue, so the audience is forced to fill in his own friends' voices instead of what he could get from voice actors. There are no representations of place besides some blurry stock photographs, so the player can more easily imagine himself in the places familiar to their ordinary lives.

Another game that gives a new perspective on an already familiar theme was 1979 Revolution: Black Friday by iNK Stories. The game tells the story of ordinary people going through the Iranian Revolution in the 1970s. As an American growing up after the Iranian Revolution, I've only known Iran as a country hostile to mine and assume stereotypes based on that hostility. 1979 Revolution presents the events of the game using an interactive format similar to that of Telltale Game Studios games. In it, a fully 3D-modeled and voice-acted cinematic plays and you are given the opportunity to intervene at a number of key points that may or may not change the narrative.

While I feel I learned something playing 1979 Revolution, I fear that its attempt to directly represent its subject matter may have hurt it. Some characters that I probably should find sympathetic annoy me because of quirks of voice acting and other likely subconscious biases. The context of knowing what happens in Iran for the next four decades means I already have an opinion on the revolutionaries. It is hard to separate from that opinion. It is also hard for me to see myself as the main character Reza, as he looks and sounds different enough from me that I can easily identify him as different. This is one area where the silent protagonists common in video games have an advantage.

1979 Revolution has greater production values but has an underlying structure fairly similar to that of Depression Quest. Despite that, the former is generally seen as more "game-like" than the latter, which is a shame. Both should be judged on the efficacy with which they execute on their goals.

Papers, Please

As a college professor and administrator, a large part of my day-to-day activities involves reading paperwork, ensuring its accuracy, and forwarding it to the appropriate bureaucratic entity. On its surface, Lucas Pope's 2013 independent hit Papers, Please doesn't seem like it would provide any kind of escape from the menial aspects of my ordinary life.

In it, you play as a low-level border guard in the 1980s for the fictional Warsaw Pact-like country of Arstotzka. Your job is to check the paperwork of those who cross the border for inconsistencies, scan them for contraband, and be on the lookout for persons of interest. You are incentivized by payment for shuffling people through the checkpoint quickly (see Figure 11.2) but are penalized for letting people through who should not be let through. That payment can be used to provide for your family's needs at the end of each day, but the payment is never enough to cover all of the needs, so it becomes tempting to take bribes and shortcuts to let more people through the checkpoint.

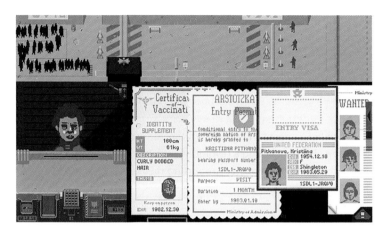

Figure 11.2 Papers, Please

Papers, Please is surprisingly fun. The narrative takes some interesting turns depending on your actions, some characters are quite memorable, and the mechanics are slightly tweaked from day to day, changing the novelty of an otherwise mundane set of tasks. Critics lauded the game. It won the Seamus McNally Grand Prize, independent gaming's highest award, at the 2014 Independent Games Festival. It was also named the Game of the Year from publications like *The New Yorker, PC World,* and *Wired.*

The entire aesthetic nails the sense of duty, drudgery, and desperation that must have been part and parcel of living life in Eastern European dictatorships of the 1980s. Or at least it measures up to the aesthetic suggested by popular literature and film about the time.

At some point in the game, you may be presented with a possible entrant to Arstotzka who does not have the needed paperwork. When you highlight the discrepancy, he will plead with you that he is only bringing needed medicine to a relative and if he cannot get the right paperwork in time, she will die. You can choose to let that person through and receive a penalty (although he may return later to reward you, hopefully), or you can do your duty and press the element that locks the booth down. When you do, pixelated representations of armed guards come in and carry the illegal entrant off screen while he pleads for leniency. What happens to him then? Who knows, you have more people in line to serve.

As a game element, this feels like a true meaningful decision. From the game design perspective purely, it should provide at least a moment of uncertainty because there are multiple desirable paths forward. But the game design perspective can only examine the situation in a vacuum. We subconsciously (or often consciously) use our perspective that we have honed from a lifetime of social and cultural cues to interpret complex events. As someone who grew up in safety and wealth in comparison to someone living through 1980s Hungary, I have the luxury of examining the game design of Papers, Please from a relative distance. Imagine how different the above scenario would feel if you grew up in a dictatorial country where you had relatives killed by the regime for trying to import medicine illicitly? Imagine how that decision would feel if you or your family were once a refugee and an immigration inspection was what saved your family's life or damned other relatives to being trapped in poverty? Now the game feels cruel.

Pope puts players in no-win situations to advance the story and, for most players, it creates a compelling combination of mechanics and narrative. Consequences are low for most players when playing Papers, Please. Getting a revolutionary killed or not is based on narrative preference at that point. Do you believe that supporting the revolutionaries in Papers, Please will direct the narrative in a better direction than obeying the central authority? That is how most players will make their calculus. But if someone's family trajectory was defined by someone else making that choice in the real world, that choice becomes obvious and likely loses its aesthetic sheen.

A Mind Forever Voyaging

Admittedly, the intersection of people who were affected first- or second-hand by the kinds of events caricatured in Papers, Please and the people likely to play the game contains only a small number of people. If the point is to make something that affects a larger number of contemporaries on a political issue, one of the first to try to tackle that goal in a commercial setting was Infocom's 1985 interactive fiction game A Mind Forever Voyaging, written and designed by Steve Meretzky.

The computer games industry was nascent in 1985, and with the low amount of computing power available to consumers (compared to today), the form of interactive fiction was a popular way to get deeper concepts in games fleshed out. The specific type of interactive fiction Infocom created was the "text adventure." Like Depression Quest discussed above, players are given blocks of text to describe the situation of their character. Unlike Depression Quest, the options available to the character were hidden. Players could type in commands that were parsed by an interpreter that would allow the game to go forward. For instance, if you wanted a description of the view out a window, you could type LOOK WINDOW. If the game had a case to handle that, then it would give you a description of what it looked like when you peered out the window at your location.

Meretzky was coming off the commercial success of the adaptation of Douglas Adams' Hitchhiker's Guide to the Galaxy into text adventure form (and earlier successes Planetfall and Sorcerer) and wanted to create something more than just an adolescent pastime. He decided to make something that would be more political in nature and leveraged his intense aversion to then-president Ronald Reagan to make something that he hoped would be both entertaining and convincing.

In A Mind Forever Voyaging, players play a character in a distressed version of the United States of America that is using a supercomputer to simulate the effects of a new senator's sweeping plan to revitalize the country. The character interacts with this simulation of a town in America called Rockvil after the plan has been put in place to report the effects over several time periods. The plan is a generic right-wing agenda that could be copied and pasted for many presidential candidates over the last generation (lower taxes, decreased regulation, strict law enforcement), with a couple of planks that seem out of place with contemporary politics like mandatory conscription for criminals.

Early in the simulation, things seem fine. There are some hints that there is trouble brewing under the surface, but largely Rockvil is doing okay. As you progress in the game and move farther into the future, Rockvil deteriorates. The increased focus on domestic law enforcement turns the nation into a police state with a mandatory curfew; a focus on religion by government officials turns into a full merger of an insidious Church with a more powerful State including "church police"; income inequality left unregulated turns into ration cards and fenced-in enclaves for the rich.

The rhetoric is pretty clumsy, unconvincing, and lacking in nuance. Meretzky's polemic attacks straw men and is hard to take seriously unless you already completely agree with his political alarmism. It leaves no out for those of opposing political persuasion and is more likely to entrench than persuade. But some of the futurism of his 1985 experiment has indeed come to pass. Luckily, zoos haven't been reduced to monkey-fighting arenas yet and the amount of street cannibalism is currently low, so we may have a decade or two.

The point of appreciating A Mind Forever Voyaging isn't to appreciate its predictive prowess or its ability to be persuasive. It's to appreciate that game designers *can even aim* to be persuasive. Game designers can aim to create something that is more than just adolescent power fantasy. Game designers can create works of art like A Mind Forever Voyaging that attempt to insert themselves into the social and cultural landscape.

One Vision

It may seem obvious, but studies have repeatedly shown we are much more likely to listen to people who resemble us. Studies in the 1970s showed that we are more willing to lend money to strangers who resemble us in some obvious way. In another study, researchers were able to get people to agree to sign a petition without even reading it just by wearing similar attire. Marketing agencies have been using this technique throughout the modern age: Person X likes product Y, you are like person X, therefore you should like product Y.

Because of this, one possible way to make a game more persuasive is to get the player to identify the protagonist of the game as like themselves. This is difficult in a sci-fi odyssey like A Mind Forever Voyaging because the protagonist is a blank slate of an artificial human. Games with a more modern design often allow for custom characters to be created. Nick

Yee's research suggests that those custom characters often resemble a slightly idealized version of the player herself. And we like the things that our avatar likes. In a 2006 study, researchers were able to observe a subject's increased preference for a fake soft drink just by creating an ad where an avatar that looked like him was holding the drink.

Italian group Molleindustria makes explicitly political interactive content and does not shy away from its hard-left perspective. What may be the most persuasive of their games is Unmanned. In the game, players start by doing some mundane tasks: hitting the alarm, thinking about the day ahead (via some text choices), shaving, keeping the car on the road through drowsiness and distraction, and of course, singing in your car as loudly as possible.

These tasks serve to create a connection with the avatar. While the avatar is not customizable and is cartoonish enough to not really look like anyone in particular, a few elements serve to foster an emotional connection to the character. First, he is doing the same kinds of tasks you do every morning. Second, the text prompts flesh out a man suffering from some malaise that may be identifiable to the audience. Third, the shaving sequence causes the avatar's face to bleed if you shave too quickly. Any cuts you create persist on the character throughout the game, creating an "Ikea effect." This is the colloquial term for liking something more simply because you've put a personal effort into it, similar to how we often have an otherwise unexplainable connection to the Ikea furniture that we assemble ourselves.

After setting up this character to be relatable enough to be like ourselves, he starts his work as an unmanned drone operator. In the drone operation, you have control. Unlike September 12 (referenced in Chapter 6, "Mechanics as Message"), you have the option to launch an airstrike or not, although the game tries to manipulate you a bit into doing so. The tension created by the uncertainty is much more relatable because Molleindustria first established this connection. It is not *the character* possibly bombing an innocent civilian; rather, now *you* may be bombing an innocent civilian.

After this, you engage in more mundane activities: smoking a cigarette, attempting to bond with your son through a video game, going back to bed. This brings the player back to empathy with that character. The scene in which the player plays a shooter with his son also contextualizes the disconnected considerations of violence. Without this second half, the game would feel more overtly manipulative. But by bringing the action back to the mundane, it rolls the whole experience back into a relatable whole.

The game has a clear political point: The use of unmanned drones in war creates a moral hazard with regard to the disconnection between the use of force and its effects. But it never needs to say it. And instead of saying it, you experience it as someone faced with that tension not because an avatar experienced that tension but because *an avatar you identify with* experienced that tension.

The risk of persuasive games is that they can trivialize their subject matter. In most games, the worst-case scenario is that you can get a "bad ending," which can be ignored because it is of no consequence to actual reality. The lives and concerns of fictional characters and systems are trivial. They don't exist. It's easier to forget this with films because we see actors who are relatable in some way to ourselves. We forget this in books because we fill in the narrative blanks of characters with our own imaginary frameworks that make sense to us. Additionally, both of these media are guided by an author whose responsibility it is to treat subject matter with respect and guide the plot into ways that do not trivialize the subject under consideration. But the freedom allowed in games can only show us the consequences of our actions within a limited framework. If the game's designer has a message to convey, but the player can act in a way contrary to that message and not feel proportional consequences, then the avatar-player relationship suggests that the consequences of similar real-world actions are also trivial. That's not the message most persuasive games want to relay.

Summary

Games are not fully explored if you only consider them as self-contained systems. Even the most abstract of games are played by dynamic humans who vary in experience and culture. Their cultural norms can amplify or deaden the impact of game events in comparison to a completely neutral theoretic player.

Designers who ignore the cultural milieu in which their games exist in do so at great risk. While many game makers have tried to leverage the cultural aspects of their game for attention (see the 1990s slate of increasingly ridiculous games that tried to out-violence each other), some are beginning the leverage the cultural to help give depth and nuance to issues that surround us.

GAMES COVERED

Playlist Game #36: Super Columbine Massacre RPG!

Creators: Danny Ledonne

Why: Let's be frank: Super Columbine Massacre RPG! is a game that swings and misses at key points. In one moment you feel you could be on the verge of a deeper understanding of a sensitive and divisive topic, and in the next moment you are mindlessly killing demons stolen from Doom. Like many titles recommended in this book, Super Columbine Massacre RPG! is interesting not because it is a particularly excellent game, but because it suggests that the boundaries can be pushed a lot further than where they currently stand. Games have the benefit over movies and books of interactivity. *We Need to Talk About Kevin* handles the topic of school violence in a much more adult and meaningful way, but Super Columbine Massacre RPG! hints that games can go even deeper, even if this one is not wholly successful.

Playlist Game #37: Depression Quest

Designers: Zoe Quinn and Patrick Lindsey

Why: Discard any baggage you may have heard about Depression Quest and play it for yourself. Text adventures often struggle when what the player wants to do exceeds what the game is programmed to handle. Depression Quest instead makes that a core element of the game itself and as such helps to increase empathy for people with depression.

Playlist Game #38: 1979 Revolution: Black Friday

Creators: iNK Stories

Why: Telltale's *The Walking Dead* series helped to revitalize a struggling visual adventure genre. iNK Stories uses the format to immerse the player in the Iranian Revolution of 1979. Many Americans have a caricatured understanding of the politics of Iran. By giving the player agency over characters in that tumultuous era, it helps to develop empathy more than reading about or seeing characters in a non-interactive setting.

Playlist Game #39: Papers, Please

Designer: Lucas Pope

Why: Papers, Please will make you reexamine your own decision making at times. The task of document processing is tricky, yet interesting. However, it could have been done with any other theme. The thematic elements in Papers, Please challenges players to understand why and how they choose to follow instructions from authority figures.

Playlist Game #40: A Mind Forever Voyaging

Designer: Steve Meretzky

Why: Meretzky intends for players to examine the ramifications of political decisions by creating a simulation wherein players enter a simulation that challenges them to examine the ramifications of political decisions. This is heady, but it is extra heady for a game that had to deal with the technological restrictions of the mid 1980s.

Playlist Game #41: Unmanned

Creators: Molleindustria

Why: A game whose main mechanics involve shaving, driving, and singing surprisingly asks us to consider our relationship with violence, both with remote warfare and simulated warfare for consumers. The mixture of the droll and the serious make for a compelling experience.

CHAPTER 12

THE CLONE WARS

"Taking something from one man and making it worse is plagiarism."

—George A. Moore

If everyone has a library of game ideas waiting to be developed, why do we see the same ideas again and again being marketed? When a new mobile game becomes a hit, why do we see a hundred facsimiles pop up as quickly as they can be hammered together? If game design itself is solving interesting problems with the end of a particular squishy human aesthetic like "fun," why would so many developers eschew the fun part of game development?

Here Comes the Flood

Making digital games is simultaneously incredibly risky and incredibly simple. Any cursory perusal of a discussion of employment in the industry inevitably turns to the high likelihood of systematic layoffs. This has been the case for many years as studios staff up highly trained workers for projects, ship the projects, and then have nothing for these expensive workers to do until the same time in the next project. The layoff cycle has become part of the expected ebb and flow of game development careers and was the case even in the best of times. At the same time, studios close at an alarming rate. There are few reliable sources for exactly how many, but anecdotal evidence is strong that game studios have a lower survivorship rate than other small businesses.

The labor market for game developers has been consistently oversupplied. A 2017 Indeed.com analysis found that since 2014, the number of open game developer positions had dropped by 65% while in the same period searches for those jobs rose by 50%.[1]

Many game developers are turning their skills to self-employment instead. It doesn't take a massive corporate structure to push out a mobile game. One only needs a developer's license and some time. As tools and available assets increase in supply and inevitably become cheaper, the barrier to entry becomes less and less.

That reduction of the barrier to entry means that the market for consumer attention is that much more crowded. In order to get something in the hands of consumers in the days of the Nintendo Entertainment System (NES), one had to be a company with a relationship with Nintendo, obtain capital for development kits and cartridges, have knowledge of tricky assembly languages, and have the means to publish and distribute a game. Thus, in the nearly 10 years of Nintendo's console, there were 822 games published for the platform in America. Today, potential developers need only a license and some freely downloadable source code to push a game to consumers. As of this writing, there are over 780,000 games in Apple's iOS App Store alone, nearly 100,000× the supply of NES games. While the gaming market has increased and prices have decreased, there still isn't the demand for that many games.

So, faced with the consumer who has an endless supply of games from which to choose, and a business survival rate that is generally perilous, what should a game studio do? It is easy for us with no stake in the game to say that every studio should swing for the fences and make the wildest, most original concept possible. Many do. But with the uncertainty in labor, in technology, and in the market, why add unnecessary design risk?

Many studios try to mitigate this to an extreme by getting as close to an already proven design as possible. Some studios try to eliminate risk in every customer-facing area they can. If their game's icon reminds consumers of another game they like, then that's one less barrier to that consumer downloading the game and handing over some money.

---

1. http://blog.indeed.com/2017/01/10/video-game-labor-snapshot/

Twitter user @palle_hoffstein posted the image in Figure 12.1 of some of the top App Store game icons, all of which seem fairly similar.

Figure 12.1 "Screaming Men" seems to be a popular genre if you judge by app icons.

No game is wholly original. Each designer works with mechanics and norms that other designers have pioneered in the past. Students and other novices routinely make games that are near clones of the games and mechanics they enjoy, simply because they don't have the deep literacy to understand the history of what has come before. It would be extremely diffi-cult for players to learn a modern game like Destiny 2 if they didn't already have a basket full of experience of systems from other games to pull from. Nonetheless, while it is a subjective measure, Destiny 2 is not considered to be a "clone."

Clones are games that are copies in all of their essential senses of another game. A clone may even be the same code reverse-engineered with only a cosmetic change on top. In this chapter, we will examine some case studies of pairs of games that are extremely similar to one another and may or may not be actual clones.

Game enthusiasts, worried that game cloning will stifle innovation and lead to fewer innova-tive games, can come down in a heavy-handed way against those they believe are engaging in "cloning." But that boundary between the acceptable and unacceptable is murky, as we will see.

What If Clones Are Necessary First Steps?

Minecraft is an unexpected cultural juggernaut. It is one of the few examples in modern video gaming of a truly independent game becoming ubiquitous. Before kids everywhere were sporting Minecraft shirts, before Microsoft paid $2.5 billion for the intellectual prop-erty, the game was a solo project of Markus "Notch" Persson. In 2009, the first mention of the game is made on the TIGSource.com forums. Persson shares the very early version with the forum, calling it "[I]nfiniminer, but it's going to move in a more Dwarf Fortress way, gameplay wise."

Infiniminer was a game from independent developer Zach Barth that used a procedurally generated voxel-like world where players could mine, build, and explore. It sounds (and looks) quite a bit like what millions of people would consider the Minecraft look today. Persson's first post to YouTube showing Minecraft is captioned, "This is a very early test of an Infiniminer clone I'm working on."

Anyone who plays Infiniminer and Minecraft today would find themselves hard-pressed to say the games were clones. Minecraft has had the benefit of nearly a decade of development while Infiniminer was abandoned after its source code was leaked. Early Minecraft was clearly a riff on Infiniminer.

Many heated Internet discussions focus on the lack of creative progress that clones foster. We will certainly get into examinations of those later in this chapter. Anti-cloning game players and many game developers insist on not financially supporting developers that clone games. However, if players truly should care about clones and do not support developers who release games that are close in execution to other available games, then Minecraft wouldn't have had the early support that turned it into the fully featured and transformative game that it ended up becoming. Would the world be better with only Infiniminer and not Minecraft?

Nintendo is often seen as a shining example of innovation in game design coupled with a mass-market focus. However, if you go far enough back, Nintendo was in the business of cloning arcade machines. A look at Nintendo in 1980, a year before the appearance of Donkey Kong, would reveal a company largely getting by on ripping off the game designs of other popular companies. Their Block Fever was a direct clone of Breakout. Their Space Fever was a direct clone of Space Invaders. If the nascent gaming community had shunned them for their cloning behavior, would we have ever gotten Donkey Kong, Super Mario Bros., The Legend of Zelda, Metroid, or Pokémon?

How Mechanically Different Can a Clone Be?

In 2014, independent developer Asher Vollmer released the mobile game Threes! on the iOS App Store to near-universal acclaim.

The game is a brilliant little puzzle. There are only four actions: swipe up, left, down, or right. When you do, all the tiles in the game move in that direction. Some tiles combine to form higher numbers when they collide. 1s and 2s combine to 3s. Then 3s combine to 6s, 6s to 12s and so on. Each swipe adds a new tile from the direction swiped. The goal is to get as high a score as possible before the grid is filled and no more swipes can be made.

Threes! elicits the reaction of "Why hasn't anyone thought of this before?" The interaction is so simple and satisfying and yet still deep. The value in the game is in its mechanics. Vollmer would later release a year and a half of emails, prototypes, and design discussions[2] to show-case the development of Threes! Given the long development cycle for such a beautiful and polished game, Vollmer's company decided to charge $3 for the game, even as the down-ward price pressure was building to a point where a game needed to be free or it would be destined to never be tried. Given the great attention to detail in Threes!, it is hard to make an argument that the game is not worth $3.

Appropriately, it took 3 weeks for the first clone to appear. Called 1024, the game copied the swiping and tile-combining mechanics of Threes! but made subtle tweaks to the mechanics to avoid being exactly the same. A fan of 1024 made an open-source version called 2048 ten days later, again making minor tweaks, releasing it on App Stores for free. 2048 quickly took off to the point where many more users recognized it than recognized Threes!, leading many users to think that Threes! itself was the clone.

2048 would not exist without Vollmer's work on Threes! That is incontrovertible. Does that mean that 2048 should not exist? 2048 (and the dozens of other clones of the Threes! con-cept) clearly cannibalizes some amount of sales that may have otherwise gone to Vollmer and his partners, even though 2048's creator chose not to monetize his app. But does that make it wrong? Is it wrong for Call of Duty to cannibalize the sales of Medal of Honor? Is it wrong only if they charge money for it? What about the people who couldn't play Threes! because it initially only launched on iOS devices and not Android devices? Should they not play a similar game versus no game at all? What about cloning a game that wasn't on the platform at all? Would it be okay to clone a PC game onto mobile, making only cosmetic changes?

In 2009, one could still make a business in publishing browser-based Flash games. Joey Betz and Chris Condon enjoyed a trebuchet game called Castle Clout. In it, the player timed a space bar press to best angle a trebuchet shot to knock down castle walls and kill the little knights inside. Betz contacted the developer of Castle Clout and received permission to make a similar game, which was called Crush the Castle. Crush the Castle included upgrades like a triple shot and bomb shots to knock down the target walls.

Before the end of the year, a new mobile game would hit the app store that directly copied many elements of Crush the Castle. This game, Angry Birds, took the core gameplay, changed the trebuchet to a slingshot, and placed it in a much more visually appealing, if somewhat thematically inconsistent package. Angry Birds would become a huge hit, spawn-ing a dozen games in the series, a television show, and a feature film.

Is Rovio's Angry Birds different enough from Crush the Castle to not be considered a clone? It looks different, it uses a different interface, and it certainly has a different user experience. But the core mechanic is the same. Crush the Castle was a mild success, while Angry Birds made millions. Is that an appropriate metric to judge the ethics of possible cloning?

---

2. http://asherv.com/threes/threemails/

One of my personal all-time favorite games is the innovative puzzle game Triple Town by Spry Fox. Clearly inspired by match-3 games like Bejeweled, in Triple Town players try to build a civilization by matching three items to create an upgraded version of the item.[3] In 2011, game publisher 6waves Lolapps released Yeti Town. While most of the games cited in this chapter have some structural difference from their antecedent, Yeti Town was mechanically identical to Triple Town; it only featured different art. Spry Fox was able to stop Yeti Town because 6waves Lolapps violated Spry Fox's "trade dress." It wasn't particularly legally relevant that 6waves Lolapps cloned Spry Fox's mechanics, as ideas cannot be protected legally. The expression of those ideas are what are protected by copyright, and a judge ruled that Spry Fox had its expression copied.

The Spry Fox ruling is not a strong enough precedent for protection against clones. DaVinci, the publisher of the successful Bang! card game, recently lost a lawsuit against a publisher that made a direct clone of their card game, while changing the name and art of their game's cards but keeping all of the effects and mechanics. This is disheartening for many designers because, had the situation been switched—that is, had a company copied the art for a game and changed the mechanics—copyright infringement would be clear.

Summary of Questions

As a leaping-off point, let's discuss questions raised in this chapter:

Is it wrong to make a cloned game at all?

Is it only wrong if you sell it?

Is it only wrong if it causes the cloned game to make less money regardless of whether you sell it?

How mechanically different must the cloned game be in order to be ethically made?

What if the cloner is more powerful and connected than the clonee—that is, is it okay for an indie to clone a Zynga game when it is not okay for Zynga to clone an indie game?

Do intentions matter? Is it okay to create a tool kit that people can use to clone a game, even if you intend for it only to be educational?

What is okay to copy? Halo's controller layout almost immediately standardized how a console-based first-person shooter game would function. But Halo was not the first game to use that control scheme. The scheme was largely panned by critics of the Alien Resurrection game just a few years earlier.

Is what is legal a reasonable barometer for what is ethical?

Is what is ethical for a game designer different from what is ethical for a game consumer?

---

3. We covered Triple Town in Chapter 9, "Challenging Complexity."

Philosophically, what should be the basis for originality in game design? Should it be a universal principle, applied a priori to its effects? Or should what is right depend on the effect that those acts or rules have? This is a fundamental dichotomy in ethics itself, so I don't think there are easy answers here.

It is not my place to preach ethics in this chapter. Instead, I ask you only to play the games listed here, and others, with the following in mind: Do we only condone copying/cloning when it is our favorite games and developers doing the copying? What is a reasonable and consistent view to have on originality?

GAMES COVERED

Playlist Games #42 and #43: Infiniminer and Minecraft

Designer of Infiniminer: Zach Barth

Creators of Minecraft: Mojang

Why: If possible, seek out an alpha edition of Minecraft and compare it to Infiniminer. Note the similarities, sure, but also note the differences. Was to wrong for Notch to start with what was an innovative base in Infiniminer even if it eventually was changed enough to become a vastly different game in Minecraft?

Playlist Games #44 and #45: Threes! and 2048

Designer of Threes!: Asher Vollmer

Creator of 2048: Gabriele Cirulli

Why: Threes! is an elegant, beautiful game. 2048 gets close enough. Subtle differences make 2048 a dynamically dissimilar experience. Play both, and compare and contrast. Also note the large number of clones made from 2048's source. Is it right for someone to carry the heavy design work only to have the market flooded with lesser copies?

Playlist Game #46 and #47: Crush the Castle and Angry Birds

Designer of Crush the Castle: Joey Betz

Creators of Angry Birds: Rovio

Why: Angry Birds was clearly copied to some degree from Crush the Castle. Many elements match the original version of Angry Birds so closely as to have been impossible to happen by chance alone. Yet Angry Birds is a better game because of its attention to aspects of user experience and feedback. Why is Angry Birds wrong to have been made if it creates a better experience? If Angry Birds had not made the money it had, would the sentiment still be the same?

CHAPTER 13

THE DISCIPLINE OF GAME DESIGN

"The best games are not those in which all goes smoothly and steadily toward a certain conclusion, but those in which the outcome is always in doubt."

—George B. Leonard

Every year, I meet hundreds of prospective game design students who come through the university where I teach. Often, they are younger and have their parents in tow. These parents tend to look at me askance and ask me what exactly it is that a game designer does. I have a stock answer ready, and it tends to satisfy the interested. But at the same time, I feel like a physicist who is asked about gravity. The stock answer is good enough for most people, yet it is an incomplete approximation of the truth. This chapter is meant to show examples of the edge cases of what it means to be a game designer.

The Worst Game Design Question

One of the worst arguments that a game designer can engage in with regard to their craft is the one over "What is a game?" It's not anti-intellectualism that makes me blanch at the suggestion that the argument is about to begin. I think a solid philosophical base is important for understanding the "whys" in life. And the "why" behind a career that will last you the better part of your life should be scrutinized thoroughly.

"What is a game?" is a worthwhile thought experiment to have if you are planning to become someone who designs games for a living. If you make homes, you should know what makes a home as opposed to a convenience store or sewer pipe. If you are planning to explore this topic further, there is a bunch of great academic reading on this widely available, and I summarize it in *Players Making Decisions*.

If it is such a rich academic topic, why shiver at the question coming up? There are plenty of topics of conversation that are inappropriate because they have an underlying subtext. For instance, it can often to be rude to ask someone where they are from as an icebreaker. The question itself is innocuous, but it carries a lot of emotional baggage: "Do I not look like I belong here?" "Is this person going to be projecting racial or cultural stereotypes on me?" "Why do I have to justify where I am from to you?" Among people you have met and with whom you have established a relationship, that question can be fine. There is acknowledged at that point no ulterior subtext. In a similar manner, the "What is a game?" question can be innocuous, or it can be used to exclude or belittle things that do not meet the question asker's fluid definition of what deserves to be held up as worthy of consideration.

The clear case study in this is Fullbright's 2013 game Gone Home. In Gone Home, players explore the objects left behind in an abandoned mansion, putting together clues about the home's former inhabitants. There are a few traditional game puzzles, but largely the experience is played at the player's pace with very little gating.

Gone Home had an extremely polarizing reception. Game critics lauded it for its innovative approach, but traditional "gamer" culture targeted it as "not a game" despite being described as such by its creators, media outlets, retailers, and critics. These objectors cite the game's lack of challenge and narrative linearity as disqualifying factors. Of course, Gone Home was not the first game to have either (or both) of those features, but it happened to do so while generating a lot of media attention in a time at which gaming culture was feeling threatened over cultural changes in the medium. Some of the more thoughtful objections relegated Gone Home to labels such as "interactive story," as if that was a distinction that somehow made it also not a game.

The most extreme objectors use "not a game" in a pejorative sense. In their eyes, games are things that make up their identity, and Gone Home does not dovetail with their identity, therefore Gone Home cannot be a game. It is a sad bit of cognitive dissonance. More often than not, "[X] is not a game" is just a way of saying "I don't like [X]." I've seen little evidence of many players who simultaneously think that Gone Home is great and also not a game.

An interesting thought experiment to take with these controversial "non-games" is to imagine what would need to be added to make the experience a game. What would need to be added to Gone Home? Would time pressure have made the experience a game? What if there were branching endings? How about a counter of rooms explored? One parody called Gun Home added Wolfenstein-inspired shooting mechanics to the setting.

In earlier chapters, we discussed many games that use untraditional mechanics, lack challenge, or have a straightforward linear narrative approach. Yet Gone Home is the game that has spawned the most "What is a game?" discussions in recent memory. I recommend all prospective or current game designers play Gone Home, not because of any technical merit the game may have, but to probe one's reactions as to what they think makes a playable thing a game.

So Then What Is a Game Designer?

New (and sometimes experienced) game design enthusiasts often take a romantic view of what it is to be a game designer. They instill the discipline with the kind of cultural gravitas that they hope will make game designer the relevant form of artist in the 21st century as musician, painter, composer, and novelist have been in bygone eras. It is certainly true that game design is very much an art form as much as it is a craft. *Art* here is synonymous with "so new and fertile that we really have no ossified processes formed yet."

Clearly, the only practitioner who can get a handle on such a complex melding of aesthetics, logic, psychology, and the hundred other disciplines from which game design samples must be a true renaissance man (or woman) worthy of the kudos of a true artist, right? There must be some beautiful intuitive process that these individuals use to turn all the right knobs in a way that evokes the correct aesthetic responses.

It may surprise you that despite spending a good portion of my career attempting to prepare and inspire burgeoning game designers (and writing a couple of books on the subject) that I don't actually believe that there is a special intuitive touch that separates good and bad game designers. I believe what separates good and bad designers has nothing to do with the initial designs themselves. What proved this to me is a game called Yavalath.

Yavalath is an abstract strategy board game, like Chess, Go, or even Connect Four. An abstract strategy game is a class of games in which athematic pieces are manipulated into some sort of winning pattern. Since they are abstract, they tend to be played with just colored stones, chips, or other plain shapes. Chess is probably the most thematic of the popular abstract strategy games. There is a small but prolific community of folks making new and interesting abstract strategy games every year. In 2007, one of those new abstract games was Yavalath.

Yavalath, like many games of its type, is a two-player game[1] in which each player controls one color of stone (usually white or black). Players alternate placing a single stone on an empty space on a hexagonal grid, trying to get four in a row. If that was all, the game would be fairly dull, as "x-in-a-row" games have been around for a very long time, Tic-tac-toe being the most popular. However, Yavalath has two interesting rules:

1. You lose if you ever have three in a row.

2. If the opponent is one move away from getting four in a row, your move must block the opponent's win.

Here's an example. In the board in Figure 13.1, the white player has two stones, a gap of one, and then another stone. If he plays in that gap on the next turn, he will win. Therefore, black must play there. However, because black is forced to play there, he will have three in a row and lose the game due to Rule #1.

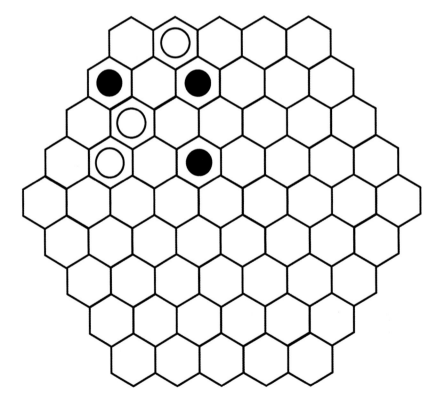

Figure 13.1 Yavalath

---

1. Yavalath has an interesting three-player variant, but that is not necessary to detail here.

The combination of Rules #1 and #2 make for a simple and beautiful dynamic. Players jockey for position, trying to judo their opponent into creating a position where they will eliminate themselves. Play involves springing traps and avoiding being caught in opponent's traps. It contains that "special sauce" that is in many great games: a simple ruleset, approachable beginner strategies, deep expert strategies, and dynamics that make the players always feel one move away from victory or defeat.

At the time of this writing, there were over 4,600 abstract strategy games listed on the BoardGameGeek.com database. Yavalath ranks in in the top 2% of abstract games according to ratings submitted by users there. It is undoubtedly a success in the niche-of-a-niche that is abstract board games. Clearly the designer had keen insight and intuition as to what makes an interesting strategy game.

Cameron Browne, a research fellow at Queensland University of Technology, could be credited as the inventor of Yavalath, but that would not be entirely correct. As part of Browne's PhD research, he created an evolutionary algorithm called Ludi that would break down abstract games into individual components and then combine those components in numerous combinations and evaluate them based on some heuristics. Ludi is the creator of Yavalath. Yavalath was a survivor of 1,389 attempted game designs created by Ludi. Algorithms that judged how interesting a game would be to human players based on various characteristics winnowed that down to 19 released games, of which Yavalath has been the most popular.

Pedants can argue that since Browne coded the ludemes into Ludi's system and created the heuristics to evaluate the games, that he ultimately is the designer of Yavalath and that Ludi is just a tool used to create that game design. I disagree. Browne had some high-level ideas of what would make a compelling game, but the N wins/N-1 loses mechanic was not something that Browne had previously compared. The "special sauce" of Yavalath was created by evolutionary algorithms. If the magic of game design is in identifying the combination of elements that make for targeted dynamics and aesthetics, Ludi did the hard work.

But if a computer algorithm can be a game designer, does the discipline lose its magic? In 5 years, will megacorporations just be pressing a "Make me a story-based adventure game" button instead of teams of creative people collaborating together to create an artistic accomplishment?[2] Will it be more efficient to design by algorithm? If that's the case, do game designers just become strange artisanal sideshows like glassblowing and weaving? I don't believe so.

---

2. I'm avoiding the cynical knee jerk response that would claim that some studios do make games by algorithm. I think that is just more sour grapes about bad processes than an objective reality.

Yavalath serves as example to question what it is that makes game design such an interesting and attractive field. What can we bring to it? Where is the value that the human touch brings? How can we ensure that it persists even through automation? By identifying these answers, we can only strengthen the practice of meaningful game design.

Accidental Game Design

If a computer can create an excellent game, then it strikes at the heart of the "auteur" model of game design—that is, that good game design can only come from the intentional practice of the convergence of a number of disciplines combined with a black box of inspiration directed toward making a particular aesthetic. This model celebrates the deliberate human task of game design. Proponents of this model can try to explain away Ludi's work as just a reflection of Cameron Browne's genius. The black box, they would reason, lies in Browne.

If Ludi challenges the "human" portion of the deliberate human-directed task of game design, then there are many examples that challenge the "deliberate" portion. Freeform play occurs in many species of creatures, and humans aren't the only creatures to transform play into experiences that could be called games, applying a structure to play. Many adults can relate the experience of a game they created as a kid from components or processes that they were already taking part in.

Sometimes, codifying an already existing process into a game is less a leap of inspiration and more a reclassification of something that existed as a game by accident. In the 1970s, Marsha Falco was working as a genetics researcher trying to understand the heritability of epilepsy in German shepherd dogs. She tracked specific elements of genetic data on index cards, creating a symbolic shorthand so that the cards were largely just symbols. How those cards could interact from a combinatorial perspective was particularly interesting. Finding patterns in the collection of randomly generated symbols was fairly fun. It was nearly two decades later when she self-published the game SET based on her system.

In SET, each card has four properties: color, shape, shading, and quantity. Each property can be one of three possible values. For instance, a card can be red, green, or purple in color. There is one card for each permutation of the properties meaning there are 3^4 or 81 cards in total.

SET has simple rules that are easier to show than to explain. Draw 12 cards to the table. If a player can find a set of three cards where each of the three cards has all the same or all different of each attribute, it is a *set*. The player announces that she has found a set, points it out, and removes those cards. The removed cards are replaced, and play continues until all players agree there are no sets (in which case more cards are drawn) or the deck runs out of cards. The most sets completed wins.

Figure 13.2 is an example of a SET game in progress. Cards are also not normally numbered but are here to aid with explanation.

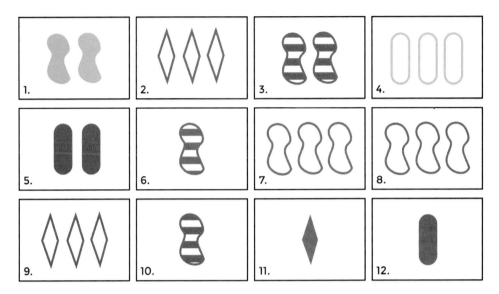

Figure 13.2 A SET game in progress

In the example, #3, #9, and #12 would make a set (see Table 13.1).

Table 13.1 SET

Cards	Color	Shape	Number	Fill
#3	Red	Squiggle	2	Striped
#9	Red	Diamond	3	Empty
#12	Red	Oval	1	Full
All same or all different?	YES	YES	YES	YES

In the example, #5, #9, and #10 are not a set because at least one of their attributes is not all the same or all different (see Table 13.2).

Table 13.2 Not a Set

Cards	Color	Shape	Number	Fill
#5	Red	Oval	2	Full
#9	Red	Diamond	3	Empty
#10	Green	Squiggle	1	Striped
All same or all different?	NO	YES	YES	YES

Finding sets is a real brain-burner despite having incredibly simple rules.[3] Strategically, the game is not complex. Every pair of cards has one and only one third card that will create a set. The game is even modular. If you use only red cards, then the set-making becomes one dimension simpler, making it appropriate for younger children.

The game's design didn't come from the inspiration that a particular aesthetic goal would need to be met. Instead, the core of the game was found by accident and only post facto was a set of game-like rules applied to it.

Write What You Love ... or Not?

I often get to listen to student pitches for their capstone projects. The subject matter of the games students want to create often correlates with what is popular at the moment. When Destiny came out, students wanted to make shooter RPGs. When Heroes of the Storm was shaking up the staid multiplayer online battle arena (MOBA) scene, students wanted to make new MOBAs. When Cuphead was new and exciting, students wanted to make difficult shoot-em-ups. It is tough to blame them. They are excited about a new thing and want to put their own spin on it. It is also likely to be economically advantageous. A new text adventure might be innovative, but there are probably more jobs and money in action games.

Common advice is to pursue something for which you could have a passion and an expertise. Thoreau was a fountain of this advice: "Do what you love. Know your own bone; gnaw at it, bury it, unearth it, and gnaw it still." Also (in paraphrase): "Go confidently in the direction of your dreams." With regard to others, he said, "Do not hire a man who does your work for money, but him who does it for love of it." Taking that advice is to encourage us to find a tiny niche of something we already love and mine it for a living.

That advice can lead you to specialize in something, carving out a niche in which you can excel. But it may also lead you to an echo chamber, where you can only copy the ideas you have already experienced. Some incredible growth can come from exploring areas in which you are not expert, where ignorance of the standard operating procedure allows you to eschew that procedure to create something new.

For example, independent designer Michael Brough wasn't a fan of making games with puzzles in them. His design philosophy was that he liked to make games that he himself would have fun playing. But if he wrote a puzzle, he would also know the answer, so puzzles just were not interesting concepts for his games. Upon some urging from another designer, he decided to try to make a game that was both focused on puzzles (of which he is not generally a fan even in games he did not make) and was interesting for him to make.

---

3. There are six sets in the example cards of Figure 13.2. Try and find the rest.

One of the lowest-hanging fruits for a 2D puzzle game is to make a Sokoban clone. Sokoban is a classic game that has been the antecedent for many game puzzles. In it, you play as a warehouse keeper who needs to push boxes onto specific spots. However, since he can only push one box and can never pull them or walk through them, the challenge is in how to position your character to push all the boxes into the correct locations without getting stuck. Literally hundreds of games followed on this exact premise to the point where it is a genre unto itself.

Brough's Corrypt looks like another Sokoban clone. In it, you push (and pull) blocks to activate switches. However, that appearance is deceiving. Puzzles get fiendishly difficult for a simple Sokoban clone early, and players are taunted by seemingly inaccessible items. I will avoid spoiling the wonderful twist that exists in the middle of Corrypt that transforms it from a solid Sokoban clone into a noteworthy game in its own right. I recommend it for all designers to show how a simple twist on standard mechanics can make a major impact without the heavy hand of loads of additional mechanical complexity or technical asset creation. By setting off on a project specifically about a genre he didn't personally appreciate, he made his breakout game, culminating in an Independent Games Festival Nuovo Award nomination.

A similar tale is seen in independent designer Zach Gage's SpellTower. Developed when there was already a massive glut of word games in the iOS App Store, SpellTower nonetheless peaked in the top 10 of paid app sales alongside more widely promoted games like Cut the Rope and Angry Birds. SpellTower started as a pet project to make a word game even though Gage himself did not like word games. SpellTower's success is largely based on a clear visual design and simple combination of mechanics. It is a word search version of something like Bejeweled (or more accurately, Drop7, discussed in Chapter 9, "Challenging Complexity"). Players create words with as many letters as possible from blocks that have various requirements (be in a 4-letter word or create a word next to this block to unlock), and those blocks disappear when used on a word, creating a cascade of other letters. It requires strategy to anticipate and maneuver in such a way that you can line up larger words. Other mechanical requirements, such as keeping a column of letters from hitting the top of the screen, give the game a more careful and strategic approach than similar games like Bookworm.

Keeping an open mind but still working in areas that challenge you can help to create an uncomfortable space that foments a great deal of creativity. For Michael Brough, questioning why people develop puzzle games helped to unlock a beautiful puzzle design of his own. For Zach Gage, questioning why people play word games helped to challenge the assumptions he held about what a word game needs to be about.

Why Rewards?

One of the common complaints with a loose definition of "game" is that if anything can be a game, then nothing can be a game. I have some sympathy for that idea. When I go to a local fast-casual dining establishment, if I scan a QR code into an app, I get points toward discounted food. But if I scan at particular times, I can gain even more points. This kind of sounds like a game, and is supposed to feel like one, but I would be hard pressed to actually call my dining purchase a game. Are the members of the marketing group that created the restaurants app actually game designers? It seems to be a poor use of terms.

The technique of applying game-like concepts to non-game activities is generally called *gamification*. Gamification advocates claim that adding these elements will turn non-engaging activities into engaging ones, will transform forgettable activities into memorable ones, and will build customer loyalty in an otherwise fickle customer. This is because games seem to create engagement, memorable experiences, and brand loyalty for the game products themselves. Desperately seeking the secret ingredient that makes games so intrinsically motivating, gamification practitioners put the body of a Ferrari on the internals of a Kia and wonder why the new Kia doesn't create the same emotional connection as a Ferrari.

This is because the "fun" (for lack of a better term) in games is not generated by any design system or mechanic in isolation, but from the balance of mastery and challenge. Buying a couscous bowl at the corner store gets me 10 points closer to free Greek fries, sure. But amassing those points doesn't give me any particular challenge and thus doesn't really give any sort of intrinsic motivation. It is a game-like veneer over an explicitly non-game activity. What gamification does do is weaponize the *extrinsic* motivators present in games toward some sort of tangential marketing goal. By this definition, gamification marketers cannot be called the same title as game designers. It would be like calling advertising copy writers novelists because both roles use words symbolically.

A great examination of this is in the Flash game by John Cooney called Achievement Unlocked. It is a simple, one-screen platform game like Lode Runner. But nearly every imaginable action in the game is giving an extrinsic reward: little achievement notifications that constantly pop up. There are achievements for moving to the left, moving to right, or jumping; there are achievements for *not* moving, achievements for playing a certain amount of time, achievements for getting other achievements, and so on. It is a joke game, but it does have a degree of fun to it in puzzling out what the 100 achievements could be in a game of such confined mechanics. Thus, the game that originally seems to be showing the emotional emptiness of achievements actually creates a system to make them intrinsically interesting.

Achievements, leaderboards, appointment dynamics, and other mechanics that can be found in "gamified" systems and games share common psychological hooks. But in different contexts, these systems can either provide motivation for activities or destroy that motivation.

The Book It! program in the United States rewards students with Pizza Hut pizzas for reading books. Research involving the program showed that students in the program read less and comprehended less after the program concluded than a control group of students. The extrinsic motivation of getting pizzas crowded out the intrinsic motivation that already existed for reading. When the extrinsic motivator was removed, there was no motivation left for students to continue reading.[4]

An early Kickstarter success was the phone app called Zombies, Run! Players start the app when they decide to go for a run in the real world. The app then creates an augmented reality layer aurally over the real world in which zombies are chasing the player. The player is then rewarded for continuing to run and must make decisions about gaining supplies at various stopping points. For many users of Zombies, Run! the extrinsic motivators (story, game resources, achievements) were just what they needed to engage in the task of running. It didn't serve to kill the intrinsic motivation of running because it was designed for people who already had no or little intrinsic motivation to complete the task in the first place. There have been a handful of studies examining this "gamified" version of exercise and whether it leads to better long-term outcomes, but results so far have been inconclusive.

It seems much more natural to call the creators of Zombies, Run! game designers than any other title. The main decision making in the activity is intrinsically interesting. The hook is that rather than interfacing with the game using standard game interfaces, players interface using the movement of their GPS signal. Contrast this to gamified loyalty programs where there is no decision making, only a quantity of interaction.

Summary

Many people have their opinions on what it means to be a game designer. Largely that view is formed by marketing and having "rock star" game designers give interviews that talk very little about the day-to-day craft and instead focus on tabloid celebrity with the subculture. But the actual discipline of game design doesn't have clear boundaries. I'm uncomfortable being the arbiter of who is or is not a game designer. I can only comment on what seems to fit the pattern. Declaring Gone Home or Zombies, Run! are not games does not change their aesthetic experiences one whit. Slavish devotion to a particular orthodoxy of what a game designer is and what the game design process is could leave out worthwhile experiences and make the world a poorer place.

---

4. This is also covered more in *Players Making Decisions,* but the best writing about the topic is Alfie Kohn's *Punished by Rewards.*

GAMES COVERED

Playlist Game #48: Gone Home

Creators: The Fullbright Company

Why: Gone Home is not the first and will not be the last game that challenged the mainstream acceptance of what features are required to be considered a game. For most designers, it really does not matter what the technical definition of a "game" is. All that matters is creating a targeted aesthetic. For what Gone Home lacks in "game-ness," it makes up for in aesthetic relevance and is worth playing for designers to understand nontraditional methods of interaction and challenge.

Playlist Game #49: Yavalath

Designer: Ludi

Why: Yavalath is a deep, yet simple abstract strategy game. It is more compelling by many measures than something like Reversi that has been played for hundreds of years. Yavalath is a great game even if you are unaware of its origins in that it was designed by an algorithm crafted to create combinations of mechanics that humans would find interesting. In this case, it succeeded.

Playlist Game #50: SET

Designer: Marsha Falco

Why: SET started as a system for codifying genetic information. Coming from that system, it is difficult to imagine it would turn into a mass-market card game with wide-ranging appeal for players of all ages. SET is a great example of a game that started as an accidental curiosity and was curated into an excellent design.

Playlist Game #51: Corrypt

Designer: Michael Brough

Why: Corrypt is a clever title that first is an exemplary example of a Sokoban-style game and then completely subverts the normal play of the genre. It has brilliant puzzle design, despite coming from a designer that specifically did not like to design games with set answers.

Playlist Game #52: SpellTower

Designer: Zach Gage

Why: Gage's SpellTower is another example of taking a genre for which a designer has a personal animus or dislike and breaking it down to find something within its conventions that interests him, building it back up to a successful entry in the genre that he originally disdained. For that alone it is a notable achievement, but it works as a well-designed word game even without that backstory.

Playlist Game #53: Achievement Unlocked

Designer: John Cooney

Why: Achievement Unlocked takes the concept of achievements to an extreme slippery-slope ending. If rewarding players for game activities is good, then rewarding players for every activity they could possibly do must be better? Past that one-note joke, the game becomes interesting to play as a puzzle experience as players try to figure out what would get them another achievement. In the game, execution is not what is rewarded, but instead understanding what execution could be rewarded is the goal.

Playlist Game #54: Zombies, Run!

Creators: Six to Start and Naomi Alderman

Why: Gamification is largely about applying game-like approaches to otherwise non-game-like activities. There are thousands of poor executions of this approach, but Zombies, Run! is one of the few successes. It applies an augmented reality layer to the world, where players have to exercise in the real world to progress the story and reach new decision points. In a decade where gamification is largely used as a soulless manipulator of consumers, Zombies, Run! stands out as a particularly well-implemented use of motivators.

CHAPTER 14

WINNING AND LOSING

"For when the One Great Scorer comes/

To mark against your name,/

He writes—not that you won or lost—/

But how you played the Game."

—Grantland Rice

There are certain elements of games that we often take for granted. Sports, for example, most often involve a team of players versus another team of players or many players all versus each other. Someone needs to win and someone needs to lose (or tie, at the very least). Sports also conjure up the implicit image of a central authority that determines the rules. But none of these things are necessarily true for all games, even if they seem to be true for most games. Exploring the edges of these ideas digs up some interesting classes of games.

Playing Together

Dr. Reiner Knizia is somewhat legendary amongst board game designers. He has at least 600 published games (and although some are just re-skins of other designs, it is still very impressive). His game Keltis won the prestigious Spiel des Jahres in 2004, and he has more games in the Top 300 on BoardGameGeek.com than any other designer.

One of Dr. Knizia's most significant contributions is his 2000 game based on *The Lord of the Rings*. In it, players work as the hobbits trying to take the One Ring back to Mount Doom. The winner is not the player who throws the ring into Mount Doom. Everyone wins or loses together, creating a vastly different dynamic than the standard all-versus-all model of conflict. Instead, players are all fighting the same game, working together toward a common cause.

Knizia's Lord of the Rings was not the first cooperative board game, but it certainly helped popularize the model. In the mid-to-late 2000s, cooperative games became their own genre with Arkham Horror in 2005, Pandemic in 2008, Ghost Stories in 2008, and Hanabi in 2010. Of these, Pandemic was the most commercially successful.

In Pandemic, players represent various public health officials trying to contain and eliminate a number of virulent diseases that are spreading throughout the world. Each player has a different role such as a researcher, a medic, or a quarantine specialist, each with different abilities. Because these abilities differ, no one player can try to monopolize the game's activities through his own role. Instead, each player has to focus on his strengths and ask for help at appropriate times. While the game can hinge on the random drawing of cards at the wrong times, often success is determined by the efficiency of the coordination of the players. Everyone has something to contribute.

This model brings new players to the table. Some players are intimidated by the possible gap in skills between players and use that as a reason to avoid certain games. I had a former colleague who was a ranked Chess master. There was no reason for me to ever play him in Chess. He wouldn't have fun because I would make too many mistakes to pose a challenge, and I wouldn't have fun because the end result was certain. But a cooperative game never needs to have that play aesthetic. While a new worry can bubble up when a player doesn't want to be a group's weakest link, the cooperative model is more inviting to this style of play overall.

Communication

A problem with some cooperative games (and is particularly exhibited by Pandemic) is what is called the *alpha player problem*. If there is no limit to communication and information known by each individual player, then the loudest or bossiest player can just tell everyone what to do on their turns, robbing them of the agency of making decisions. As there are no limits to communication or information known in Pandemic, this is often used as a negative toward the play experience. Groups have to be vigilant to avoid usurping the decision making of other players.

There are multiple ways to solve the alpha player problem. One way is by limiting communication by making it impossible for the alpha player to control the game. Some games, like Space Alert, use a timer to enforce this. If you have only 10 minutes to do your actions, then you likely won't have time to commandeer others' actions.

Another method is by limiting what is allowed to be communicated. In Antoine Bauza's Spiel des Jahres–winning game Hanabi, players work together to put on a fireworks show. They hold a hand of cards and must play those cards in sequence 1 to 5 for each color. If players play cards out of sequence 3 times, they immediately lose. This would be trivial if players had perfect information and could communicate. However, each player holds her hands in reverse, with the information side facing every other player. Thus, the person playing the card may not actually know what card she is playing.

Players are limited in their communication in Hanabi. The group has a certain number of hint tokens that can be used to give players information about the colors or numbers in their hands. No player can dominate this cooperative game because the rules explicitly limit the players' ability to communicate.

One of the challenges of playing Hanabi is that communication is not always direct transfer of information and it is not always done voluntarily. Saying that you are about to play a card and then hovering your fingers over a card allows you to watch the faces of your other players and see if any expressions clue you to the wisdom of playing that particular card. It isn't spelled out in the rules not to do this, but it is certainly against the spirit of the rules. As humans have myriad ways to communicate, apt letter-of-the-law cheaters can make a game of Hanabi a less-exciting challenge.

Of course, cheating itself is not a black-and-white issue. Making a gasping sound when a player is about to play a card that they shouldn't is a fairly direct transfer of information that feels like it should be against the rules. But what about creating a system in which the decisions that you make key the other players in to extra information? Should that be allowed?

Having found a website where I could play Hanabi online, I was pretty excited. In my very first game, my partner asked me whether I *finesse*. Knowing that word doesn't appear in the Hanabi rules, I was confused. The player then said he only played with people who knew how to finesse and left the game.

After doing some Googling, I found out that finesse was one of many conventions that online Hanabi players use. First, cards are ordered in a player's hand from newest to oldest.

Next, you assume that if someone gives you a clue about a card and it isn't apparently obvious what that clue was for, it means you can safely play the card. Finesse, then, can be explained with the diagram shown in Figure 14.1.

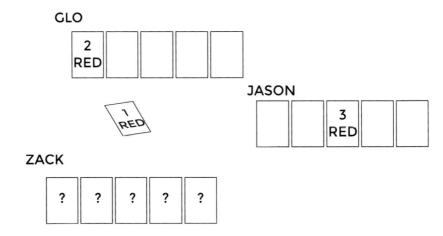

Figure 14.1 Finesse in Hanabi

In it, Zack, Glo, and Jason are playing. It is Zack's turn and he sees that Glo just picked up a 2 Red on her last turn. There is a 1 Red already on the table. Instead of using his hint token to tell her that she has a 2 (which would imply that it is a 2 that she can play), he tells Jason that he has a 3.

Jason, seeing that Glo has a 2 Red knows that his 3 must be Red because, otherwise, why would Zack have given him that information? Glo, seeing Jason's 3 Red knows that Zack must be telling him that because she must have the 2 Red—otherwise, why would Zack tell him about the 3 Red? Thus, she can safely play her newest card and Jason can play his 3. All this information was given with only one hint.

Like finesse, other conventions are used by online Hanabi players. *Reverse finesse* does the finesse trick out of order. *Bluff* is an even deeper trick that lets a player think a finesse is happening but allows them to play a different card legally. It's all very confusing to the novice!

Are these conventions within the spirit of the game? Is a rule that says I need to play this card when I give a hint that meets such-and-such requirements any different from saying, "When I raise my eyebrows, play your leftmost card"? The former is encouraged in high-level play, but the latter is forbidden. Bridge is a much older game with a cooperative element in player partnerships. It has numerous conventions that allow implicit communication much like Hanabi, and yet nonetheless has a robust tournament scene that fairly adjudicates these communication issues.

Diplomacy

After all, what is allowable? Is it breaking the rules as written, or is it an amorphous breaking of unwritten social conventions? One game that tests this to its limits is Diplomacy.

Diplomacy is a board game from the 1950s that still has an active player base and tournament scene. A world Diplomacy championship featuring national champions has been held since 1992.

Diplomacy is a fairly simple simulation of the First World War. Players take control of one of seven national powers and place supply centers, armies, and fleets in order to take control of the most territory. Combat is incredibly simple, with no heavy lookup tables or random elements. The intriguing part of the game is that all players play simultaneously; orders are written down and placed in the game box and then revealed simultaneously. Players are free to plan and wheedle on their own. As no agreements are truly binding, backstabbing is an integral part of the game.

What makes Diplomacy of further interest is that it has almost no socially implicit rules. Take Monopoly, for example. While the rules never say that you cannot steal from the bank,[1] it is socially accepted that this is against the rules. In Diplomacy, whatever you can get away with is fair game. If you want to sneak an extra army on the board when no one is watching, go ahead. Just don't get caught. Want to shift an opponent's supply center one space over? If he doesn't notice in time, tough luck. Want to eavesdrop on a private conversation? Go ahead. Or maybe you want to forge another player's orders and submit them as that player's own? There's no way to enforce it.

Because of this, Diplomacy is a mean, cutthroat game that appeals to a niche of a niche. Games of Diplomacy can cause terrible hurt feelings more than any other similar game. And individual sessions can be long. An in-person game can take an entire day. The 2012 online championship of Diplomacy went so long that the real-world calendar read 2016 when it was finished.[2] But it is nonetheless consistently played.

What makes Diplomacy evergreen is its purity. Sure, it is a nasty game that is sure to lose you friends, but any means of victory is encouraged. Not only do you have to have a military mind to position your units effectively (which many, many other games do well), but you must also have a political mind to build a framework that not only encourages alliances but gives you enough advantage that they can hold until you no longer need them.

Political philosophers use the prisoner's dilemma to model a particular type of direct conflict. In it, two players who would benefit from cooperation are both incentivized to

---

1. Except in the 2018 Monopoly: Cheater's Edition. Yes, that is a real game.
2. And in game, World War I extended into the 21st century!

betray each other so each ends up in a worse position. The iterated prisoner's dilemma is a model in which that direct conflict repeats and players can retaliate for another's betrayal. Political scientist Robert Axelrod once ran a famous (in the political philosophy literature, at least) tournament that challenged people to come up with strategies to the iterated prisoner's dilemma. The winner of his tournament was a strategy called *tit-for-tat* that essentially trusted people, and was not envious of other players, but punished them when they betrayed. Diplomacy is a massive seven-player iterated prisoner's dilemma in which the complicated strategies like tit-for-tat only work if you are around long enough and remain strong enough to retaliate, making the decision of when and how to betray incredibly nuanced. Thus, when and how to lie and cheat is the core of the game, something few other games can emulate.

Informal Rules

In Chapter 7, "Requiem for a Pewter Shoe," we discussed Nomic and other games that use their rules as the game's essential mutable characteristic. Regardless of whether a game has a variable win condition (meaning it can be changed), it is nonetheless defined and is something the players are consciously working toward. There are many forms of play that are a kind of may-fly game: an activity that has a bunch of little sub-games in it.

When I was in high school, my friends and I liked to play Hackey Sack. Also called *footbag* by some, players stand in a circle and kick a small woven ball loosely filled with small beads. The only formal rule is that once the sack hits the ground, you have to start over. An informal rule is that you can't use anything from the elbow to the fingertips to keep the sack in the air.

Hackey Sack is hard. It's especially hard if you are not coordinated or flexible. Nonetheless, because the activity has very few formal rules, the informal rules and structure of play end up creating small games that are customized for the group's skill level. At first, we tried to achieve simply having everyone touch the hackey sack at least once before it hits the ground. Once that became somewhat easy, we started adding tricks. There is no shortage of stunts you can pull in a Hackey Sack game. The goal then became an amalgam of discrete precision (keep it in the air) with style (how you keep it in the air). The degree of each of these goals was individualized for every member of the circle.

While the activity of Hackey Sack is a fairly old folk game with numerous variations, others have tried to formalize games of that nature into something to stand in contrast to other more well-defined and conflict-based games. In the 1960s, a counterculture spin-off called *New Games* developed. New Games were much more like Hackey Sack and much less like Diplomacy; the games were often cooperative rather than competitive (an early predecessor to games like Pandemic, perhaps?), where winning is minimized or undefined, and play is participatory rather than simply to be watched (some games could handle hundreds of players).

Inclusion is an integral part of the New Games Movement. As modern games become more and more toxic, the idea of inclusive spaces seem more relevant. Hackey Sack can be an example of a type of what New Games pioneer Bernie DeKoven called a "well-played game." In some Hackey Sack circles, it is discouraged to apologize when dropping the sack and ending the current round. The idea behind this is that apologizing puts focus on the failure and may intimidate players of lesser skill. It is this kind of playful and empathic spirit that makes many folk games such a joy to play. Modern commercial games should work to encourage such a feeling, but first designers need to be placed in play spaces that evoke that sense of community.

Summary

Play involving winning and losing is important developmentally. It is a part of most games. However, the head-to-head winner-take-all framework of play is really only one way to play games. Designs that eschew this conflict model sometimes stray into really interesting territory and have the opportunity to develop entirely new play aesthetics.

GAMES COVERED

Playlist Game #55: Pandemic

Designer: Matt Leacock

Why: Pandemic is one of the most popular cooperative games, a model where players succeed not by playing better than their opponents, but by helping their peers to play better. This model generates a bunch of aesthetic differences to the standard competitive model.

Playlist Game #56: Hanabi

Designer: Antoine Bauza

Why: Hanabi is a unique cooperative game where communication is limited, but coordination is required. The simple design innovation of having your cards face the opposite way as is expected opens up myriad opportunities for unique play.

Playlist Game #57: Diplomacy

Designer: Allan Calhamer

Why: Diplomacy is a tough game to recommend. It is long, brutal, and emotionally draining. It has a theme that has been used in hundreds (if not thousands) of games. Yet it is the most pure game about alliances in a zero-sum state that has ever existed. The fact that it has still has a devout following 50 years after first being published attests to its depth and staying power.

Playlist Game #58: Hackey Sack

Designers: Unknown/Folk

Why: Keeping a fabric-covered sack in the air with only your feet sounds too simple of an activity to teach game designers anything, but that knee-jerk (pun intended) reaction would be wrong. The amorphous game space that is created within a group based on a variety of attributes (player skill, environmental layout, end goal, etc.) make for a great exercise in player-determined game spaces. Go get some fresh air.

CHAPTER 15

INPUTS AND OUTPUTS

"One's destination is never a place, but rather a
new way of looking at things."

—Henry Miller

When we think about playing games, there is often an archetype that
comes directly to mind. Perhaps it is a player, seated on a couch with
an Xbox controller gripped tightly. Or maybe it is a group of friends
seated around of table, each clutching a hand of cards. Or maybe you
just picture a commuter tapping on his cell phone with one hand while
hanging onto a subway strap with another. While these are certainly
common abstractions, thinking about different input methods can open
up entire new types of designs.

Mimicry

The game that probably has the widest recognition despite nontraditional inputs would have to be Dance Dance Revolution. The game challenges players to step on arrows on a platform or pad to sync with a song, approximating dance. As public arcades are much more prevalent in Japan than they are in the West, games like Dance Dance Revolution had more of a market to blossom there in the late 1990s. When the game was brought to Western home consoles (and our more limited arcades) in the 2000s, it was a hit. People wanted to dance in their homes. Multiple competitors popped up. Schools even integrated it into physical education curricula using it to promote healthy play.

Arcades were fertile grounds for innovation in inputs as technology increased. Before powerful home consoles, economics dictated that only arcades could afford the expensive technology to push interesting game experiences. Home consoles could approximate the experience but were limited by hardware costs. For example, the Atari version of Pac-Man is a strange interpretation of the arcade version, limited by the console hardware. But as home consoles came to parity with what arcades could provide, game makers had to give players an experience they could not easily replicate at home.

The *rhythm* genre made the transition to the West fairly easily. Dance Dance Revolution had worldwide popularity, spawning competitors. Just as important may have been a partnership between a small peripherals maker called RedOctane and an independent music game developer called Harmonix. Their game Guitar Hero was an interpretation of the Japanese game Guitar Freaks. Both games involved using a plastic guitar peripheral to time button presses and "strums" of virtual strings to match falling notes on screen. It is not coincidental that this is a minor riff[1] on the interaction in Dance Dance Revolution. In both games, players mimic a real artistic activity by timing their movements with on-screen prompts.

While players certainly can dance while playing Dance Dance Revolution, the act of playing is not itself dancing (see videos of "freestyle" performances of Dance Dance Revolution songs for impressive dancing while playing the game). Likewise, success at Guitar Hero was not playing guitar. Other games in the genre were just elaborate dressings to make players think they were doing a task when they were just play acting: Players of PaRappa the Rapper weren't rapping, players of Beatmania were not mixing original compositions, and few who played Tony Hawk: Ride could transfer standing on a skateboard controller into real-world shredding.

This is not surprising. Games are not often meant to be analogues of real-world activities. But what surprised many is how the use of interesting input devices didn't only serve to engage the players of the game but served to engage spectators. Rock Band, the spiritual successor to Guitar Hero, in its best moments involves people sharing the same room, singing, drumming,

---

1. Pun definitely intended.

and strumming together. *Guitar Hero* and *Rock Band* require talent that is directly applicable to their real-world antecedents. More interesting are games that take the same performance qualities that made games like Rock Band so successful and recreated them without mimicking a real-world activity.

Jousting

The PlayStation Move controller is a strange-looking device. Sony attempted to capitalize on the success of Nintendo's Wii system's motion controls by implementing a device that could replicate the Wii's acceleration sensing with a position sensing enabled by cameras that tracked a glowing ball on the top of the controller. The result looked like a futuristic lollipop. Like many new technologies, it suffered a chicken-and-egg problem. As it wasn't packed in when consumers bought a PlayStation (as the Wii's controllers were), a very small percentage of players would own them. But because few players owned them, few developers would risk developing for them.

The "killer app" for the device would come not from Sony's headquarters, but from a few small independent developers and PhD students in Denmark. In Johann Sebastian Joust, players each hold a Move controller. When the game begins, music (Bach's *Brandenburg Concertos*) begins playing. As the music plays, players can move slowly. The accelerometers in the controller will be able to tell whether the player makes a sudden movement. After a certain amount of movement, a sound goes off in the controller and the player is eliminated.

The object of the game is to be the last player standing. Players are encouraged by the game's dynamics to slowly sneak up to other players and smack their controller hand to get their controller to register vibration and eliminate them. Periodically the music will speed up, offering a brief period of lower sensitivity on the controllers. The faster music wordlessly communicates that players can move faster and attack more aggressively without being eliminated.

No rules are supplied to the player. The game doesn't require players to look at a screen. Inevitably, players will attempt various strategies. I've seen players try to act as a human shield, lying on the ground with a bubble protecting their controllers. I've seen players try to sneak off and hide their controller somewhere still in the Bluetooth range so they could either pretend they were not playing or aggressively attack other players. But most games act like slow-motion knife fights. It is hilarious to watch and just as entertaining to play.

Unfortunately, the game did nothing to buoy the business prospects of the Move controller. But the game can still be played with various motion controllers on other platforms as part of the Sportsfriends game package. As *esports* becomes a more recognized term, it nonetheless describes an activity that has a lot of the same decorations as sports, but little of the actual interactions. Johann Sebastian Joust provides a different interpretation of what a symbiotic relationship between electronic games and sports can be.

Another Dutch developer, Game Oven, released a phone app called Bounden in 2014 that reinterprets what a *dancing* game could be mechanically. Previously, dancing games were of two designs, either the aforementioned Dance Dance Revolution games where players simply press buttons on a large controller to simulate dance, or games like Just Dance that use a combination of cameras and motion controllers to match poses to keyframes. While both of these archetypes had multiplayer modes, players were largely dancing solo.

Bounden is a dancing game for pairs. Each player holds the end of a phone placing a thumb on the screen and must rotate the phone together to meet the various cues. The game is only possible to complete by the players spinning and twirling in an actual dancing pattern. The Dutch National Ballet helped with the choreography of a number of the game's songs. Inevitably, players will get entangled in a way that is simply not a dynamic in nearly any game but Twister.

Both Bounden and Johann Sebastian Joust use verbs that appear in many other popular game franchises, but they do so in a mechanically different way that suggests even the most worn game verbs have a chance to be reinvigorated by innovative mechanics.

Life as Game Inputs

Game designers Katie Salen and Eric Zimmerman cribbed from Dutch historian Johann Huizinga when they defined the term *magic circle* in their book *Rules of Play.* Huizinga's magic circle was an example of a space in which a game is played, in which a temporary world exists on top of the real world where the rules are enforced and where dispositions can be altered to fit the needs of the game. The magic circle exists as a realm separate from the real. Only clueless politicians seem to think that there is an imminent risk of the activities within the magic circle seeping into the real.

But the circle's boundaries are not always so clear. Some truly innovative game scenarios have been born from experiments to use the real world in real time as the inputs for a game. The converse has been common for a long time: Games would be inputs for events in the real world. Gambling is an ancient version of this, but gold-farming operations in massively multiplayer games are a more recent export of the virtual into the real.

Protean *real-world* games have been with us since before the Internet. Fantasy sports have been played since at least the 1950s. In a fantasy sport, players act as general managers of their own sports teams. Game events are not simulated by a system but are instead provided by the real-world version of the player's on-field accomplishments. Fantasy sports increased in popularity as sports statistics became more varied and available than just the box scores in the daily newspaper. Now fantasy sports are a multibillion-dollar industry, toeing (and sometimes crossing) the line between games of skill and gambling.

Virtual stock exchanges have been used to educate students on the workings of financial markets for many years. Here, students use money that exists only in the magic circle to buy imaginary shares of companies that fluctuate in value based on real-life fluctuations. A clever adaptation of this idea is the Hollywood Stock Exchange.

In this game, players use imaginary currency to buy similarly imaginary financial products that fluctuate in value based on the box office returns of films and actors. Hollywood Stock Exchange feels more immediate and interesting than a traditional stock market game as the subject matter fluctuates on a much shorter cycle and the market doesn't operate as efficiently as one where real money is on the line, allowing for opportunities for smart play rather than just blind guessing.

Perhaps one of the subtlest examples of a game requiring the involvement of real-world dynamics was the 2008 Facebook game Parking Wars. Created by Area/Code (also the creators of Drop7 from Chapter 9, "Challenging Complexity") as an advertisement for a television series about traffic enforcement (meter maids, in the colloquial), the game eschews the reality TV spectacle of the subject matter for a more nuanced strategic experience.

In the game, you control parking spaces and cars. Your cars must go on the parking spaces that belong to your friends. Each parking space has a requirement. For example, a space may only allow red cars. Players gain money the longer their cars are parked (up to a cap). To gain the most money, players must log on to move their cars periodically. They will also want to check often as the requirements can change. What may have been a safe spot for your yellow car this morning may now be illegal. If you catch an illegal car on your street, you can ticket it for a huge payoff straight from your friend's account. It is often impossible to place all your cars legally, so you must choose between gaining no money or being a scofflaw by parking illegally on someone else's street.

On its surface, Parking Wars seems like a simple but novel use of a social network to provide a loosely thematic experience. However, to excel at the game requires a bit of social engineering. For instance, when I was playing with my friend who was living in Japan at the time, I knew that he was 14 hours ahead of me. This put my play time right in his sleeping hours. I could park illegally on his street with impunity as long as I remember to move my cars before he got up. This was a lucrative plan until one night he decided to check on his game because he couldn't sleep and he ticketed all of my cars.

It could be a valid criticism of Parking Wars that the game is less interesting the more it is watched. A social experiment based on the game Pokémon Red did just the opposite: create a version of Pokémon that could be played and watched by hundreds of thousands of people at a time.

Using the streaming website Twitch, the aptly named Twitch Plays Pokémon was a set of scripts running on top of an emulated copy of Pokémon Red. Twitch has a chat feature and so viewers of the stream could send a command using the chat window that would then be interpreted by the script and executed in the game. For instance, if I typed "right" in the chat room, then it would be just as if I pressed the "right" direction on the gamepad. With one player, a game could theoretically be completed quickly, if somewhat laboriously. But as players flooded into the chat, the game became a confused mess. At its peak, 120,000 players were sending commands to the game. Imagine two football stadiums full of people all smashing the buttons on a single Game Boy. Nonetheless, the community completed the game in just under 17 days.

Whether the real-world events used to power these games have to be anticipated as in fantasy sports, manipulated as in Parking Wars, or are acts of spontaneous order as in Twitch Plays Pokémon, real-world events serve as a rich repository of potential candidates for new and exciting game mechanics.

Waiting Is the Hardest Part

A truly strange genre of games that emerged in the mid 2010s is the *clicker* genre. In a clicker, players automatically generate resources over time that can be invested in various game elements that help increase the rate of resource generation. Thus, the decisions players make are largely based around how to most efficiently wait. Progress happens while the player is not interacting with the game. The name *clicker* comes from the construction that players' early resources are often awarded at one each time the player clicks. But early in the game, players buy an element that allows the player to gain resources over time rather than clicking for every single resource earned.

As with many new genres, a name hasn't been truly settled. Clickers may also go by *incremental games* or *idle games*. Idle games as a genre is a bit broader, as it goes back to games like Farmville where progress was generated by *not* interacting with the game (e.g., waiting for plants to grow before they could be harvested). But the waiting is a small part of the entire play aesthetic of Farmville, whereas in a clicker, it may be a large part of the play experience. Cow Clicker (covered in Chapter 6, "Mechanics as Message") is also a foundational idle game.

To explain the mechanics of clickers, it is best to go through examples. The title that helped popularize the genre was 2013's Cookie Clicker by Julien Thiennot. When you start the game, you simply have an image of a cookie on the screen with an inviting sunburst pattern behind it. Since players already know the name of the game, no use of tutorials is needed for the first interaction. Players click the cookie and it animates. Players then see their counter of cookies increase.

To the right of the area with the cookie is a panel labeled *Store.* The two items there are obscured, but their prices (15 cookies and 100 cookies, respectively) are displayed, encouraging players to click enough to unlock them. Once the player gains 15 cookies, the first item, *Cursor*, becomes purchasable. This item clicks automatically once every 10 seconds, whether you are playing the game or not. Players can buy additional cursors, investing the cookies earned from the first cursor to buy additional cursors. When the player reaches 100 cookies, she can unlock a *Grandma* who will make one cookie per second whether the player is playing or not. This increases the player's cookie production to the point that the player needs to only wait. Clicking is just one vector to getting more cookies.

From here, cookie production increases exponentially with more and more efficient upgrades always reinvested until the player needs to use scientific notation to best represent the number of cookies being made. The player decision making after the initial steps involves calculating return on investment (ROI): How long will it take for an upgrade to pay for itself?

While watching a counter increment is not particularly exciting on its own, the mystery of upcoming upgrades and variations on the core play experience keep these games engaging. A particularly interesting variation on the clicker formula that continually opens up new mechanics is Candy Box by French designer "aniwey."

Candy Box starts like any other clicker with the exception that we skip the step where a player needs to click enough to start generating resources automatically. The player starts generating one candy each second. After a short time, the player can choose to throw some of his collected candies on the ground or eat all of the candies. A little later, the player meets a lollipop merchant who will trade lollipops for candies. Eventually, the merchant will sell the player a wooden sword. Then the player can go on quests, cultivate lollipop farms, and do a bunch of other actions that frankly seem ridiculous from the basic loop of automatically collecting a candy every second.

Inspired by Candy Box is the clicker A Dark Room. Like other clickers, A Dark Room starts with a very simple interaction. The player is told she is in a dark room with a fire and is given the opportunity to stoke the fire every few seconds. The player can then gather wood to help with her fire and explore the surrounding area. As part of the pleasure of enjoying these games is the discovery, I will limit what I explain about the game. However, A Dark Room is an excellent merging of the mercenary aspects of the clicker genre (e.g., maximizing ROI and watching a meter fill) with a compelling story structure that gives that interaction meaning. While visually spare, A Dark Room provides one of the finest examples of transcending a simple mechanic to create a full aesthetic experience.

Verbal Communication as Game Inputs

We are used to playing games by using handheld controllers. If you were to commission an icon representing games, it is likely that one of the early candidates would be a representation of a controller similar to that used on the PlayStation or Xbox One consoles. Of course, game inputs predate video game controllers by a vast amount as sports are games without controller inputs that date back to first human civilizations. Nonetheless, when we think about the inputs of games, we tend to consider discrete enumerated messages like a button press and ignore the rich field of possible inputs that we use in day-to-day communication.

The party game Mafia was designed by Dmitry Davidoff, a Russian professor in 1986. It was rethemed by game designer Andrew Plotkin in 1987 as Werewolf and remains more popular by that name today. In it, a large number of players get together in a room with a non-playing moderator. The players are all assigned roles secretly. In Werewolf, some players are the titular werewolves, whereas other players are simple townsfolk. The moderator asks all players to close their eyes and then asks only the werewolf players to open their eyes. Silently, the werewolf players choose a villager to "eat," which eliminates a player from the game. Then everyone else may open their eyes. The moderator announces who was eliminated. Then the remaining players (villagers and werewolves alike) can discuss who they think is a werewolf and can vote to eliminate a player. These two steps (*night* and *day*) repeat until the villagers have eliminated the werewolves or there are as many werewolves as villagers.

Since the villagers do not know the identities of the werewolves but the werewolves know each other, there is an asymmetry of information that helps to make up for the werewolves' lack of numbers. As a villager, during the daytime discussion, you may have clues or suspicions as to who the werewolves are. But do you say them aloud? If you do, and the other villagers fail to eliminate that player, then will the werewolves choose to eliminate you on the next night because you pose a threat? Or if you are wrong, maybe the real werewolves will eliminate you just to throw everyone off their track? The dynamics of a game of Werewolf are very nuanced, especially in groups that play often. Play is enhanced by adding additional roles that can change votes, get extra information, or have alternate win conditions.

There are flaws in Werewolf's design: The first round offers no real information for the villagers, player elimination is no fun for those being eliminated, and final rounds can play out in a scripted way. But even with those limitations, the vast amount of player communication that can happen with just language, posture, and tone makes for a very entertaining social dynamic.

Werewolf has spawned an entire genre of games, *social deduction,* that attempt to fix the original's problems and/or expand the range of play possibilities.

Social deduction games use verbal communication as a game input for one specific purpose: to figure out a player's role. But the role of verbal communication as a game design tool can go well beyond that. A particularly compelling example of verbal communication as a main mechanic is Keep Talking and Nobody Explodes.

Originally conceived as (and best played as) a virtual reality game, Keep Talking and Nobody Explodes puts players in two asymmetric roles. One player, wearing a virtual reality headset, is a bomb technician attempting to defuse a ticking bomb. The other player or players is/are the bomb technician's team, using a paper manual to help the technician decide which buttons to press and which wires to cut on the bomb. Because the technician is wearing a headset, the assistants cannot see what the technician sees and are forced to communicate verbally. Of course, the game is designed in a way to make that verbal communication difficult. For instance, a particular module on the bomb may have a display and four buttons. The technician reads out what the display looks like and reads. The assistant looks in the manual and sees that if the display shows a 3 then the player has to hit the button marked "4." Often, with time sensitivity being an issue, a question is mistaken for a statement. The technician says, "3?" but the assistant thinks he is reading off #3 instead of confirming the last number read, pressing the wrong button and detonating the bomb.

As the game scales in difficulty, technicians have to juggle modules that demand the players switch their focus constantly while maintaining effective communication, all without ever being able to see what the other players see. While technically, the interaction with the game is based on very straightforward digital gates (button presses, discrete number/password entries, and so on), the real interaction comes between players and their ability to figure out effective shorthand that allows the technician to defuse the bombs in time. It is quite unique in that aspect and shows the breadth of possibilities for game designs about the ambiguity of language for game control.

Summary

There is not enough space or time to do a full appreciation of games that use strange inputs to create a new experience. In a period of just two months in 2017, one designer presented a suite of edible games at the Experimental Gameplay Workshop at the Game Developers Conference and another presented at the CHI Conference on Human Factors in Computing Systems a virtual reality game in which players have to eat to progress (microphones were used to detect the players' chewing sounds). Whether any of these games have any use beyond their own novelty is not nearly as relevant as what innovative solutions they can inspire for future games.

GAMES COVERED

Playlist Game #59: Johann Sebastian Joust

Designer: Douglas Wilson

Why: Real jousting is dangerous and requires a hefty amount of specialized equipment. While PlayStation Move controllers are specialty equipment, Johann Sebastian Joust converts a device made for solo gaming in front of a screen into an active, communal play experience. It's only a little dangerous.

Playlist Game #60: Bounden

Creators: Game Oven

Why: The old board/party game Twister is often name-checked with regard to Bounden. Both are experiences about contorting your body in the presence of others. But Bounden involves the beautiful aesthetics of dance whereas Twister is just meant to be a cluster of bodies.

Playlist Game #61: Hollywood Stock Exchange

Creators: Max Keiser and Michael R. Burns

Why: Playing the stock market responsibly is boring. Billions of dollars' worth of industry has been built to ensure that they are faster at profiting from market inefficiencies than you can ever be. And companies keep their prospects close to their chest. Any uncertainty is priced into securities immediately. But entertainment isn't boring, almost by definition. Hollywood Stock Exchange allows players to use entertainment vehicles as imaginary securities. Not only are they much, much more volatile than business securities, but most find the latest Marvel movie more worthy of conversation and speculation than the recent movements on the board of International Paper.

Playlist Game #62: Parking Wars

Creators: Area/Code

Why: Games about driving have been popular almost since the beginning of video games. Games about parking, however, have not been as well examined. While Parking Wars is ostensibly about parking, it is more about social engineering and was one of the first Facebook games to leverage the social aspects of the platform for something other than forced virality.

Playlist Game #63: Cookie Clicker

Designer: Julien Thiennot

Why: Click and get a cookie. How many cookies can you get? This sounds like a terrible premise, but quickly the game eschews clicking for investing. The vast upgrade tree in Cookie Clicker (along with the others listed here) helped to spawn an entire genre of clicker games. Soon after starting, large number values like "octillion" and "decillion" will be second nature to you.

Playlist Game #64: Candy Box

Designer: aniway

Why: Candy Box is a clicker game that starts like any other as you click to attempt to gain as many candies and lollipops as possible. Soon though, the play stretches into new and strange interactions. Candy Box's surprises make it one of the most interesting examples in the genre.

Playlist Game #65: A Dark Room

Creators: DoubleSpeak Games

Why: Like Candy Box above, A Dark Room subverts the normal clicker expectations to evolve the play of the genre. Instead of simply collecting a ludicrous number of things, A Dark Room focuses on RPG mechanics toward exploration and survival.

Playlist Game #66: Mafia/Werewolf

Creators: Dmitri Davidoff/Andrew Plotkin

Why: Mafia (or Werewolf) spawned a genre of social deduction games. The original has its flaws but remains a pure example of the large-scale social dynamic only possible in games of this style.

Playlist Game #67: Keep Talking and Nobody Explodes

Designers: Allen Pestaluky, Ben Kane, Brian Fetter

Why: Keep Talking and Nobody Explodes should be used in every team-building and communication seminar. It shows the signal loss in attempting to communicate verbally and under time constraints better than anything else I've ever experienced.

CHAPTER 16

WHOSE STORIES?

"Stories are the creative conversion of life itself into a more powerful, clearer, more meaningful experience. They are the currency of human contact."

—Robert McKee

Games are a really complicated way to tell stories. It is much easier to write stories on a notepad or word processor. Sure, you have rules of grammar, but out-and-out "bugs" are rare. To reveal an unpopular opinion of mine, the story of something like Final Fantasy VII isn't that interesting: The characters are one-dimensional, the world lacks nuance, and the plot hits a fairly conventional rhythm. So why do games provide a peculiar connection when it comes to stories?

Negotiated Storytelling

Dungeons & Dragons is, of course, the standard bearer for many elements in game design. Including it in this book at all seems unnecessary because of how ubiquitous it is among active game designers. For those who may still not be familiar with it, however, I will give a brief introduction.

Dungeons & Dragons is a role-playing game. In it, players work together to meet some fantasy objective with the help of another player (called the *Dungeon Master*) who acts as a narrator and mediator of conflicts. Often Dungeons & Dragons scenarios are based around fantasy tropes such as a group of wizards and fighters entering an area guarded by goblins and orcs to liberate a treasure. The players decide how their characters will act, and the Dungeon Master responds by controlling all of the non-player characters (NPCs) and events with the help of a random number generator (usually dice).

Where Dungeons & Dragons differs from general strategy games is the flexibility of the options for players. In a strategy game, the player actions are often limited and the scope of them is fully known. In a game like Dungeons & Dragons, campaigns often take on unexpected turns based on creative thinking from the players and/or the Dungeon Master.

This makes Dungeons & Dragons a game not only about strategy and tactics, but also about discovery and improvisation. There is no shortage of rules in the Dungeons & Dragons universe; publisher Wizards of the Coast produces volumes and volumes of rules supplements and scenarios every year. But unlike in a traditional board game, those rules are not necessary to play the game. The rules are whatever the Dungeon Master chooses to enforce and are applied however the Dungeon Master feels.

This is a difficult balance. The Dungeon Master's goal is to be a real-time game designer. It is simple to crush the characters ("A dragon appears out of nowhere and eats you. Game over.") or allow them free reign ("You find a chest with a magic wand that provides unlimited wishes!"). But neither of these extremes are much fun. The fun comes from keeping the players in flow. But doing that when the options are nearly endless such that a Dungeon Master cannot reasonably be expected to prepare a scenario that perfectly balances challenge and skill is extremely difficult.

The stories that emerge from a great session of Dungeons & Dragons are rarely wholly planned by the Dungeon Master or a third-party scenario writer. Instead, Dungeons & Dragons involves what I call "negotiated storytelling," not unlike that involved in improvisational (improv) comedy. In improv, one of the cardinal rules is called "Yes, and...." What this means is that players in improv should never shoot down another player's contributions; instead, the player should accept them and build upon them.

Let's look at an example from Dungeons & Dragons. The Dungeon Master has crafted a main NPC and written tons of dialogue and plot points around her, making her a key figure in the game's worldbuilding. The first time the player characters encounter her, something about the character's behavior sets them on edge and they end up fighting and killing her. The Dungeon Master didn't anticipate this and had to make up combat attributes for the character on the fly. The Dungeon Master here now has a few options:

- Not allow the players to kill her, conjuring up some sort of deus ex machina to save her such as other NPCs rushing in to save her, or using a magic force field conjured by a powerful wizard to protect her at the last minute.
- Let the players kill her and throw away the work.
- Allow the players to do what they had decided but create consequences for their actions. Save the work and assign it to different NPCs, or edit it based on the player's actions.

The first option is unsatisfactory for the players. They want to do a thing and the game system (represented by the Dungeon Master) will not let them. This is similar to when a video game provides an unopenable door or invisible wall to direct player navigation. It takes players out of the world created by the system by providing an unlikely yet coherent explanation for an external effect.

The second option is unsatisfactory for the Dungeon Master. No one likes to throw away work, especially for a reason external to the work itself. It wasn't a flaw of the Dungeon Master's that made the work obsolete; it was actions of the uncontrollable players! Worse, this would lead the Dungeon Master to not create interconnected content in the future out of fear of wasted time and effort.

The third is the most satisfactory for both parties. The players continue with whatever line of motivation caused them to take their actions in the first place; the world remains consistent. The Dungeon Master must take pains to improvise but can rework plot points and elements into future encounters.

Both sides "win" by negotiating the outcome in good faith. The players may not be aware of this negotiation, but by acting within the scope of the rules of the world the Dungeon Master provides, they agree to the negotiation. After all, in a system where anything is possible, the player could choose to sit and do nothing or choose to do things clearly not in line with the story. But his cooperation allows the experience to continue. This is unique because the Dungeon Master has the flexibility to change the rules at will, not for the end of a win or a loss, but for the end of an experience.

Automated Dungeon Masters

The first computer role-playing game was 1977's Colossal Cave. Its designer, Will Crowther, was an active Dungeons & Dragons player and modified the experience of playing that game into a more constrained digital form. Colossal Cave was the first work of interactive fiction (which we covered as a genre in Chapter 4, "Piecemeal Perspectives").

Looking at Colossal Cave and its much more commercially distributed genre mate Zork shows the first nascent steps at building an automated Dungeon Master. The player's options are limited only by their ability to express their desired actions. The limitation comes from the text parser's (the Dungeon Master's) ability to understand them within the context of the world. Interactive fiction often suffers from this "parser fighting," where a player wants to do a thing but the system does not understand what that thing means. In some, saying, "pick up the silverware" is incomprehensible because the system is looking for "take fork." Humans have a much better handle on the ambiguity needed for effective Dungeon Mastering.

In the 40-plus years since Colossal Cave, developments in AI and machine learning have made promising strides toward an automated Dungeon Master. Interactive fiction stalwart Emily Short announced the production of Versu, a storytelling engine, with developer Richard Evans in 2012. Versu focused on creating believable behaviors for AI characters such that the NPCs could improvise in a contextual way, allowing for a story where a character was able to be courted or killed with the remaining characters acting appropriately based on those choices. The company behind Versu was bought by Linden Labs, which ended up shelving development of the project. A later agreement allowed bits of fiction using Versu to be released, but it stands as abandonware at this point.

One of the key works in adaptive storytelling is Façade, a 2006 work by researchers Michael Mateas and Andrew Stern. In it, players attend a cocktail party hosted by their friends Trip and Grace. Immediately, the writing infers that there is a domestic problem between the two. Players can then converse with Trip and/or Grace using text prompts and the characters respond in meaningful, contextual ways. Two identical statements can be interpreted by the characters in different ways based on the character's emotional state or from earlier remembered elements of conversation. The result is a surprisingly real (at least in comparison to traditional digital storytelling) feeling of interacting with dynamic individuals.

This dynamism is what makes negotiated storytelling feel more realistic than standard hypertext fiction. An example of hypertext fiction would be a "Choose Your Own Adventure" book. In these, players read to a point and then make a decision, which determines the page to which they turn next. While these narratives allow for more agency than a standard narrative, they are also extremely constrained by the combinatorics in hypertext. For example, if you have a hypertext that allows the player to call up one of three friends, each of which presents three different activities to do, and each of those has three different outcomes that may occur, the author of the experience has to explicitly make 27 outcomes even though the player is likely to only ever experience one. This doesn't provide bang for the development buck. A negotiated storytelling approach doesn't require the author to know the destination of the narrative, only to understand the context of player decisions. It is much harder to architect, but when this problem is solved, expect leaps forward in interactive narrative.

Symbolic Worlds

There is usually a distinct tradeoff between representational fidelity and flexibility. The 2001 film *Final Fantasy: The Spirits Within* featured groundbreaking computer graphics for its time. The characters in that film looked more photorealistic than any characters that came before. However, at the time, no computer could render those impressive graphics in real time. Thus, to create that level of representational fidelity, the creators had to aggressively plan every angle and every effect that would be shown to a minute scale. There was certainly no room for improvisation.

At the other end of the scale is 2006's Dwarf Fortress. Dwarf Fortress' representation of its world is limited to ASCII text characters. However, a hefty computer is required due to the depth of behaviors of the characters in the game.

In one particularly memorable bug report, players were confused as their cats kept dying without having any record of being involved in combat. When examined, the only strange status in their description was that they were covered in vomit. As cats roamed around the titular fortress, they encounter many drinking dwarves (as drinking is a popular activity for dwarves). In doing so, there is the chance that a cat walks through a puddle of spilled alcohol or has alcohol spilled on them. While cats did not have a behavior that would allow them to drink alcohol, they did have a behavior to clean themselves. Since the game simulated drinking alcohol by number of pints, when cats cleaned themselves, they ended up drinking an entire pint of alcohol (as that was the smallest possible unit), thereby giving themselves alcohol poisoning and dying. A later update patched that behavior, but that is just a small example of the depths of the simulation and the unintended consequences of emergent systems.

This is only possible in Dwarf Fortress because the representation is so crude. A cat is simply represented by the character "c." The game spends the vast majority of its resources checking elements *about* the cat rather than displaying how the cat should look (which is an astonishingly difficult computational task only made possible by powerful graphics cards, the complexity of which we take for granted).

Even the lowly "c" can slow modern computers down. A Dwarf Fortress phenomenon called a "catsplosion" can happen when a critical mass of cats adopt owners. The owners bond with the cats and become reluctant to kill any cat. This causes a quick overpopulation as these dwarves will also not let other dwarves kill any cats. The exponential growth can cause a vast slowdown on the player's computer.

Dwarf Fortress's consideration of so many elements creates unexpected emergence. It is a deep well for innovative combinations of mechanics that can inspire any potential designer.

Who Are You?

A particularly interesting side effect of the agency that interactive entertainment affords is the grey area when talking about the identification of a game's avatar. For instance, it is quite natural to say, "I landed on Boardwalk" in Monopoly, even though the "I" in this case is represented by a pewter top hat. Since there is no personification of the top hat, it is tough to have any qualms about that statement. However, in many games, players identify with fleshed-out and anthropomorphized characters that are not wholly under the player's control. When I make Lara Croft jump in Tomb Raider, I can just as easily say, "I jumped" or "Lara Croft jumped." Yet seconds later, Lara might be in a cutscene killing bad guys where the player has no control. Do we still say, "I killed the bad guys" or must we switch to "Lara killed the bad guys"? I certainly wouldn't identify with the person on screen in a movie (Luke blows up the Death Star; I don't blow up the Death Star), yet we are comfortable doing it in games even when the happenings are not a direct result of our own agency.

Where this becomes worth discussing is when the player's avatar does something that is incongruent with what the player would do. 2007's Bioshock gave characters a standard voiceless first-person avatar. In cases like that, it is easy for players to identify the avatar's actions as their own (e.g., "I used the crowbar" versus "Gordon Freeman used the crowbar"). However, later narrative devices lock the player into a kind of mind control where there is no way out of the avatar doing things that may be against the player's desires. That creates a dissonance for the player in terms of story. Up until that point it is easy to consider yourself in control of the narrative. When that control is taken away, it raises questions about the player's total agency in the experience and confuses further participation.

Another technique that can cause dissonance is when the avatar needs to know things that the player does not know. One of the axioms of drama is that the characters in the drama have a full life outside of the drama that is not directly revealed to the audience. This gives characters depth. However, if the character is literally the audience in the case of player/avatar synergy, then what happens when the player needs to know something that the avatar would clearly know? The player can improvise and fake it, of course, but depending on the stakes of the decision that may not be enough.

A great example of this is the interactive fiction The Warbler's Nest by Jason McIntosh. In it, the player occupies a rural pastoral setting and must complete a ritual. Over the course of the game, the player's perception of the meaning of the ritual changes. By the end of the game, assumptions made at the beginning of the game are completely amended. I dance around the content of the plot as I want players to experience it for themselves. It is free to play on McIntosh's website. However, if the player knew what the avatar knew at the beginning of the game, there would be no sense of shift in perception and the game would be a drudging affair of simply walking around and collecting objects.

Contrast this approach to something like Quantic Dream's 2010 game Heavy Rain, in which one of the controllable characters has a significant shift in allegiances during the course of the story that cannot be controlled by any interventions from the player. In this case, as in The Warbler's Nest, significant information is kept from the player. However, in Heavy Rain, earlier actions under the control of the player do not make much sense after the revelation. The player ends up feeling used by a narrative sleight of hand as something external forces a change in perception about the game's characters instead of the player being the agent of the change in perception.

Summary

Stories are clearly important to consumers as we continue to spend more and more on fiction books, movies, and narrative-driven games. Games have a unique opportunity to allow players agency within artificial worlds, but that is a very difficult task in terms of both design and implementation.

A 2010 study showed that almost 90% of players, when given the opportunity, chose to make their game avatars resemble a (possibly idealized) version of themselves. It is important to understand then that to most players, avatars are not just game characters. Instead, they are a special class of game characters that have to be allowed to drive elements of the story but must not have anything happen to them that would jeopardize the bond between the player and his avatar.

GAMES COVERED

Playlist Game #68: Dungeons & Dragons

Designers: Gary Gygax and Dave Arneson

Why: Dungeons & Dragons is simply the most important game ever to have been created. While traditional sports like soccer have more reach to a greater population, no game has influenced the quantity of other games that Dungeons & Dragons has. Even Madden NFL, a game with a vastly different marketing profile from Dungeons & Dragons, uses a similar skill-checking system for determining stochastic skill results. Dungeons & Dragons' reach cannot be underestimated.

Playlist Game #69: Zork

Developers: Infocom

Why: Zork expanded on the genre created by Colossal Cave and was an extremely successful first step in making games in which players could be immersed in a narrative rather than using narrative as set dressing. But Zork isn't important just for its historical value. Watching players struggle with the text parser can be a lesson in how different players attempt to solve problems. As much as designers can allow players to solve problems in their own way, the more the consistency of the world remains solvent. Solutions that may be obvious to one player may be unimaginable to another. How do you design to accommodate that?

Playlist Game #70: Façade

Designers: Michael Mateas and Andrew Stern

Why: Mateas and Stern's work stepped beyond the standard list-lookup method for interactive fiction and treated in-game characters as rational agents rather than states in a world. Playing Façade after Zork shows a clear progression in the development of digital storytelling, regardless of whether you are interested in the narratives of either the caverns in Zork or Trip and Grace's party in Façade.

Playlist Game #71: Dwarf Fortress

Designers: Tarn and Zach Adams

Why: Dwarf Fortress is an amazing achievement in simulation fidelity that designers should appreciate. The game's steep learning curve and inscrutable iconography can make it difficult to enjoy, but potential designers should appreciate the vast degree of consideration given to each game object.

Playlist Game #72: The Warbler's Nest

Designer: Jason McIntosh

Why: Normally, hiding critical information from the audience is a cheap trick. Consider the trope of the amnesiac protagonist who is only an amnesiac so that the player can slowly learn about his or her world. The protagonist in The Warbler's Nest is not an amnesiac, but crucial information is hidden and released by the character's attention and actions. This agency over the revelation makes The Warbler's Nest clever rather than contrived.

CHAPTER 17

CHEAT CODES

"If you're not cheating, you're not trying."

—Eddie Guerrero

I'm admitting now, ahead of you reading this chapter, that I am about to cheat. There is nothing you can do about it except close the book and walk away. But why would you? You are so close to being done!

I built each of the previous chapters around a concept. That part was not difficult; the world is so bursting with worthwhile games to play! However, as I mentioned before, I have to cheat. This final full chapter has no overarching theme. There are just a number of really excellent games that I wanted to share. So here they are, piled up in the back. But just to make it formal, let's talk a bit about cheating.

On Cheating

Baseball is a sport built for statisticians. Most of the action happens in discrete, codifiable chunks with only two players contributing to the play at any one time, which makes the game easy to break down into analyzable data. Twenty-four-hour sports networks fill the airwaves with questionably held opinions about the worth of players in hypothetical situations. Mining the great database of sports statistics helps to make that argument.

The Baseball Writers Association of America is an organization of sportswriters whose most newsworthy job is to decide who gets inducted into the National Baseball Hall of Fame each year. The National Baseball Hall of Fame is a museum that immortalizes the best of the best players in professional baseball. To be inducted, 75% of the sportswriters must vote you in. It's a high bar, certainly.

What evidence should sportswriters use as their guide in comparing players who may not have played at the same time in the same league? One metric that informs a player's offensive capability is called the "on-base plus slugging average" or, more reasonably, the OPS. The OPS measures two things: a player's on-base percentage (how often they are able to get on base) and the slugging average, which is a metric that measures how many bases a player reaches per at bat. Sum these two metrics together and you get the OPS.

Babe Ruth was the first player to ever record above a 1.250 in OPS, and he did it 6 seasons in 8 years. Ruth was also in the first class inducted into the National Baseball Hall of Fame. Ted Williams recorded an above 1.250 OPS both before he served in World War II and the Korean War and after he returned, recording the highest career batting average ever. Williams was an easy choice for the Hall of Fame when he became eligible in 1966. No other player reached this mark in all of baseball's history until 2001 when a player recorded 4 years in a row above 1.250 OPS, including the all-time high OPS of 1.422.[1]

This player should also be a shoe-in for the Hall of Fame. However, in 2013 when he became eligible for the Hall of Fame, he received only 36.2% of votes. This was well short of the 75% threshold required. In 2018, in his sixth year on the ballot, he received 56.4% affirmative votes. While certainly better, it was still well short of the 75% threshold. If he does not reach 75% by 2022, barring any rules changes, he will be removed from the ballots permanently.

Fans of baseball will know that the player I am talking about is Barry Bonds. Bonds was an all-star player for the Pittsburgh Pirates in the 1990s, but he smashed records in the early 2000s on the San Francisco Giants after gaining roughly 40 lbs in size. Bonds played in what is now known as the "steroid era" because many of the greats of the time have been accused (and in many cases, indicted on charges) of using performance-enhancing drugs.

---

1. Thanks to Jon Bois of SB Nation and his "Chart Party" video series for these statistics.

Would Bonds have been a Hall of Fame player without the steroids? He was voted the National League's Most Valuable Player for 3 years in the period of 1990–1993. His performance was solid throughout the late 1990s and skyrocketed in the early 2000s. From 1993 to 1998, in his so-called lagging period, he was never worse than third in the National League in OPS. It's likely that he could have kept up production that would have made him an easy choice for the Hall of Fame.

Many of the member sportswriters who vote for Hall of Fame induction refuse to cast votes for anyone known to have used performance-enhancing drugs. In 2013, when the first class of the so-called steroid-era players became eligible, the sportswriters sent a message by electing no one to the Hall of Fame in that year.

There is a pro-Bonds argument to be made. "He was only doing what everyone else at the time was doing," it goes. If he did not use drugs, his performance would look artificially deflated compared to those who did. Anger about the means used to hit all those home runs does not invalidate that those home runs happened or that the San Francisco Giants won those games. If those games are invalid, what do we do with entire seasons of baseball where we know someone cheated? They clearly happened, so why pretend that they didn't?

Philosopher Bernard Suits, writing about the essential nature of games says, "The end in poker is not to gain money, nor in golf simply to get a ball in a hole, but to do these things in prescribed (or perhaps more accurately, not to do them in proscribed) ways: that is, to do them only in accordance with rules. Rules in games thus seem to be in some sense inseparable from ends.... If the rules are broken, the original end becomes impossible of attainment, since one cannot (really) win the game unless he plays it, and one cannot (really) play the game unless he obeys the rules of the game."

This is a contentious view in the philosophy of games and sports, but it is worth considering. If a game is made of rules, someone acting outside those rules is not playing the game. Since the "winner" of the game must be playing in order to win, cheaters are not even playing the game.

I have been an official for high school football games in the state of Florida for the past 10 years. If you really want to learn to appreciate the structure of a game, train to become an official. One of the early lessons that shocked me in my training class was a command to **not** call every violation of the rules that you see. At its face, that lesson combined with Suits's definition above means that no high school football game has ever been successfully played.

The reason behind that lesson became clearer as I became more experienced: Football is a difficult game to play by the rules. At any time, there are 22 players on the field[2] pushing and shoving and trying to gain a physical advantage. There are many illegal methods to gaining

---

2. Or more if there is cheating!

a physical advantage, such as holding a player who does not have the ball. An official could call a penalty for offensive holding on every play of every game at lower levels. If he did, the game would never finish and no one would be satisfied.

The direction for young officials is to only call violations that directly affect the play of the game. It may say in the rulebook that a player cannot grab the jersey of another, but if a player is doing that 20 yards to the side from where the ball is, what effect is that having on the game? In that case, it is wise to keep the flag in your pocket and save it for violations that directly affect the game or pose a safety risk for players.

The rulebook never says to only call violations that meet an arbitrary standard of meaningfulness with respect to the game. Instead, the rulebook provides a ceiling on what can be called and leaves it to experienced officials to manage the game in a way that is satisfying for players and fans alike.

Baseball's viewership continued to rise throughout the steroid era. Fans packed stadiums to watch athletes knock balls out of the park. Is the satisfaction of players and fans the true metric of success in a fan-driven sport? If so, what does that say for other games? At what level of popularity does a game stop being intrinsically meaningful based on its rules and turn into a black box that produces entertainment for spectators?

Katamari Damacy

I'm always surprised when Keita Takahashi's 2004 masterpiece Katamari Damacy is unknown to students. Most video games are explained primarily by some verb. For instance, Halo is a shooter. *Shoot* is the primary verb. Mario Kart is a racing game, the verb there is *to drive.* Super Monkey Ball's primary verb is *to tilt* or *to roll.* While at its surface, Katamari Damacy may involve rolling, quickly it reveals itself as so much more unique.

In it you play as the diminutive *Prince of All Cosmos* who is directed by his father the *King of All Cosmos* to rebuild the sky as the King happened to have knocked all the stars from it. This is done by the Prince rolling a strange ball called a katamari. The katamari adheres to elements with which it collides that are some degree smaller than it. As the katamari grabs objects, it grows and thus the threshold for objects that can stick to it grows larger.

Stages start by the player rolling up small elements like pencils. As the katamari grows, players can roll up larger objects like people and cows and eventually large land masses. Nearly every element in a stage can be eventually rolled up.

The thematic elements are no doubt a large part of Katamari Damacy's charm. The absurd humor is embraced wholeheartedly, the low-resolution of the graphics allows for the world to be constructed as a cohesive whole technically, and the soundtrack is one of the best of all time.

The mechanic elements are largely straightforward. The Prince simply rolls the katamari around. As each level is timed, player decision making hinges on a simple set of criteria: Can I reach that thing? If so, can I roll up that thing? And then, finally, is that thing big enough to make a difference?

It's such an oddly compelling set of player decisions that there simply is not another title that has ever combined its whimsy, humor, and sense of challenge. There are certainly other wacky games that play with the environment in clever ways. But games like Goat Simulator or Catlateral Damage seem to try to build a game around wackiness whereas Katamari Damacy is a game that satisfies on a mechanical level that just happens to be wacky.

When designers insist that games are just tweaks of the same tried and true verbs, Katamari Damacy stands out as a notable counterexample.

Terry Cavanaugh

Irish independent designer Terry Cavanaugh is responsible for a number of underappreciated titles. His unpronounceable 2010 game VVVVVV is a masterclass in level design. VVVVVV is a platforming game (like Mario, for instance) with the absence of a jumping mechanic. Instead of jumping, the player can at any time flip the y-direction of gravity, causing the character to fall upward instead of downward. Since players can do this as often as they like, with skillful maneuvering they can jump in the x-direction a long way without ever hitting the ground by flipping gravity often. VVVVVV uses that simple mechanic and takes it to its limit, creating a difficult yet fulfilling puzzle-platformer that would help popularize the genre within the indie community.

In 2013, Cavanaugh released Super Hexagon, a highly twitch-based survival game. In it, the player's avatar rotates around a hexagon while walls close in from the edge of the screen. If the avatar touches a wall, the game ends. Challenge comes from the rotation of the entire game arena, camera movements and color changes that distract the player, and increases in speed and complexity of the walls.

The sense of flow in this game is particularly effective. It will take novices a good deal of time to learn to survive just 30 seconds. However, even genre novices will find themselves getting better and better over time. This is unlike *masocore* games that misuse flow by always erring on the side of frustration over ease. While Super Hexagon can be extremely frustrating, it never seems unfair and it never seems as if there was no way forward. This serves to keep players playing, feeling they are always just out of reach of their possible skill ceiling. If I could reverse engineer that feeling into other games, I'd have solved game design.

Dream Quest

Every year graphics cards get smaller and more powerful. With that power, video game companies weaponize the aesthetic. They offer fancier and fancier graphics tricks. For a long time, the holy grail was *photorealism*. 2001 shooter Max Payne was credited for its photo-realistic look in many reviews, but a modern eye (less than 20 years later!) laughs off that assessment. Nonetheless, companies spend more and more of their development budget making a game look lifelike, while spending money on the mechanics does not necessarily warrant the same investment. It can be clear why: The marketing machine that makes these multimillion-dollar titles possible relies on using pictures and videos to show off the games. Good mechanics do not come through in a screenshot or video.

Many games have been purchased due to fancy videos, slick magazine images, or well-composed App Store preview shots only to find a shallow, tedious game underneath the surface. Media-literate game players are often aware of that bias. But what tends to be ignored is the comparatively ugly game with deep, beautiful mechanics.

In 2014, Peter Whalen released Dream Quest to the iOS App Store. To say that the art of the game looks amateur is an understatement. Dream Quest is a combination of permadeath dungeon exploring games like NetHack mixed with the deckbuilding mechanics of Dominion. In it, you explore a dungeon, battle monsters, and find new cards to customize your deck for further dungeoneering. The deckbuilding and dungeon exploring offer deep customization for both strategic and tactical decision making. However, the art on the cards and the art for the monsters are literally stick figure drawings. While those in glass houses shouldn't throw stones, it is nonetheless impossible to not comment on the crudeness of the presentation.

If you are able to look past the surface-level concerns, you will find an extremely well-thought-out system that challenges players over many plays. Whalen eventually accepted a role on Blizzard's Hearthstone team after many players at the Blizzard studio enjoyed playing Dream Quest. A spiritual successor is being developed by an indie team called Slay the Spire with, thankfully, a more traditional presentation.

Desert Golfing

Desert Golfing is a simple golf game in an avalanche of games of increasing complexity in the mobile space. Desert Golfing is simple: You drag your finger to set an angle and power for your stroke in a 2D environment and try to get the ball in the hole. Simple physics provides the rules. The main mechanic difference is that the game never restarts. It has a seemingly endless progression of holes and the score doesn't reset.

While the holes are procedurally generated, they display the same for every player. My hole #1234 is the same as your hole #1234. The game lacks ornamentation. There are no menus. Visual interest is carried by a very gradual shifting of the color palette. A hole that features a cactus becomes visually striking after hundreds of holes with nothing extraneous. A hole with a cloud feels special and meaningful.

For a while, a natural cap to the game was thought to happen at hole #2866. The hole exists in an alcove that seems impossible to reach. But eventually, a player found a small bit of real estate off-screen that could be used as collision to conquer the unbeatable hole. The algorithm that designer Justin Smith used to create the holes begins to create flat, simplistic levels around the 3000th hole.

As players demanded more content, Smith changed the algorithm to remove the flat and "impossible" holes. Eventually, he gave up. Around hole #21,700, an ocean appears. You can hit the ball into the ocean for eternity but can never progress. It is an end without fanfare for a game that explicitly relinquishes any opportunities at fanfare. In a climate where designers feel it is important to externalize every action into a quantitatively rewarded achievement, Desert Golfing stands out as happily against the grain. It offers only itself.

Summary

It has been wonderful watching the popularity of independent games ebb and flow throughout the past decade. As tools development decreases the barriers for people to make and distribute games, we can expect to see more and more innovation in the space. The sheer volume of game releases means there will always be something interesting to play, whether you want to roll up the world or putt your way across it.

GAMES COVERED

Playlist Game #73: Katamari Damacy

Designer: Keita Takahashi

Why: Katamari Damacy holds a place in my heart for being so unabashedly unique and yet so satisfying as an experience. Usually uniqueness implies some sort of feeling-out period as your tastes are informed and modified by the new experience. But Katamari Damacy is digital joy right from the get-go. It is a game all designers should both play and analyze.

Playlist Game #74: VVVVVV

Designer: Terry Cavanaugh

Why: It is often said that creativity is fed by constraints. VVVVVV's limited action selection of moving left, right, or flipping gravity is fodder for a beautiful set of level designs. Where it may have been tempting to introduce many new elements to this formula, variations on the mechanics are spaced apart far enough that it really feels like the idea space was well explored and refined.

Playlist Game #75: Super Hexagon

Designer: Terry Cavanaugh

Why: Super Hexagon is frustrating not because of any tricks up the developer's sleeve (like a masocore game), but because you simply aren't good enough. Only a few moments in Super Hexagon require superhuman reflexes. The rest of the experience is an example of living and playing in flow. While flow is hard to describe objectively, handing someone Super Hexagon to play for a few minutes seems to serve as a useful alternate definition.

Playlist Game #76: Dream Quest

Designer: Peter Whalen

Why: Whalen's Dream Quest looks like the placeholder art for an otherwise amateur production. One could understand this, assuming that the underlying game was similarly low effort. That assumption would be incorrect. Dream Quest provides some of the most satisfying dungeon crawling mechanics of any game to that point.

Playlist Game #77: Desert Golfing

Designer: Justin Smith

Why: Golfing is only "a good walk spoiled" if you take it seriously. Taking as a meditative exercise, it can be quite fulfilling. Desert Golfing takes that a step further, eschewing many of the assumptions of what makes a mobile game compelling. It serves as an enduring counterexample against the needs of extensive tutorialization and hand-holding or the piecemeal spoon-feeding of extrinsic rewards.

CHAPTER 18

CONCLUSION AND FINAL PLAYLIST

I had the opportunity to discuss 77 games here in this text (and a few more tangentially), but that is by no means a definitive list. Even if there was a way to enumerate all of the great games designers should play, it would be obsolete by the time a book about them went to print. The majority of games I discussed here were released in the past 15 years. In the time between the first draft of this book and the final edits, at least six more games will come out that I'll feel sad about not including. As it goes.

Mindset

To me, one of the most important figures in the world of psychology is Dr. Carol Dweck. She has worked her entire career studying how mindset affects motivation and achievement. I read her book *Mindset* when I was a frustrated junior designer at a massive international game developer. *Mindset* is not a self-help book by any means, but it almost acted as one for my career.

Dweck's research places people on a continuum between two extremes. Those with a more "fixed" mindset believe that success is based on innate traits. I have this discussion all the time with students who say, "I can't do programming," as if it was encoded into their DNA and not a teachable skill set. Fixed mindset people dread failure because that failure is a reflection of how their innate abilities did not stack up. The opposite side of the spectrum is the "growth" mindset. A growth mindset individual believes that success is based on constant improvement. Failure for them is just a signal as to how they can improve.

I still struggle with my mindset when faced with failure, but by understanding the dynamic, I know it is something I can work on. When I began to look at success and failure through this lens, it was really encouraging. The truly skilled designers I knew all seem to exhibit growth mindsets. It is hard to imagine how a fixed mindset designer can survive in an industry whose technology, markets, and business plans change as often as they do in games.

One of the ways that designers can grow and continue to learn is to be exposed to innovative games. Everyone doesn't have to like every innovative game (there are even a few in this book I actively dislike as a player), but openness to new experiences allows you a toolbox from which you can leverage good experiments into your own creations. Designers who shy away from new things end up making the same things over and over again and repeating the same mistakes. You can be successful doing that, perhaps, but I can no longer imagine being content with stasis in a field where there remains so much potential.

What did I miss? Let me know. I'm always looking for clever things to enjoy!

Zack Hiwiller
May 2018

Final Playlist, Divided by Platform

In cases where a game is on multiple platforms, I used discretion to sort them into the platform on which it was popularized or on which it provides the described experience best. Titles are boldface if they are freely available at the time of writing without the purchase of any additional materials or equipment beyond the system or device listed.

Mobile

- **2048** (#45)
- **Angry Birds** (#47)
- Bounden (#60)
- Desert Golfing (#77)
- Dream Quest (#76)
- **Drop7** (#29)
- **Pair Solitaire** (#31)
- SpellTower (#52)
- Super Hexagon (#75)
- **Threes!** (#44)
- **Triple Town** (#30)
- VVVVVV (#74)
- Zombies, Run! (#54)

Consoles

- Bioshock (#19)
- Dark Souls (#13)
- Katamari Damacy (#73)
- Mega Man X (#34)
- Night Trap (#7)
- Super Mario Bros. (#33)

PC

- 1979 Revolution: Black Friday (#38)
- **Achievement Unlocked** (#53)
- **Candy Box** (#64)
- **Cookie Clicker** (#63)
- **Corrypt** (#51)
- **Cow Clicker** (#20)
- **Crush the Castle** (#46)
- **A Dark Room** (#65)
- **Depression Quest** (#37)

- **Dwarf Fortress** (#71)
- Event[0] (#10)
- **Façade** (#70)
- Gone Home (#48)
- **Hearthstone** (#26)
- Her Story (#8)
- **Hollywood Stock Exchange** (#61)
- **I Wanna Be the Guy: The Movie: The Game** (#12)
- **Infiniminer** (#42)[1]
- Johann Sebastian Joust (#59)
- Keep Talking and Nobody Explodes (#67)
- **The Marriage** (#16)
- **A Mind Forever Voyaging** (#40)
- Minecraft (#43)
- Mu Cartographer (#24)
- **NetHack** (#14)
- Orwell (#9)
- Papers, Please (#39)
- **Parable of the Polygons** (#21)
- **Parking Wars** (#62)[2]
- **Passage** (#18)
- Portal (#35)
- **September 12th** (#17)
- **Super Columbine Massacre RPG!** (#36)
- Super Meat Boy (#11)
- Undertale (#15)
- **Unmanned** (#41)
- **The Warbler's Nest** (#72)
- **Zork** (#69)

---

1. Infiniminer is technically abandonware at this point, but the source code is available.
2. The original Parking Wars is defunct, but Parking Wars 2 is available and provides a similar enough experience to include.

Analog

- 7 Wonders (#28)
- Can't Stop (#5)
- Diamant/Incan Gold (#6)
- Diplomacy (#57)
- Dominion (#27)
- Dungeons & Dragons (#68)
- Go (#1)
- Hackey Sack (#58)
- Hanabi (#56)
- LCR (#2)
- Love Letter (#32)
- **Mafia/Werewolf** (#66)
- Magic: The Gathering (#25)
- Mate (#3)
- **Nomic** (#23)
- Pandemic (#55)
- SET (#50)
- The Settlers of Catan (#4)
- Yavalath (#49)
- Zendo (#22)

INDEX

Credits

Photo by marvent/Shutterstock

VIDEO TRAINING FOR THE **IT PROFESSIONAL**

LEARN QUICKLY
Learn a new technology in just hours. Video training can teach more in less time, and material is generally easier to absorb and remember.

WATCH AND LEARN
Instructors demonstrate concepts so you see technology in action.

TEST YOURSELF
Our Complete Video Courses offer self-assessment quizzes throughout.

CONVENIENT
Most videos are streaming with an option to download lessons for offline viewing.

Learn more, browse our store, and watch free, sample lessons at
informit.com/video

Save 50%* off the list price of video courses with discount code **VIDBOB**

the trusted technology learning source